Dirk Meyerhoff, Begoña Laibarra,
Rob van der Pouw Kraan, Alan Wallet (Eds.)

Software Quality and Software Testing in Internet Times

With Contributions of

Ståle Amland, Walter Bischofberger, Arnim Buch, Astrid Dehnel,
Tessa Döring, Stefan Engelkamp, Thomas Fehlmann, Elmar Fichtl,
Stephan Friedrich, Ulrich Hasenkamp, Dirk Huberty, Paul Keese,
Dirk Kirstein, Andreas Kramp, Jens Lehmbach, Claus Lewerentz,
Martin Lippert, Christoph Mecke, Michael Meyer, Trevor Price,
Werner Schmitz-Thrun, Katrin Severid, Frank Simon, David Singleton,
Jarle Våga, Erik van Veenendaal, Michael Vetter, Steve Willis,
Jan-Gerold Winter, Heinz Züllighoven

Springer

Editors

Dirk Meyerhoff
SQS Software Quality Systems AG
Stollwerckstr. 11
51149 Cologne
Germany

Begoña Laibarra
SQS Software Quality Systems S.A.
Avd. Zugazarte 8, 1
48930 Las Arenas, Vizcaya
Spain

Rob van der Pouw Kraan
SQS Software Quality Systems B.V.
Van Voordenpark 5A
5301 KP Zaltbommel
The Netherlands

Alan Wallet
SIM Group Ltd.
Systems Integration Management
Albion House, Chertsey Road
Woking, Surrey GU21 1BE
United Kingdom

With 70 Figures and 13 Tables

ISBN 3-540-42632-9 Springer-Verlag Berlin Heidelberg New York

Library of Congress Cataloging-in-Publication Data applied for
Die Deutsche Bibliothek - CIP-Einheitsaufnahme
Software quality and software testing in internet times/Dirk Meyerhoff; Begoña Laibarra,
Rob van der Pouw Kraan, Alan Wallet (eds.). With contributions of S. Amland ... - Berlin;
Heidelberg; New York; Barcelona; Hong Kong; London; Milan; Paris; Singapore; Tokyo:
Springer 2002 ISBN 3-540-42632-9

Cover design: Künkel + Lopka, Heidelberg
Typesetting: perform, Heidelberg from author´s data
Printing and binding: Mercedesdruck, Berlin
Printed on acid-free paper SPIN 10852726 33/3142XT 5 4 3 2 1 0

Preface

Software quality and software testing have for decades been decisive topics in software development. However their potential and their influence on the economical side of software development and operations has been understood more clearly only in the last years. This is illustrated by the increasing number of books such as this one and conferences such as SQM (Software Quality Management Congress) and ICSTEST (International Conference on Software Testing).

The era of the commercial Internet has brought about new requirements and new challenges for software quality and testing experts. They must cope with new technologies, but more importantly with new project structures where for example the marketing department takes on the role of software buyer, general IT service companies are awarded development outsourcing contracts and IT generalists provide IT infrastructure and the application framework, and untrained customers become users of the software systems. Also, tougher economical conditions and narrow time frames make software development more challenging today.

This, the third volume in Springer's series "software.quality@xpert.press", is a collection of articles which focuses on these challenges. The authors are well-known experts of national and international reputation. They have described their current practices and experience taken from a variety of IT projects in large organisations.

After an introductory overview of today's software development as well as software quality and testing challenges, the first part of this book deals with project management. It highlights practical experience with recent approaches successfully applied using object-oriented development, in most cases Java-based.

The second part introduces two extremes, namely extreme programming and its influence on quality and testing as well as the processes designed for a portfolio of Internet applications in a very large IT organisation.

Testing from the user's perspective is discussed in the third part. Detailed concepts for testing the relevant business, experiences with end-to-end integration testing and a general procedure for testing usability are introduced. The last article in this part presents the problems of testing intelligent dialog software, namely bots and avatares.

The challenges of technical testing are introduced in the fourth part. These range from the automated testing of legacy back-end systems to security testing, monitoring of website operation and performance testing. Finally, the potential of and current experience with source code-based quality assessments of the architecture, design and the implementation of large object-oriented systems are presented.

The final part of the book highlights experiences made in test automation.

We would like to thank all the authors for their great interest in this book project and their outstanding support in its realisation. The enthusiasm and interest that the authors have in their relevant subjects is apparent in their articles. They convey clearly the issues they have encountered, and perhaps more importantly the lessons they have learnt from them. This book is an opportunity for us to learn those same lessons without repeating the mistakes of the past. Without the support of these authors, it would have been impossible to compile this high quality collection of highly practical examples from software development projects. Unfortunately one of the authors is no longer with us. David Singleton died shortly after completing his article. However we know that SiteConfidence are continuing to successfully implement Dave's ideas with an increasing number of sites.

We would also like to thank Bob Bartlett, Heinz Bons, Alex Cummins, Kai-Uwe Gawlik, Andreas Golze, Paul Keese, Michael Kuß, Rudolf van Megen, and André Welling, who greatly supported our editorial work.

Dirk Meyerhoff, Begoña Laibarra, Rob van der Pouw Kraan, Alan Wallet

SQS-Group

Table of Contents

Part II: Processes

Michael Meyer, Astrid Dehnel, Elmar Fichtl
Designing Processes for User-oriented Quality Engineering

Martin Lippert, Heinz Züllighoven
Using Extreme Programming to Manage High-Risk Projects Successfully

Software Quality
and Software Testing
in Internet Times

Springer
Berlin
Heidelberg
New York
Barcelona
Hong Kong
London
Milan
Paris
Tokyo

Part III: Testing from the User´s Perspective

Erik van Veenendaal
Low-Cost Usability Testing

Michael Vetter
Quality Aspects of Bots

Part IV: Technical Testing

Trevor Price, Werner Schmitz-Thrun
Securing e-Business

David Singleton

Website Performance Monitoring

Arnim Buch, Stefan Engelkamp, Dirk Kirstein

Applying a Control Loop for Performance Testing and Tuning

Frank Simon, Claus Lewerentz, Walter Bischofberger

Software Quality Assessments for System, Architecture, Design and Code

Katrin Severid, Jan-Gerold Winter
"The Back-End Side of Web Testing": Integration of Legacy Systems

Part V: Test Automation Techniques and Tools

Christoph Mecke
Automated Testing of mySAP Business Processes

Part VI: Appendix

Systems Development in Internet Times – Overview and Perspectives

Jens Lehmbach, Ulrich Hasenkamp
Philipps-University Marburg (Germany)

Abstract: This article provides an overview of essential aspects of systems development, including quality assurance and testing, in Internet times. Both areas – systems development and the Internet – are dramatically changing and are closely interdependent. Induced by the Internet, systems development faces new challenges, especially new response time and quality requirements. Approaches like object, component and agent orientation, application mining, open systems development and the new lightweight development models must prove their suitability to solve the new kinds of problems. Two important technological developments in this context, namely peer-to-peer computing as well as the implementation of the so-called Web services, are introduced and their potential influence on systems development is analysed. The article concludes with a look at the resulting impacts on software quality and testing.

Keywords: Systems development, Internet, object orientation, component-based software engineering, agent-based systems, reuse, application mining, open systems development, Extreme Programming, peer-to-peer computing, Web services, .NET, software quality, testing

1 Introduction

Systems development and the evolution of the Internet are interdependent in many ways. This article focuses on requirements, opportunities and special aspects of systems development in regard to the evolution of the Internet.

First, Internet applications or Internet-based applications must obviously be developed, just like any other application. Even though in a Web environment, systems development is often done "on the fly" and without any formal methodology, larger and especially strategic applications require a sound methodological base that supports processes and assures quality. New requirements for Internet applications generate a need for systems development research, e.g. in the areas of method application, time-to-market, quality aspects etc. [cf. e.g. [HOWC00], [BAUE00]]. Not to be ignored is the need for concepts to integrate new Internet applications into existing IT solutions and infrastructures.

Second, the Internet itself can function as an enabler for new ways of systems development. Of special interest in this context is the discussion on open source software and free software development which arose after some extraordinarily successful projects like the development of the free operating system *Linux* and the open Web server *Apache*. The major question is whether projects of this kind are based on a model of software development that can be generalised.

Third, systems development is a living discipline that evolves gradually, with or without the requirements stemming from Internet applications. Nevertheless, the Web is almost always a relevant context variable of systems development, at least indirectly. The relatively new "lightweight models" of systems development – especially a variety of prototyping approaches and *Extreme Programming* [BECK99] – are promising candidates for Web environments [see also the article by Lippert and Züllighoven in this book].

Finally, both fields together – systems development and the Internet – are influenced by technological progress, their evolution fostering each other. The Internet is a fast moving environment and new technologies are becoming available almost daily, and any methodology supporting the development of Internet applications must evolve with the Web. Two of the most important technological advances in recent times (both of them not yet completed) are platform concepts for so-called *Web services* (especially Microsoft's *.NET platform* and Sun Microsystem's *ONE – Open Net Environment*) on the one hand, and the rebirth of peer-to-peer computing on the other.

1.1 Evolution of the Internet

Since the beginning of the 1990s, the Internet has developed extremely rapidly and is becoming *the* medium for information retrieval, communication and transaction for more and more people. In spite of a recent decrease in business-oriented Internet euphoria, there is undoubtedly a continuous increase in the social and economical importance of the Internet.

Whereas in the early stages of the Web the mostly passive consumption of static information was predominant, the focus is now on Web-based transactions like seat reservation, ticketing, purchasing, etc. The Web becomes more and more a platform for application development [CLAR01, p. 16]. Buzzwords in this context are Customer Relationship Management, Supply Chain Management or Application Service Providing (see section 3.2). All that the users see is the user interface and the easy-to-use functionality of the new applications – typically via their browser window. A view behind the scenes, especially from the viewpoint of systems development, does not always show just positive aspects.

Over a short period in the beginning of the World Wide Web static *HTML* pages were satisfactory. As a consequence there was no question about formal development methods or quality assurance. However, as soon as the idea of dynamic generation of Web contents came up, there arose a need for user input, database calls and programming logic, either client-based (in the Web browser) or server-based.

Today the boundary between traditional and Internet applications is becoming fuzzy. The requirements imposed on the processing logic of Internet applications are at least as high as with any other application – maybe even higher because the system complexity in the era of e-business has increased again. Internet applications often have to be accessible for an undefined number of users anytime (temporal aspect) and anywhere (local distribution aspect), and there is little room for compromises regarding quality, especially for security and reliability reasons – just think of the consequences of a faulty online-banking application! As long as programming was restricted to *graphical user interfaces (GUI)* and *CGI* scripts, quality was not that important because the code became obsolete rather quickly anyway [FISC01, p. 65]. However, as soon as strategically important applications were to be re-implemented for or provided via the Web, a defined quality standard became an absolute necessity.

Unfortunately, the Internet and e-business hype of recent times led to something like an e-contamination: a collection of half-done *C++*, *Java*, *JavaScript*, *VBS*, *Perl* and other code. The large demand for Web applications forced companies to produce suitable applications. However, the limited workforce of qualified software developers or the reluctance to engage expensive software engineers made compromises necessary. Usually there was not enough time for detailed analyses and architectural concepts. This situation was reflected by the results.

The problem is getting bigger because the developers are permanently confronted with new technologies around the Internet, with new programming languages (Java, C#, Ruby, VB.NET), communication protocols, middleware structures (*COM*, *DCOM*, *COM+*, *CORBA*) or whole frameworks for systems development (Microsoft *.NET*, Sun *ONE*), among other things. All of these are not predictable regarding their development cycle and future existence. Today, after *Java* and *XML*, the *Web services* trend is making its way through the development departments world-wide. The question of which technologies will have significant impact on the development of the Internet remains open. Every development project in the Internet environment is characterised by a high degree of uncertainty.

1.2 Challenges for Systems Development

Both practitioners and researchers in the field of systems development are facing new challenges every day. As mentioned, a large part of these challenges is induced by developments in the Internet environment and by the introduction of electronic business, recently also by mobile business:

- Increasing importance
  Information technology has taken on much greater significance in organisations and society today. Systems are not used merely to automate well-established tasks and processes but also to redesign business processes, reinvent organisations and even to create entirely new businesses and industries [YU01, p. 124].

- Growing complexity
  The complexity of the projected systems and software has increased and is still increasing for multiple reasons. The number of tools and technologies that are employed for the development process is getting larger – in many cases they are not compatible with each other. For example, the traditional programming languages like *COBOL, C* and *C++* are continued to be used beside newer languages like *Java, VB.Net* or *C#*. The multitude of available platforms opens up more design choices in systems architecture. This increases the importance of the integration of heterogeneous systems (the buzzword is EAI, Enterprise Application Integration) and the management of interfaces associated with them. Last but not least, the complexity of systems is increasing due to new and additional application areas and because more complex problems are being addressed. Complex tasks ask for complex and more comprehensive software [BALZ98, p. 29].

- Increasing quality requirements
  Because IT systems are applied in more important and critical areas than before, the failure of such a system can result in serious economical and material damages, up to dangers for health and life [BALZ98, p. 30]. Therefore, the quality of IT systems has increased in importance. Especially quality features like security (access control, authentication, encryption) and reliability (availability, failsafeness, correctness) must be essential parts of a Web service environment today.

- Demand backlog and bottleneck
  The demand for more flexible, adaptable, extensible, and robust Web-based enterprise application systems accelerates [GRIS01, p. 37]. Regardless of their market niche, most companies are feeling the pressure to release software faster. The development cycles of the past decade, typically 24 to 36 months, have been compressed to 12 or 18 months for non-Internet-related companies. For companies involved in electronic business and the Internet environment, the cycle can be as short as three to six months [BASK01, p. 51]. Until recently a major problem was the lack of good developer capacities which led inevitably to a demand backlog. Due to the breakdown of many dot-com companies there are now more developers available. But it is still doubtful that the recent displacement of a number of developers will be a solution to the limitation of development resources of many companies and organisations in the long run. On the one hand studies reveal that only 30 to 40 percent of software developers are skilful enough to develop successful applications [CLAR01, p. 17]. On the other hand the tech-

nology change rate especially in the field of the Internet is still accelerating, leading to a greater demand for experts with up-to-date knowledge. Furthermore the current decline of business with software and services will not last very long because the high-tech industry remains the driving force of economic growth.

- Burdening legacy systems
  Millions of programs have been produced in the last three decades. A large part of the productive systems of these days is many years old and is written in *Assembler*, *FORTRAN*, *COBOL* or *C*. As the application environment of these systems changes in the course of the time, the systems have to be updated, adapted or redeveloped [STAH99, p. 326]. More than two thirds of the activities of software developers and programmers deal with maintenance (bug fixes and optimisation) of and services (adaptation and extension) to existing systems [BALZ98, p. 969f.]. Currently there are efforts in many companies to open existing application systems up for an Internet access.

2 Problem-Solving Approaches of Systems Development

Systems development as a discipline faces the task to find solutions for the problems mentioned above. There is a tension between

- the excessive demand for application systems, especially for Internet-based applications,
- the tremendous time pressure for application development (time-to-market),
- increasing quality requirements and
- the limited development resources.

What are the solution paths?

In most cases, the limited development resources seem to be a bottleneck that in total cannot be influenced, at least not in the short run. This restriction is a limiting factor for all other variables of the given problem. This finding can be phrased as „nowadays resources determine requirements" [MELL01, p. 4].

How is the remaining conflict between the targets *short time-to-market* and *essential quality requirements* to be solved?

A study in the United States revealed that the time factor in Internet-oriented development projects has top priority: time is the primary driver that causes attributes like performance, cost, and even quality to become low-priority in comparison [Baskerville et al. 2001]. Within the resulting frame there are different solution strategies that aim at reducing the development time and at the same time not falling below a certain quality standard:

1. Moving up to a higher level of abstraction in systems development, e.g. by using powerful development tools and program generators.
2. Employment of object-oriented or even component-based development methodologies that ensure modularity and reusability of the systems under development.
3. Using approaches for the reuse of existing, well-established business logic, e.g. application mining.
4. Introduction of social and organisational measures, like the application of lightweight models, e.g. Extreme Programming, or distributed forms of open systems development.
5. Solving the problem without any in-house development. Instead, adapting a standard software package or commissioning a specialised service company (outsourcing). Of course, the core problem continues to exist and is only shifted from one company to another.

2.1 From Object Orientation to Agent-Based Systems

The employment of object-oriented methods has gradually become a standard in systems development [BALZ98, p. 328f.]. Even traditional procedural programming languages like COBOL or Pascal have meanwhile been enhanced by object-oriented principles, and also script languages like Perl, PHP or Ruby [WYSS01, p. 78], that are often used for Web application programming, support object orientation.

The consequent application of object orientation leads to better modularity and therefore greater flexibility and maintainability as well as to better reusability of program modules [FISC01, p. 62]. In view of software projects that become constantly more complex these advantages gain importance. The next higher level of construction of modular software structures is reached by the application of component orientation.

Component-based software engineering (CBSE) offers an attractive alternative for building Web-based enterprise application systems. It works by developing and evolving software from selected reusable software components, then assembling them within appropriate software architectures [GRIS01, p. 37]. A component is a unit of independent deployment that interacts with its environment through its well-defined interfaces while encapsulating its implementation [GRIS01, p. 37].

In this approach, instead of detailed programming software development can rather be described as the compilation of several reusable components. Critical for the quality level of the resulting system is the underlying architectural concept which should be agreed upon at the beginning of the development process. The quality of the individual components has ideally been tested separately in advance.

The hope in using a component-based software engineering approach is to achieve the following goals, which are relevant especially in an Internet environment [GRIS01, p. 37]:

1. The reduction of development costs and time-to-market by assembling the application systems from a set of reusable components rather than programming them from scratch.
2. The enhancement of the reliability of application systems because each reusable component undergoes several review and inspection stages.
3. The improvement of the maintainability of application systems by allowing higher-quality components to replace older, low-quality ones.
4. The improvement of the quality of the application systems as a whole because the individual components as well as the combined total product can be developed by individual experts in their respective fields.

The next evolutionary step in following this approach is the application of agent-oriented software development [YU01, p. 123]. Whereas the components in the approach mentioned above have a capability to encapsulate extensive functionality, they are in principle not intelligent but have to rely instead on the intelligent control performed by some central feature.

An agent instead is an intelligent, autonomous, proactive software component that dynamically interacts with its environment and other agents. It therefore offers greater flexibility and adaptability than traditional components [YU01, p. 123], [GRIS01, p. 38]. Central control has in this environment been replaced by decentralised self-control by the individual agents.

For this reason agents could be seen as next-generation components and agent-oriented software engineering as an extension of conventional CBSE [GRIS01, p. 38]. Agent-based systems provide a lot of flexibility and promise to be more effective at handling the resulting software's evolution, distribution, and complexity. This style of software engineering seems to be promising especially for developing and maintaining Web-based enterprise systems at Internet speed [GRIS01, p. 43].

2.2 Application Mining

In response to increased requests for Internet-based solutions, diverse systems have to be linked to each other. That is a great challenge since the changes from one technology or interface generation to the next occur faster and faster. IT managers have to ask themselves whether a new development is necessary with each technology change or whether the fundamental goal should be to make existing processes available via new technologies.

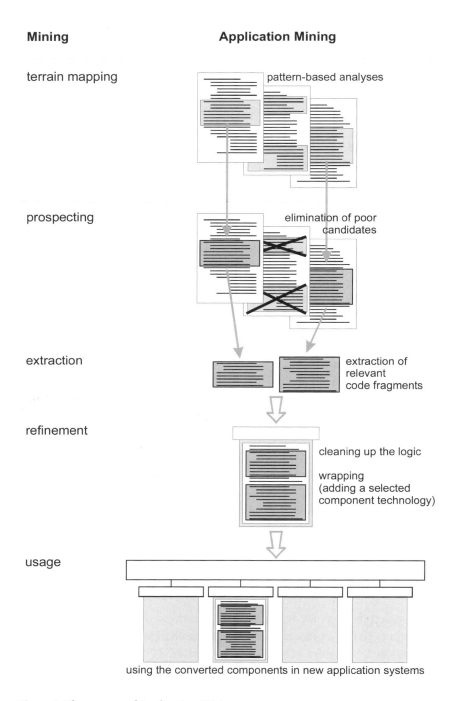

Figure 1: The process of Application Mining

In contrast to the approaches described in the previous section, older software systems have usually not been designed for possible reuse. Nevertheless many legacy systems contain well-established business processes that can be used also with new technologies. However, in order to be able to reuse parts of these systems the existing software must be reusable [BALZ98-a, p. 639]. If this is not the case, then one has to try to identify and to augment reusable components of the software firstly. The methods to be employed are reverse engineering, reengineering and redevelopment [BALZ98-a, p. 640].

A suitable term for the tasks to be performed in this context is Application Mining (Figure 1). Its goal is to extract business logic from existing and successful applications, to encapsulate that logic and to make it available within a component architecture (Section 2.1). Several steps are necessary to achieve this [MOOR00, p. 1]:

1. To search for valuable code sections using analysis tools that for example search for certain arithmetic command sequences. The goal is to analyse systems to uncover critical business processes and interdependencies.
2. To extract relevant code sections from the existing systems in order to encapsulate them in separate modules. The goal is to harvest mission-critical business logic so that it can be leveraged in new development efforts.
3. To complement the generated business modules with the selected component technology, usually CORBA, DCOM/Com+ or EJB.

Finally the converted components – just as newly developed components – are ready to be used in new application systems that are nowadays usually based on an Internet-oriented architecture.

Application Mining can, if employed correctly, help bridge the gap between the conflicting goals of short time-to-market and the necessary quality level. One should not underestimate the effort necessary to harvest reusable business components from legacy systems. However this effort is justified by the proven quality level of the resulting components.

2.3 Open Systems Development

Open source software such as the operating system *Linux* or the *Apache* Web server has in a few years created much attention as an alternative way to develop and distribute software [LJUN00, p. 501]. The underlying style of software engineering seems to be a successful way to create high quality software with little cost and there is no doubt that it has impacts on the commercial world. An interesting fact is that large IT vendors like IBM and Hewlett-Packard have turned to open source software.

The roots of open systems development lie in part in the hacker culture of the early Sixties [LJUN00, p. 501], in another part in the government-funded research activities in the United States which leads to publicly available results, namely open source and in a third part in the GNU project of Richard Stallmann, initiated in 1984. He can be viewed as a pioneer in free software development [STAL01], [LJUNG00, p. 502].

Stallmann referred to the concept of the *public good* to justify his project. Indeed, especially software must be at least partially in accordance with the criteria of a public good [SAMU98]. Otherwise there would not be a widespread problem of illegal software use:

1. Non-rivalry in consumption: The quality of the good software does not suffer (exception: bottleneck in the IT infrastructure) from the increasing number of users – quite frequently a large number of users will enhance the quality of the good overall, take the example of swapping or electronic markets.
2. Inability to restrict users from consumption (non-excludability): The distribution of software is – especially in the Internet era – practically effortless. The attempt to keep persons from using software illegally (e.g. by dongles, copy protection or need to register) are often without result.

The Internet played an important part in open systems development already at an early stage and can therefore be viewed as an enabler of this approach [LJUN00, p. 503]: "Internet and email had been used by the free software community for quite many years before the public discovery of the Internet". It served as communication and exchange platform for the developers engaged in a distributed project. Some authors even claim that open systems development, as a decentralised process based on the voluntary participation of numerous independent and location-indifferent co-workers, is in the Internet era superior to any other organisational structure.

The question is whether this model can be generalised for systems development.

In the pure form, the model of open software development is certainly suitable only in certain areas and in certain projects. Some researches name security-sensitive systems as an example. It may be doubted whether the accumulation of reputation is a sufficient motivation for experienced developers to get involved in an open source project. "In this respect, the typical motivation is too weak and the business of delivering software in accordance with the specification and in time too difficult" [FISC01, p. 64]. This style of software engineering is best suited for improving on existing systems, but essential difficulties of software development remain.

Some elements can, however, be employed in systems development models, as is shown by the example of *Extreme Programming* (XP) below – at least when it comes to testing and improving the software.

2.4 Lightweight Models, especially Extreme Programming

In Internet times the fast delivery of software products becomes increasingly important. Therefore it is inevitable to speed up the software development process. Traditional process models for systems development like the V-model [V-MOD01] or Catalysis [ELTI01] are very detailed and formalised. They have originally been designed for large projects. Development projects in a Web environment that are characterised by a tight time-to-market schedule can benefit only to a limited extent from these models.

Exactly this shortcoming is addressed by the so-called lightweight models, like Kent Beck's *Extreme Programming (XP)* [BECK99], that aim at especially short development cycles. XP does not have a detailed analysis phase and focuses on the core process of software development, namely programming, whereby systematically planned and performed tests play an important role.

The major steps of an XP project are release planning, iterations of coding, and testing of the individual releases (Figure 2). In order to ensure proper results in spite of the low level of formalism, the concept of so-called practices has been introduced. The most important practices are:

- Release Planning
  First, the scope of the next program version has to be determined. The desired functionality of the program is discussed with the customer (the future user of the software) including the decision on which part of the function can actually be implemented. The customer chooses the most important tasks that can be completed by the next release. The volume of the individual development releases should be kept relatively small. The release intervals are typically just one or two months long (short release cycles). This way the customer gets rather early a product that serves at least part of its purpose, and he has a chance to express comments and wishes for changes. It has to be noted that any extensions that the customer might wish later in the process are ignored at this stage. Only those extensions are considered that are needed for the current task.

- Pair Programming
  The actual development work is done by teams of two. One team member is responsible for the actual coding, the other develops strategies for further implementations, specifies test cases and elaborates design simplifications. The resulting code is owned by all programmers collectively. Therefore everybody has the right to change anywhere in the code and to run test cases. There is obviously a strong need for automated test procedures and a pool of common programming rules.

- Continuous Integration of Code
  On a test computer environment, each new piece of software is integrated into the overall system by their respective production teams and is checked with all test cases.

- Testing
  Quality assurance in XP is essentially done by testing. The programmers have – before starting to code – to determine all relevant test cases that are run automatically later on. After the integration of a new function, all the existing tests are performed again to ensure the proper functioning of the overall system after a modification.

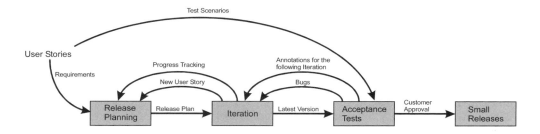

Figure 2: Extreme Programming

When looking at these practices in detail, it is clear that they resemble the open systems development as discussed in the previous section. These two methodologies overlap in some areas . Both approaches often have short release cycles, adding only a few features and rapidly integrating user feedback. Both have a user-driven focus, continual code review, tight feedback loops and rely on a culture to add features and fix bugs. It may well be doubted that these similarities are accidental. We rather have the impression that proven principles from the open source movement are systematically adapted by professional systems development.

However, the new lightweight development models like XP should not be exempt from critique. On the contrary, there are a large number of aspects to be criticised. Therefore it is doubtful that these models – at least at the current stage of evolution – can actually be the solution to the dilemma of software development.

Lightweight models seem be suited by their structural design primarily for small projects. The low level of detail can be a problem in large projects. For example, the tasks of project management are hardly described with XP. Furthermore, there is no notion of configuration management or versioning, which would be the basis for a development activity distributed in distinct locations. The required level of qualification of the involved team members is not addressed. Quality assurance is restricted to the application of automated tests which is by far not a guarantee for all quality measures. The neglect of non-functional requirements [STAH99, p. 265], like robustness or performance, can later lead to the situation that the software will not be used.

The major point for criticising XP is Kent Beck's assumption that the effort to be spent for modifications is at a constant level throughout the whole software development process. This is in contrast to the common doctrine which postulates that errors in early phases of systems development can be corrected in a later phase only with an over-proportional effort [ELTI01, p. 189f.].

3   Technology-Driven Developments

3.1 Peer-to-Peer Computing

Peer-to-peer is a class of applications that take advantage of resources – storage, cycles, content, human presence – available at the edges of the Internet [SHIR01]. It can be defined most easily in terms of what it is not: the client-server model. In peer-to-peer, an application is split into components that act as equals [SING01, p. 4]. From this point of view the term peer-to-peer seems to be anything but new. Taken literally, even servers or mainframes talking to one another have a peer-to-peer relationship, and the *USENET* and *FidoNet* from the early eighties are considered to be the first peer-to-peer applications in the modern sense.

Presently a rebirth of peer-to-peer computing seems to take place. Peer-to-peer networks are regarded as the next step in the evolution of the Internet. This technological approach is not limited to exchange platforms like *Gnutella* or *Morpheus* but is rather a potential basis for business solutions. Virtually all of the key players in the IT business like *IBM*, *Intel*, *Microsoft* (*Farsite*-Project), *Sun Microsystems* (*Juxtapose*-Project) or *Lotus* are working on peer-to-peer-based applications for the commercial sector.

Peer-to-peer computing is expected to help exploit the vast performance potential of the Internet. Up to now, normal client computers on the Internet use only a small fraction of their processor and storage capacity, a large part is idle. Therefore it appears to be promising to develop peer-to-peer applications that can exploit the unused resources, aggregate them and provide a vast computational power for example for research and development projects (*Intel* has proposed to use peer-to-peer computing for leukaemia research).

A peer-to-peer architecture can be employed in many areas. Therefore the approach bears a large potential for systems development. There are interdependencies and possible synergies with component and agent-oriented systems development (Section 2.1), with open systems development (Section 2.3), and with the concept of Web services (Section 3.2). Furthermore peer-to-peer computing offers not only an implementation option for application systems under development but can itself be used as basis for a development platform that supports especially distributed forms of systems development (like *USENET* as an example supporting the development of *Linux*).

3.2 Web Services: the Future?

As we mentioned at the beginning, the contents of the Internet become more and more active. Ideally the functional capabilities of many different Web sites are integrated without any seams. This way, the Internet is going to change from a media space for documents and simple transactions to a comprehensive infrastructure for services that can become extremely complex. The technological foundation of this vision are the so-called Web services (Figure 3).

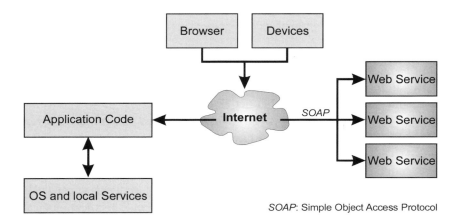

Figure 3: The usage of Web Services in Internet-based applications

Web services are program modules or black-box functions that are provided on the Internet via protocols and can be compiled to form complex Web applications or portals [STAL01, p. 72]. Companies can snap Web services for accounting, inventory, logistics, marketing and much more into their B2B Web systems to create dynamic, customised business Webs, or B2B Web marketplaces. For example a company can use a special Web service for cargo tracking which offers shipment and tracking information via the Internet to customers and agents, 24 hours a day. Web services can also serve as ideal basis for application service providing (ASP), a phrase which denotes the offering of dynamic services on the Internet in exchange for payment.

The realisation of Web services requires certain infrastructural prerequisites:

1. A communication protocol in order to provide functions and data via the Internet,
2. a directory service that enables Web applications to search and retrieve the requested services dynamically, and
3. a documentation protocol for the standardised description of all the services offered.

Furthermore, some other fundamental problems like authentication, data management, system administration etc. have to be solved. The overall job is to provide a complete Web infrastructure. Several large IT vendors, among them *Microsoft* and *Sun Microsystems*, are working on frameworks of this kind – with competitive approaches.

Microsoft's approach is called ".NET". It is praised to introduce a completely new paradigm. .NET is Microsoft's future platform for the development of Internet applications and is based on open standards like HTTP and XML. The .NET platform consists of the four components *Framework and Tools*, *Building Block Services* (= pre-manufactured Web services to be linked into applications), *Enterprise Servers* (to provide the infrastructure) and *Mobile Devices* (to support the growing segment of mobile computing).

For developers, the component *Framework and Tools* of the .NET platform is especially interesting. The core of the .NET platform is made up of the so-called *Common Language Runtime (CLR)*. The compilers of the framework – at present *VB.Net*, *Visual C++* and *C#*, all from Microsoft – do not generate native code anymore but rather translate the source code into an intermediate language, the so-called *Microsoft Intermediate Language (MSIL)*, which is later executed with just-in-time compilers under the supervision of the *Runtime*. All compilers that produce MSIL can have this code be executed under control of the *Runtime*. This way, a new level of language integration and freedom in the selection of the development language is achieved. The integration of different languages is located on the code level in this model and not on the binary level, like in the earlier *COM* approach. The intention is to be able to program object classes in just any language and use or reuse these classes with other languages, including for example inheritance across languages (Figure 4).

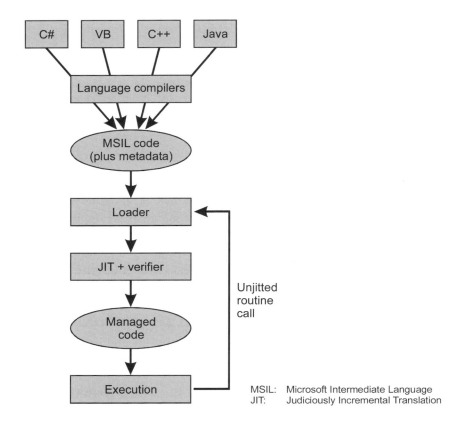

Figure 4: The Microsoft .NET program execution model

If the approach can really deliver what it promises, it could mean a huge benefit for systems development. On the one hand, the freedom of choice of the development language relieves the problem of the scarce development resources since there is no dependency on certain specialists anymore. On the other hand, new opportunities for software reuse can open up. Legacy source code could, if necessary, be modified and recompiled into MSIL. It would then be ready to be reused on development projects (cf. sections 2.1 and 2.2). Furthermore there are new chances for platform-independent development, e.g. for improved portability [STAH99, p. 88]. To give an example, there is work on .NET implementations for Linux and Apple OS X going on.

Sun Microsystem's Web services platform is called *ONE (Open Net Environment)*. It is based on Java as well as numerous other standards from the Web and XML environments. This guarantees almost complete independence of specific platforms, but requires a close connection with other companies and standardisation bodies. Sun Microsystem's approach is certainly more open than Microsoft's *.NET* and can rely on the market power and maturity of Java in the development industry. The disadvantage of

ONE is the current incomplete state of this architectural puzzle and the impression that is still in a conceptual phase.

Technologically the development of the Web services can be understood as an advancement of the component idea in the context of the increasing importance of networks . In contrast to existing component technologies like *CORBA* or *DCOM/Com+*, which build upon object-specific protocols, Web services are based on Internet standards and are therefore not limited to specific platforms.

Certainly a lot of effort will be put into the idea of Web services in the time to come. Especially the involvement of the big players of the IT industry gives reason to expect that it is not just another hype subject that will disappear soon without any permanent impact. It will be exciting to watch if and when the current problem-solving approaches will move from the development stage into the maturity stage. In case they become ready for the marketplace, the impact on both the Internet and systems development will be dramatic. Some of Gartner's market researchers believe 80 percent or more of Web applications will in the future be based on either Java or Microsoft.Net products [CLAR01, p. 17].

4   Impacts on Software Quality and Testing

Quality requirements for software highly depend on the range of use of the relating IT system. The greater the strategic and commercial relevance of an IT system for a company or an organisation is and the more damaging the consequences of system's failures are, the more important an effective quality assurance becomes. Increasing quality requirements turn out to be a problem if systems development has to take place under restrictions of short time-to-market and a limited workforce. Due to these restrictions connected to software development in Internet times, the highest quality risks need to be identified, and the priorities of the different tasks of quality assurance and testing are planned.

Under current conditions, especially under such enormous pressure of time, an exhaustive testing seems impossible. In many cases it will be necessary to switch to samples, whereby limiting the tests is threatening software quality. Especially the multiplicity of quality requirements (like availability, accessibility, security, compatibility and performance) of Internet-based applications leaves a risk when relying on samples. Because of this problem testing should be based on a risk analysis.

Another solution path is the automation of testing and the use of test tools [see e.g. the article by Mecke in this book] as implemented in the concept of Extreme Programming. Quality assurance in XP is realised by testing. The evolutionary character of developing in XP – that means the short cycles of implementing and integrating new functions – makes it necessary to run all test cases automatically. When using XP or other lightweight models for the developing process it is important not to neglect non-functional quality requirements, which are of special interest in Internet environments (e.g. performance).

The illustrated object and component-orientation in systems development also has impact on software quality and testing behaviour. The testing process is divided in different sections: Individual objects or components can be developed by respective experts and tested separately in advance. At this lower level it should be possibly to ensure a relatively high standard of software quality (also with regard to a potential re-use of the object or component). At a higher level there is the increasing importance of integration testing [see also the article by Keese in this book]. As the overall quality of object and component-based systems highly depends on the underlying IT architecture, adequate efforts should be spent on the architectural design.

Open systems development and test outsourcing remain as further alternatives to improve software quality and testing. Open systems development seems especially suited for developing security-sensitive and high quality software. This is a result of the short feedback loops, the continual code review and the specific culture of bug fixing integrated in this approach. In turn open systems development itself is enabled by Internet technologies and especially concepts like peer-to-peer computing. On the downside open systems development is only possible in areas where companies can afford to let the world share its sources, a situation rather rare in today's competitive markets. Test outsourcing does not have such restrictions and has proven to be very successful.

5   Summary and Perspectives

This article has elaborated on the many interdependencies between systems development and the Internet as well as selected impacts on software quality and testing.

The linking points between systems development and the Internet are increasing in number which makes it more and more difficult to view them as separate. Especially when thinking of future solutions and applications there is no sense in studying one area without taking the other into consideration. The technological progress affects both areas at the same time and forces their unstoppable evolution to pick up speed. Currently we are not able to foresee the outcome of this process.

Object-oriented approaches, methods and tools have become state-of-the-art. They are well-suited for handling complexity in the development of application systems. Component orientation seems to be on the same track. The R&D activities in the field of Web services give additional evidence for this assumption. Web services have the potential to be the future platform for non-trivial component-oriented Internet applications. Unfortunately it is not foreseeable which of the different solutions will find its way into the market. Almost every IT vendor is developing their own, sometimes proprietary, solution. The influence of the important standardisation bodies will be decisive.

Peer-to-peer computing will play a role in the Web environment as it is a distinctive architectural approach with several advantages over classical client-server architectures. Since all the computers in a peer-to-peer network are in principle equal, the system avoids performance bottlenecks and reduces the impact of single-point failures. The architecture opens up a chance to realise richer interaction models.

Systems development, including quality assurance and testing, must evolve with this dynamic environment and provide adequate solutions for changing requirements. Even "exotic" approaches like open software development can be useful as has been shown by the example of the principles of *Extreme Programming*. We have to admit, however, that research has not yet delivered the necessary input, as can be seen with the newer approaches for the development process. There are still many experiments with different systems development models to be undertaken, especially in Web environments, in order to determine their suitability in Internet times.

Part I

Managing for Optimal Time to Market

Managing High-Speed Web Testing

Jarle Våga
TietoEnator Consulting AS (Norway)

Ståle Amland
Amland Consulting (Norway)

Abstract: Ever felt that you were lacking both the time and information you needed to do a proper job? Or rather; have you ever had complete information about the system you were going to test, and there was never a question about time? I didn't think so. Neither have we.
The following describes a web portal with a publishing tool where little testing had been done in advance, and we were given two days of testing before the system was to go live. It was a small project, but still very interesting in nature.
This is a case study. We tell the story of how pair-based exploratory testing was tried by two rather inexperienced test managers in order to cover as much as possible of a web application where time was a commodity in short supply, and specifications where non-existing. And it worked. It really worked. So read on, and we'll tell you all about it.

Keywords: Internet test, exploratory and pair test, test management, Internet-based applications

1   Project Background

The project used for this case study was a development project for a new corporate web site. "The Company" is a merger of several large companies into one of Europe's leading IT consulting companies. The objective of this project was: "One Company – One Message".

The project was fairly simple: a tool to publish multi-language corporate information and an advanced search facility, i.e. no e-commerce. The features to be tested were the functionality of the publishing tool and the search facility. This had to be tested on Internet Explorer and Netscape version 4.0 and up, running on Windows 98, 2000 and Windows NT.

The web development was done by a subsidiary ("the Developer") of the Company - which caused an interesting attitude towards quality and software testing: "We're buddies. We will sort this out. There is no need for quality assurance or testing. We will help each other."

A few months down the line, the Company's project manager starts getting worried; there is no evidence of the Developer having planned any quality control, configuration control of software testing. Therefore, the project manager initiated a test plan review (in accordance with TPI as documented by Pol et. al. 1999).

The review confirmed the project managers concerns. He then decided to initiate a user acceptance test. There was very limited time for preparation, documentation and planning – the question was how to find the errors before the customers did?

2 "High-Speed" Methods and Preparation

A small analogy. When I was a kid, I sometimes stayed up after bedtime by half an hour at a time just to see how much I could stretch the limits before my parents got angry. I discovered that my mother started commanding me to bed before my father did, meaning those two "systems" had a different tolerance rate. I just tried to see what happened. I believe I was doing my first exploratory tests. Once or twice, I teamed up with my brother in doing this. We had the benefit of being a pair, and felt stronger. This made us stretch the limits a little further, even though the outcome usually was the same. It's much the same with software testing. You know the system should stop you from accessing restricted information – but does it really? Pairing up often gives you more ideas.

An over-simplified example of course, but it still stresses the point. Neither exploratory nor pair testing are new and revolutionary methods. Nevertheless, implementing them into a system, using them in planned, structured software-testing sessions proved to give surprising results.

2.1 Exploratory Testing

The ideas of using pair and exploratory methods came originally from James Bach and his articles on www.satisfice.com. As James Bach sees it, exploratory testing is in actuality a teachable discipline, where success depends on the skills of the tester and the test manager. He uses the term "exploratory", since "skilled ad-hoc" doesn't seem to get the point across. Exploratory testing relies on the knowledge and creativity of the testers. Without this, it is rather meaningless. The plainest definition of exploratory testing is test design and test execution at the same time. To the extent that the next test we do is influenced by the result of the last test we did, we are doing exploratory testing. We become more exploratory when we can't tell what tests should be run in advance of the test cycle, or when we haven't yet had the opportunity to create those tests [BACH01].

Exploratory techniques are used more frequently than most people seem to recognise, both in planning, scripting and in execution. Even when making detailed test scripts, people often adopt an exploratory approach to familiarise themselves with the software before developing the scripts. The difference between completely scripted testing and completely exploratory testing ("bug hunt") can be visualised on a scale, where the ends represent the extreme of both practices. In the middle, you'll find different levels of exploratory testing.

2.2 Pair Testing

Pair testing is, as the term indicates, two people working together on one computer. The major benefit of this is that testers become more confident and creative. Confident, because they have the ability to discuss ideas and viewpoints during the test, and they can back each other up. Creative, because two brains are better than one. Suggestions from one can spark new ideas from the other, and vice versa. To quote Cem Kaner: "We noticed several instances of high productivity, high creativity work that involved testers grouping together to analyse a product or to scheme through a test or to run a series of tests. We also saw/used it as an effective training technique." [KANE01]

3 "High-Speed" Test Planning

In Norway, we have a saying that goes: "Well started means half finished". But to get started proved difficult. The system was poorly documented, and the documentation available consisted merely of user manuals and "white papers". In addition, people with knowledge of the system and the development were difficult to reach. The project manager seemed to realise this, as this was one of the reasons for him to advocate the acceptance test we had been asked to do. We started out with a standard, non-exploratory approach with plans and scripting. A lot of time was spent "trying out" the portal and the publishing tool prior to writing the actual test execution plan. The system was in actuality not that big, so this seemed to us like a doable task. What caused many problems during this phase was the fact that the developer kept doing sudden changes in the code without anybody knowing it. This became quite an office joke after a while; we kept guessing each morning how the system would work today.

The acceptance test plan was written already in the first week, before we actually knew too much about the system. This was a good thing, because we were able to separate out what to test and, more important; what not to test. Responsibilities and acceptance criteria were also stated here. However, the section with "Approach" was written rather superficially. After "trying out" the system for some time, we started writing test scripts, but soon realised that this would get us nowhere. We simply didn't have enough information, and the system kept changing all the time. From our manager we got some information about some new methods called exploratory testing, and testing where two testers teamed up (www.satisfice.com, 2001). This seemed immediately like an interesting approach, since we became much more flexible both when writing the execution plan/"scripts" and in the actual execution of the test. In addition, we could use the experience and creativity of each tester in the test. However, how in the world should we set up such a test, execute it in two days and be sure of covering everything?

This was in many ways a very special test assignment, and we soon came to see that our way of managing the test would be one of the most important factors of success. Perhaps even more than the actual methods used. One of the managerial issues we were puzzled with was reporting and documentation. Both our manager and mentors were concerned about this problem, and stressed the issue well in advance. What we came up with was a simplified deviation form, which would be easy to write. In addition, we planned a close monitoring of each pair to assure ourselves that reports were actually written. After each session, we collected and read the reports while the testers were on a break, so that any questions with the reports could be raised while the session was still "fresh in mind".

We were also short of time, and had to use every minute efficiently in order to get things done in time. We were promised a test lab after our own specifications, where everything should be "ready to rock". But we still brought with us installation files for all browsers, including back-up plans B, C and D, just in case. And we did come to use some of them. At least this taught us a thing or two – never completely trust a man on the phone. If you want something done in a certain way, you had better check it yourself. We had allowed ourselves two hours in the morning to check the test environment, and we had to spend them well. But thorough preparation and risk analysis saved the day. For example, we needed Internet Explorer (ie) 4.0. However, software from Microsoft is meant to be upgraded, not downgraded. Therefore, if every machine has ie 5.0 installed and one wants 4.0, one had better know what to do to get around the error messages.

"In the fields of observation, chance favours only those minds which are prepared."

This was once written by Louis Pasteur, and is just as suitable in software testing as in medicine. Even when doing exploratory testing, one needs to plan, motivate, guide and monitor. So be serious about your preparation, and remember that well started means half finished.

4 "High-Speed" Test Execution

By "high speed" we refer to the pace of testing, and not to performance testing in any way. And high speed it had to be. In two days, we were to conduct an acceptance test of a system not formerly tested. When arriving at the test lab, few, if any, of the computers were ready.

Back-up plans and installation discs came in handy. By 10 am, the testers had arrived, and we were ready with the test environment. These were mainly end users of the software who had completed a two-day training course prior to the test. This would later prove very useful when conducting the exploratory test.

When organising the pairs, one should preferably have some knowledge of the people and personalities one is working with. This was not possible in our situation, and we had to team up the tester according to profession and his own wishes. When the testers arrived, there were 14 of them. This meant seven pairs, for each of which we had prepared a folder with the most essential information. Our briefing was a 20-minute session in which we explained the folder, some of the important areas of the test plan (what to test, what not to test etc), and what we should be doing during the next two days.

On the first day, we performed the functionality test of the publishing tool and how the pages published could be viewed in the web portal. To cover all browsers, operating systems (OS) and user groups (Content Creators, who write the information to be published, and Topic Managers, who must approve the information before it is published), we developed a set of matrixes. These matrixes explained when each group should use a certain browser and OS, and what identity they should use to log on to the system. This attempted to verify whether pictures and text published with Internet Explorer 5.5 could be viewed with Netscape 4, etc. The folders explained how the pages should be published, and at which level in the structure, pictures and files should be embedded. Apart from these guidelines, the testers could experiment with their own choice of text size, font types, frames, html and links. It soon became clear that the publishing tool didn't perform any control of the input given before it published the information. This produced some rather strange results in the web portal. This also trigged discussion and exchange of ideas between the pairs, and the discussions were far greater than we had anticipated. The testers tended to forget the test guidelines, and instead focused on just finding "bugs". They turned from a structured exploratory approach to a "bug hunt", which was unfortunate. We were therefore challenged with the task of structuring the testers once again. In order to ensure that all functionality and browser-options were covered, we relied heavily on written test guidelines and matrixes on the first day, in addition to an exploratory approach to test management. The guidelines were important when considering how to document the test in the test summary report.

Due to the short time span of the test, no tool of any kind was implemented. We instead used an Excel sheet to log the deviations found.

On the second day, we started a less structured exploratory approach, where we depended more heavily on the knowledge of each tester and the experiences gained the first day. Pages published on the first day were used to test the search-functionality in the web portal. We also did a more extensive browser test, in which every piece of functionality in the portal was tested in all browsers. This produced rather interesting results, as layout and frame sets sometimes were altered in Netscape 4.6 and 6.0, and colours changed when using Internet Explorer 5.5. This proved once again how important it is to use different browsers when web testing. How embarrassing it must be to exclude 20-30% of the market just because they couldn't view your page with their Netscape browser.

After exploring the functionality according to the planned test guidelines, we were able to document coverage of the features to be tested. Therefore we tried to spend the last hours of the test session on pure "bug hunting"- again based on knowledge and experience of the individual testers. Exploratory testing taken to the extreme!

5   The Web Testing Experience

The test project documented a total of 200 deviations including duplicates. Approximately 150 deviations were reported to the Developer who accepted 65 of them. The remaining deviations had to be postponed to "next release", and the system had to go into production with limited functionality – 3 months delayed. So the test was considered a success by the project team. We stopped a system with too many "bugs" from going into production and leaving the problems to the customers.

The analogy we referred to earlier was meant to show that everybody has used some form of exploratory or pair techniques at one time or another. But it takes skills to do it right. So what does it take? What kind of useful experience did we gain?

Some would say none. They would argue that the project was far too small and "hasty". We had little time for preparation of the pairs. We did not have a well-defined measurement of coverage. We used exploratory techniques as a "way out", since we didn't have enough information to use traditional test scripts. Conclusions can therefore not be drawn from this project.

Others say we did learn a lot: About exploratory testing, about pair testing and about managing high-speed web projects, in which documentation is scarce. A situation which sadly occurs more often as time to market is all clients are concerned about. This was also the first time we tried a concept of testing where pair and exploratory techniques were "formalised", and not only a project add-on, an ad-hoc approach to keep the testers busy. And in many ways it gave us more than we bargained for.

As James Bach states, when doing exploratory testing, the testers need to be "trained" beforehand in exploratory testing. Our testers had been on a two-day introduction course prior to the test, which was fortunate. To ensure good coverage, we also did do a more or less formal functionality test on the first day. This not only gave the testers an even better understanding of the software, it also gave them an indication of where faults could be hidden in the system. This was important, as exploratory testing is all about using what you know. One problem that did occur is that when many faults were found in a small part of the software, all the pairs started exploring that part. We therefore needed to direct the pairs in different directions to improve the coverage of the test, since they were not trained in exploratory testing. An aspect that perhaps should be taken into consideration already in the planning-phase.

Many questions were raised by colleagues as to how we kept such an unstructured test session under control. How did we make sure the deviation reports were filled out when a "bug" was discovered? How did we know whether the testers did stick to the test plan? How did we make sure they were productive at all? Did we walk around the room constantly? We didn't walk around the room, we "ran" between three different rooms (as we had Windows 95, 2000 and NT in separate rooms). The hard thing wasn't to get the testers to test, but to keep them away from testing things outside the test plan. As we flew between the rooms, we got a fair picture of what the testers were doing (there were only 14 of them, so it wasn't that exhausting). As soon as we saw one group working on areas not in the plan or with faults already reported by others, we simply gave them small hints, like "Have you tried this..." or "What happens if you do that..." This was all we had to do in order to keep everybody "on track". Whilst working in pairs, one of the testers always sat with a pen and a deviation report. This was a simple form, which was easy to fill out, but good enough to reproduce the bugs. In each break (between the 90-minute sessions) we read through all of the reports, together with the project manager if possible, to make sure we understood the writing, and that we had enough information to reproduce the bugs. In addition, we always talked to everyone during each break and gathered everybody in one room three times a day for a short briefing.

We were probably lucky with the pairs. Usually, one should know the testers in advance, and possess a little bit of "human knowledge" to get the pairs right. We didn't have time for this, so we teamed them up according to profession (not two developers in one pair), nationality (to improve communication) and their own wishes. This worked fairly well. But we also had experiences where pairs had to be altered after two days. This was easy and quick, and everything seemed to work fine afterwards. This might be a sensible approach; you often have to "try out" the testers before you find pairs that are effective and co-operative.

One of the challenges with exploratory pair testing was to ensure feature coverage during test execution. The follow-up of the pairs required extensive resources and hands-on management from the test managers. More suitable test management tools and techniques could possibly overcome this. Few tools we have seen support this kind of test planning and execution, but an exciting technique called "session-based test management" is now being developed as a way of measuring coverage and improving the effectiveness of management without destroying the creativity [BACH01].

We did find a lot of deviations and bugs during the bug hunting, but many of them were also duplicates. We sent the testers off on a wild chase across the entire system, and many pairs found the same bugs. Next time we'll tell each pair to concentrate on one particular section. After a while, we'll then switch pairs and sections.

6   Warning!

There is a time for exploratory testing and there is a time for scripting. It is a challenge to balance the two.

We are not saying that exploratory testing can be used for any type of testing of all kinds of software systems. However, it appears to us after looking into exploratory testing (and pair testing) in more detail, that exploratory testing has nearly always been an important part of projects in which we were involved – but it has not been called exploratory testing.

We think it is important to plan for this type of testing in any project. It is better to do "planned ad-hoc testing" instead of ad-hoc testing without any planning, unless you have testers with the planning skills to do it well.

7   Acknowledgements

We would especially like to thank James Bach and Cem Kaner for valuable input on Exploratory Testing and Pair Testing, and James Bach in particular for reviewing and discussing the article. We would also like to thank Johnny Heggestad, the project manager who initiated the test project. Another contributor was Harald Lind. His experience and recommendations improved the execution of this test project. And last but not least; Synnøve Brendryen's effort as co-test manager made all the difference. Without her this project would never have been a success.

Using QA for Risk Management in Web Projects

Steve Willis
Barclaycard (UK)

Abstract: Every company seems to want to have a presence on the Internet. Most companies expect to increase their speed to market and to capture an increased share of customers and profits. This rush to the Web has created huge competitive pressures and is generating a marked change in the attitudes of some customers. Customers want an instant buzz. They want what they want, when and how they want it. If they don't get instant satisfaction they are off in an instant to spend their time and money with another company.

Risks that were once of limited concern now assume new and greater importance. Poor service in the only shoe shop in town had to be borne but now the Internet means that every shoe shop is in town and every salesperson is in every web-enabled household. To the avid web surfer the only queue that exists is the one where they're at the front because they no longer wait to be served. Web developments and e-business in general have to identify and assess these risks. This assessment and management thereof must be performed during development because word of any inadequacies is published world-wide, and to be found wanting in the Internet age is the death-knell of any business. One does not have to search too hard to uncover inadequacies. There have been a number of publicised instances of personal credit card information being unintentionally disclosed to all and sundry via various websites.

QA and testing can and should be used as a risk management technique during e-commerce projects. QA and testing can be defined during the identification and assessment of risks and will usually uncover new ones. The definition and assessment of risks must be an integral part of all e-commerce projects throughout the development life cycle. Testing and QA apply the due diligence that will discover many of the gaps in risk management and provide evidence that web applications are fit-for-purpose. This article provides an insight into how QA and testing can be used as a risk management technique in e-commerce projects.

Keywords: Internet testing, Web-based applications

1 Increased Visibility of Application Failure

In the not too distant past when computers were things of mystique hidden in air-conditioned rooms away from the gaze of the masses, the public face of companies were the sales people and switchboard operators. Systems were discreet in as much as members of the public rarely interfaced directly with an application and errors or non-availability of functions were hidden behind manual workarounds or the tendering of apologetic statements of, "I'm terribly sorry. It's the computer!"

The advent of e-commerce has increased the direct visibility of application functionality in the living rooms, bedrooms, telephones and palm-tops of the customer. Customers can be other businesses, internal users or individual end-consumers. Mistakes can no longer be easily hidden or glossed over with excuses and the adverse impact materialises in terms of time, cost and reputational damage to the business.

Globalisation of whole industries has been aided by the drive towards e-business. Profits in many sectors have been squeezed by the advent of many new aggressive players or have become regulated by governments seeking to create greater competitiveness and better value for money for consumers. Consequently, the pressure has grown upon businesses to improve the quality and immediacy of products and services. The pressure is upon business to deliver new products and services to the market place faster than their rivals. It is, therefore, no coincidence that the acceptable times for software deliveries are now expected to be weeks rather than the months and years of the recent past.

However, regardless of the impact of Internet technology it remains fundamentally true that the customer is still King and for that reason it is imperative that the customer experience is considered during the planning and execution of testing for e-commerce projects. (For the purposes of this article the 'customer experience' equates to the on-line activity in which the customer indulges and the error handling or contingency processes to which a customer is subjected when systems fail to work as expected.) A creativity technique that can be adapted to help the test manager understand the customer experience and the risks encountered is examined in this article.

2   Risk and Management Thereof

Testing always has been a viable risk management technique and it continues to be so when applied to minimising the business and delivery risks attached to e-commerce projects. To ensure success it is helpful to adopt some quite simplistic governing principles:

1. Risks are things that **may** happen.
2. Risk management is something that **should** happen.
3. Risks & risk management functions are a basis for a number of valid test requirements.
4. Understand that 'failure' is an opportunity to learn and improve.
5. Risk management is akin to first aid: It stops something getting worse and helps to stabilise the patient (incident) in readiness for recovery. Finally, it seeks to stop the accident (incident) from occurring again.

If testing is to be used to minimise the risks to business functionality and project delivery it is helpful to follow some iterative steps in order that the potential risks can be identified and understood. The steps are summarised as:

1. Identify the risks – what it is, the cause of the risk, where it is most likely to be found and the symptoms that it displays.
2. Quantify the risk – the probability of its occurrence and the impact upon the business or project.
3. Manage the risk – action that needs to be taken to prevent or minimise the risk and impact.
4. Communicate the risk – ensure that probability and impact are understood to gain commitment to the proposed risk management approach. It also enables assumptions to be tested and fed back into the test planning process.
5. Monitor the risk – to ensure proactive control.

2.1 Identify the Risks

Identifying and understanding risks will help to shape decisions about the types and priorities of testing that will be used to ensure that the overall business and project delivery risks are overcome.

In an ideal world the test manager will have been involved from the earliest possible point in the project life cycle. In e-commerce projects this may prove to happen more frequently than in traditional developments but equally the test manager will have a much reduced time frame within which to identify risks and the testing that can be used to minimise their impact. Previous development experience will offer an almost immediate list of key risks: inadequate requirements, lack of skills or resources, insufficient test data, late delivery of hardware and software components, poor performance.

It is, however, worth taking a little time to understand and consider the potential risks from the customer perspective by adapting a creativity technique that is sometimes known as Problem Perfect. Full details of this technique can be found in [CLEG99].

2.2 Problem Perfect

The Problem Perfect technique can be performed by an individual but better results are obtained by involving a 'cross section' of people. Try to imagine yourself as the end customer or user of the e-commerce product or service that the project is intending to deliver. Consider the processes that will also be used to support the e-enablement.

On a flip-chart or A4 paper sketch out the 'Nightmare Scenario' of all of the things that could possibly go wrong during the customer experience. The 'Nightmare Scenario' can be drawn as pictures or words or as a mixture of both. The key thing is that all of the problems and risks captured by this process are treated as being equally valid.

The next stage after the 'Nightmare Scenario' has been completed is to list out as bullet points all of the problems and associated risks in order that they can be quantified and prioritised.

In addition there are many other means of identifying risks, e.g. metrics from similar projects, current project data such as the rate and completeness of planned testing, slippage of project milestones, or the 'top 10' production issues from the IT or business support teams. Do not confine yourself to considering only 'in-house' data. Consideration of data from external bodies is also a reasonable source of information that can highlight reasons for poor defect removal and other significant risks. It is also a good idea to walk through the transaction process. By 'becoming' input data and travelling through the application the contingency that is needed to manage failures can be planned. Appropriate tests can be incorporated into the test plan.

Whichever method is used it is important to identify the cause of the risk. If the cause can be isolated by testing or inspection this will save far more time and money than simply finding and confirming the symptoms.

2.3 Quantify the Risks

Identifying risks means that you can end up with a list that is longer than your arm and you are unlikely to have the time or resources to actively manage every risk. It is necessary to quantify and prioritise the risks in order that you can focus upon actively managing those that are most appropriate. Risks may be quantified by asking a series of questions for example:

- If the risk materialises what will it cost in terms of (1) lost opportunity, (2) reputational loss, (3) time delay, (4) customer confidence, (5) criminal/malicious infiltration, (6) breach of regulation or statute, (7) higher costs/lower profitability?
- How probable is it that the risk will arise?
- How acceptable is the adverse impact of the risk if it materialises?
- How quickly can the business recover from the risk?

This is not an exclusive list but it does give a flavour of the type of issues that need to be considered when quantifying risks. When the risks have been quantified they should be mapped into a grid that has two axes: (1) Impact, (2) Likelihood. This enables the risks to be prioritised through a range of severities from Major down to Minor.

2.4 Manage the Risks

After the identified risks have been quantified and the severities assigned to each, known actions are assigned to minimise the likelihood of occurrence and the impact of the risks. The assessment and risk management activity priorities should be used to assist the design and prioritisation of testing. Appropriate testing will help to prove those elements of an application and supporting processes where either a major risk has been identified or a risk management activity has been incorporated to reduce the probability of an adverse impact occurring.

2.5 Communicate the Risks

It is essential that the risk management assessment and control activity is communicated to all relevant project and business staff in order that they can understand and question the outcomes. It also provides a further opportunity to test the assumptions made during the process. Feedback should be encouraged and input to test planning where relevant.

2.6 Monitor the Risks

The risks and planned management activity need to be regularly monitored. Threatened manifestation of incidents arising from risks will need to be escalated to the appropriate control points to ensure that remedial or controlling action is taken. New risks will be identified and require active management some of which may require amendments to planned testing. Testing may in turn also identify risks that had not previously been considered.

2.7 Examples of Risks

The range of risks that can be identified can be appear to be quite daunting until such time as assessment and prioritisation have been completed. This section lists a range of potential risks that might be identified and that can all be minimised by carefully planned testing of application software, hardware and processes. This is not an exclusive list but it does offer a reasonable starting point for anyone wishing to use testing as a risk management technique in e-commerce projects. Each example lists 'risk cause' and the 'symptoms' that can be generated.

1. Poor communication: Unavailability of appropriate resource and environment. Crisis management. Loss of confidence in the project and its delivered outcomes.

2. Inadequate server capacity: Symptom poor performance/response. Transactions abandoned or time-out. Loss of existing customer base.
3. Over-complex site design: Difficult to navigate across the site. Transactions abandoned. Few repeat user hits. Loss of existing customer base.
4. Site content breaches regulations/statutes: Complaints by regulator, customers, and competitors. Fines or rework costs incurred.
5. Inadequate security: Loss or malicious amendment of data. Unauthorised publication of personal data. Loss of market reputation and consumer confidence.
6. Inadequate audit trail: Fraud. Attract unfavourable regulatory interest. Loss of reputation and consumer confidence.
7. Inefficient code: Poor performance. Higher transaction costs.
8. Unreliable data: Data mismatches preventing customer transaction e.g. registration, purchase, information requests. Multiple or nil information being dispatched to the customer e.g. multiple investment statements to the same address, information sent to the wrong address or recipient.
9. No business recovery process/facility: The company is unable to transact during a major systems failure or cannot recover quickly from it. Lost customer transactions. Regulatory/statutory penalties incurred. Loss of reputation and consumer confidence.

2.8 Additional Factors that Impact upon Risk

There are also a number of very specific 'project management 'factors that will create additional pressures that will increase the potential for these risks to occur. These factors include:

*   Speed to market: Internet development projects are usually time-boxed to deliver within 3 to 12 weeks. This means that very often requirements are developing in parallel with coding and the final delivery may not be fully scoped.

*   Pioneering experimentation: The technology may be new to the development organisation and consequently the requisite skills, experience and development infrastructure may not be fully in place.

*   Cultural naivety: In organisations where there is limited experience of Internet technology the commitment to e-commerce may not be matched by the proactive culture and processes that are essential to ensuring speedy delivery and ongoing development. This may take the form of slow authorisation to proceed at key points, unnecessary bureaucracy, unavailability of key staff and an unwillingness to learn from failure. It will be difficult for such organisations to move from the concept of development Phase 1 (12 months) followed by Phase 2 (24 months) to a mood of Delivery 1 (4 weeks), Delivery 2 (6 weeks), ... Delivery 15 (8 weeks).

Each of the nine examples of risks (listed above) is probably familiar to most businesses across the world. The opportunity for each of them to arise can be minimised by using planned software and hardware testing. The next section will illustrate how well-planned testing can be used as a risk management technique in e-commerce projects.

3   QA as a Risk Management Technique

QA and test managers are familiar with the 'Testing V' where the work on requirements and functionality carried out during analysis and design find their 'alter ego' in user acceptance testing and system and integration testing. It is reasonable to treat the risks and risk management functions identified during the risk assessment process as subsets of the business and functional requirements for the project. QA and testing should be planned against the risks and risk management identified. The probability and impact of each risk must be factored into the prioritisation and dependency of the planned tests.

3.1   Simple Prioritisation of QA and Testing against Risk

Although the priorities of risks themselves seem to be very much project-dependent the structure of a simple test prioritisation for a typical e-commerce project might be similar to the one following. This example prioritisation summary was successfully applied during the development of an online financial portfolio management application:

Priority 1: Screen navigation.
- All screens are navigable from end to end, forward and back.
- All field tabbing works as intended.
- Intended levels of access security proven.

Priority 2: Accuracy of displays.
- All calculations are correct.
- All fields offer full display without truncation of results.
- All date processing is accurate.
- Numeric, alphabetic and alphanumeric fields have full validation including checks for special characters and appropriate error handling.
- Protected fields demonstrate protection/security/confidentiality.
- Zero spelling errors.

Priority 3: Performance.

- Scroll speed meets requirements.
- Table look-up speed meets requirements.
- Screen navigation speed meets requirements.
- Links and data transfer meet volume and speed requirements.

Priority 4: Support process.

- All help screens fulfil requirements.
- Call centre processes and service levels in place and proven.
- Problem and audit support procedures in place and proven.
- Business/disaster recovery in place and tested.

This simple prioritisation can be used to guide the construction of test plans and strategies. The speed of Internet developments will invariably reduce the time available to produce such documents and it may not be possible to produce test plans and strategies to the depth that many testers would like. In a situation where testing is being planned alongside development it is conceivable that the prioritised list set out above may be the only formal guidance available to testers. Even in this scenario the prioritised list will pick up the risks identified in this article:

TEST PRIORITIES=>	Priority 1 Screen Navigation	Priority 2 Accuracy of Displays	Priority 3 Performance	Priority 4 Support Process
RISKS:				
Poor Communication		☺		☺
Inadequate Server Capacity	☺		☺	
Over-complex Design	☺		☺	☺
Content Breaches Regulations		☺		
Inadequate Security	☺	☺		☺
Inadequate Audit Trail	☺	☺		☺
Inefficient Code	☺		☺	
Unreliable Data		☺		☺
No business Recovery				☺

The priorities used in the example follow a very simple rationale. Risks associated with screen navigation were set at priority 1 on the basis that if the website cannot be navigated customers are unable to use the site. Its functionality will not be accessible and it therefore fails to meet its business requirement.

Risks that impact the accuracy of display were set at priority 2 because if the customer is provided with incorrect information this means that:

- Customers will make decisions based upon incorrect data that may lead to legal proceedings against the website owner.
- Damage of reputation and consequent loss of customers will ensue.
- Regulatory authorities may close the website leading to a loss of business.

On the basis that navigation and data accuracy are assured the next most likely risk to the success of the website is poor performance. In the case of one website around 6% of visitors left within one minute and 15% left within two minutes. If poor performance proved to be the principle cause of such brief visits it is a simple step to imagine the lost business opportunity that results. Performance was therefore allocated a priority-3 rating in comparison to navigation and accuracy.

Finally, priority 4 was allocated to risks that adversely impact the support processes. Failure of support processes, e.g. customer call centre, help-line, e-mail etc., is likely to result in a loss of customer retention. If these processes are not up to standard they can also result in an inability to successfully respond to complaints and cause damage to business reputation.

It is worth clarifying the use of the terms 'severity' and 'priority'. When used in relation to an assessment of defects the term severity relates to the impact that the defect has upon the application/website. A defect that brings either development work or the live website to a halt will have a higher severity rating than one that either prevents a part of the application/website from functioning or can be circumvented by a work-around. Alternatively, a defect that does not adversely affect the working of any part of the application or website will have a lower severity than those mentioned previously.

Priority may, but does not necessarily, relate to the impact of a defect or risk. The priority is the stated order of precedence in which work relating to a defect, risk or other activity will be performed. In setting a priority one will assess a combination of factors including:

- The impact upon the customer, business activity and reputation.
- The overall piece of work or functionality.
- The dependency and timing of related pieces of work or functionality.
- Costs and benefits.
- Probability and impact of the consequences of not performing remedial activity.

In consequence it is possible that even where a defect or risk has been allocated a severity, it may not gain a high enough priority for remedial work to be undertaken.

The risk assessment and simple test prioritisation, along with any known/agreed requirements for the project, should be considered during the preparation of the test strategy and supporting plans.

3.2 The Role of the QA and Test Strategy

Even within the short duration of e-commerce projects there is a role for the QA and test strategy. It provides the high-level direction that ensures that those risks that are to be managed by QA and testing will be included in the planning process. For e-commerce projects the QA and test strategy will probably be fairly simplistic and limited to a few pages providing summary information about the following:

- Test objectives and success criteria.
- The test environment.
- High-level approach, test priorities, key responsibilities and assumptions.
- Defect management and escalation thereof.
- A bibliography of related project documents e.g. Scope, Feasibility, Requirements, and Plan.

This information is essential to successfully managing testing for any project. It ensures that the detailed test planning is designed to address clear objectives and that responsibilities, timing and dependencies are clearly understood by the whole project team.

The test objectives and success criteria can include reference to the management of specific risks. Identified risks may also be picked up within broader test objectives and criteria, e.g. the outcome of testing on the development project must:

- Meet defined and agreed business requirements (including control of known risks).
- Successfully run 100 % of all planned tests.
- Implement without any outstanding defects at level 1, 2, 3.

The test environment section will define the specific test environment. The process of producing this definition may also identify new risks and dependencies that will need to be managed. The environment definition will cover information such as unit test environment components as well as elements of the system, integration and user acceptance test environment including data and external/internal interfaces. It should also specify test capacity requirements and force consideration of the post-implementation growth forecasts initially specified in the requirements. (This may turn out to be the first point at which anyone has considered production capacity. In which case, this is probably the last chance to do so and to manage the risks of poor system performance.)

Creating and communicating the statement of high-level approach, test priorities, key responsibilities and assumptions is an excellent way of ensuring that everybody associated with the project, including the 'customer', is aware of the risks that have been identified and the way in which testing will be used to help manage those risks. It also ensures that commitment to the approach and the timely provision of resources is tested and confirmed.

In e-commerce developments efficient defect management and escalation thereof is an essential aid to risk management. A clear statement of defect categories incorporating target times to fix will ensure that:

- Progress with testing is monitored and can be proactively managed and reported.
- Focus is maintained upon doing the important things first.
- Risks and the development's ability to manage them are always visible.

An example of defect severity categories used on an e-commerce project is shown below:

Severity 1:   Total loss. Target time to fix = within 1 hour of occurrence.
Characteristics: Total loss of access to system.
Security breach.
Regulatory requirements breached.

Severity 2:   Serious defect. Target time to fix = half working day.
Characteristics: Partial loss of access to system.
Inaccurate data.
Incorrect functionality.
Performance outside of target service levels.

Severity 3:   Moderate defect.Target time to fix = one working day.
Characteristics: minor errors but system still operates
Screen layout incorrect.
Field sizes inappropriate.

Severity 4:   Cosmetic defect. Target time to fix = 3 working days.
Characteristics: Not affecting the functional operation of system
Incorrect shade of screen colour.
Spelling errors.
Help text incorrect.

Simple escalation rules (set out below) were applied to ensure that target times to fix were met which in turn helped to reduce the risk of the project being delayed during bug fixing.

Escalation: Defect definition agreed by project analyst and lead business user. Defect referred to Project Manager at the expiry of the target time to fix, who can authorise:

1. Closure of defect.
2. Escalation to a higher category of defect.
3. Retention of defect open at the currently assigned category.

Publishing the bibliography of project information ensures that everybody knows where to find relevant, up-to-date information and reduces the risk of delay caused by not being able to do so.

Armed with the test strategy, risk assessment and other requirement-related information, testing is then planned against the known requirements and risks.

3.3 QA and Test Planning Against the Identified Risks

This section provides an overview that the reader can use as a starting point for their own test planning.

Due to project time or resource constraints it may not be possible to produce a comprehensive test plan. In this scenario, prioritising testing against the known risks will improve the project's chances of delivering an application with acceptable test coverage and clearly understood, proven levels of functionality and performance. For example, the testing that could be applied to minimise the risks identified earlier in this article are:

RISKS:	QA and testing activity applied to manage risks.
Poor Communication	1. Involve all relevant personnel (this usually extends beyond the recognised project team). 2. Test accuracy and clarity of displays. Record defects on project test log. 3. Walkthrough (role play if appropriate) support processes including manual workarounds and other contingencies. Record defects on project test log. 4. Record and publish risk assessment, test strategy, test plans & other appropriate project documentation. 5. Record and publish test results including: tests planned vs. tests successfully completed, defects reported, defects fixed and defects outstanding. 6. Record and publish issues, risks and management thereof. 7. Celebrate success and share learning from failure across projects.

RISKS:	QA and testing activity applied to manage risks.
Inadequate Server Capacity	1. Involve all relevant personnel. 2. Check the impact of other planned developments that may be hosted from the same server. 3. Check capacity forecasts (or perform for the first time). Plan against best post-implementation projections. 4. Confirm capacity availability and time-scales. 5. Test or simulate capacity scenarios using appropriate automated test tools. This simulation must include transactional loading as well as typical number of concurrent users. Record all defects on project test log. 6. Test, data transfer, reporting and backup and restore scenarios. Record all defects on project test log. 7. Test speed of online navigation with a range of users and transactions. Perform at different times of day/week. Simulate navigation at peak periods of day or system cycle. 8. Ensure that third-party contracts are reviewed and amended to ensure that any new requirements identified are incorporated.
Over-complex Design	1. Involve all relevant personnel. This should include real users representing a range of skill levels from novice through to expert to exercise end-to-end system navigation (include manual process walkthrough where necessary). 2. Employ critical-design reviews if time constraints permit. Focus upon areas of key process and transactional complexity. 3. Utilise code reviews especially for complex or high-value/volume transactional code. 4. All proposed changes to be managed via the project change management process. This may mean that proposed changes are included in future deliveries rather than being immediately incorporated.
Content Breaches Regulations	1. Legal and regulatory expertise needs to be factored into the project and testing from Day 1. 2. Ensure that legal and regulatory expertise is applied to a screen-by-screen walkthrough of all content. This includes help text, guidance notes or illustration. 3. Legal and regulatory expertise must also apply diligent scrutiny to any supporting literature, processes and audit trails. 4. All defects to be recorded on the project test log.
Inadequate Security	1. Ensure appropriate security expertise is available to the project. 2. Examine known security risks that have been experienced in other projects and factor these into testing. 3. Test access-level entry, end-to-end navigation, encryption, invalid inputs, destructive testing, error handling, malicious penetration e.g. virus protection, external and internal access, backup/restore, processes (including reporting alerts and access denial), documentation/administration/input/output controls and business recovery.

RISKS:	QA and testing activity applied to manage risks.		
Inadequate Audit Trail	1.	Ensure appropriate audit expertise is available.	
	2.	Ensure that the input, validation, processing and output of information can be tracked (including at archive and business recovery.)	
	3.	Ensure that audit information cannot be changed or deleted by unauthorised or untracked transaction.	
	4.	Test that any regulatory audit requirements are fulfilled.	
	5.	Ensure that all appropriate audit processes are in place and work.	
Inefficient Code	1.	Apply code reviews. Focus upon the most-used code paths.	
	2.	Utilise code-automated analysis tools if these are available.	
	3.	Record all defects on the project test log.	
Unreliable Data	4.	Build test data to match the business and transaction scenarios set out in the requirements and risk assessment documents.	
	5.	Any manual input during testing should be a mix of valid and invalid data to test validation and error handling.	
	6.	Consider the need for any data cleanup prior to implementation and ensure that process and plans are in place to achieve this.	
No Business Recovery	7.	Ensure that the scope of recovery and support processes is clearly defined and documented.	
	8.	General support processes including day-to-day call centre and IT activities are walked through as part of any testing.	
	9.	Check that incident management and escalation procedures work.	
	10.	Ensure that an up to date business recovery plan is in place and test it. (Check that key business recovery test triggers e.g. major organisational change, major system change, elapsed time period or key personnel changes, are clearly understood and in place.)	

The risks identified in this section could generally be applied to most client-server projects or to those that use web technology. There are several other points to be considered from an e-commerce perspective:

- Encouraging visitor traffic to websites.
- Website "stickiness" i.e. keeping visitors at the site.
- Conversion rates.
- Management information statistics (MIS).

The rationale for selecting these four points is that:

- Insufficient traffic to the best website in the world means the business that relies upon its success will fail.

- Inability to keep visitors throughout the customer journey reduces profitability because they do not reach the stage at which browsing can be converted into a profitable 'sales' transaction.

- If there is inadequate or inappropriate management information about the way in which the website is used it is unlikely that decisions taken about its future development or use will optimise profitability, lower costs, or increase customer retention.

It is inadequate to only consider these factors during the test phases of the project. Consideration must begin early in the development life cycle and should iterate throughout testing and post-implementation. Knowledge obtained needs to feed back into plans for the ongoing maintenance and future development of the website and associated business activities.

The table below indicates where that consideration and QA or testing thereof should occur:

Relevant Life Cycle Phase Activity	Analysis	Design	Unit & Link	System & Integration	User Acceptance	Post Implementation (&/or Pilot)
Area of Risk	Research & Predict		Test and Improve		Review & Plan Improvements	
Traffic	☺	☺	☺	☺	☺	☺
Stickiness	☺	☺		☺	☺	☺
Conversion	☺	☺		☺	☺	☺
MIS	☺	☺	☺	☺	☺	☺

It is acknowledged that a web project will overlap phases and be time and/or cost boxed but it remains absolutely critical that such business requirements, as are available, relating to site traffic, stickiness, conversion capability and management information are incorporated. One way of ensuring that this occurs is by including project success and business benefit criteria that incorporate these requirements so that they are measured and reported as part of any post-implementation benefit capture.

If insufficient attention is paid to these areas of risk then the following symptoms and causes may become apparent with any e-commerce proposition. Suitable QA/test remedial action is also noted.

Possible Symptoms	Potential Causes	QA/Test Remedy
<ul><li>Low volumes of traffic to the website.</li><li>Complaints to Call Centre.</li><li>High transaction failure rates reported in MIS.</li></ul>	<ul><li>Website not publicised</li><li>Target audience web browsers architecture does not support the website.</li></ul>	<ul><li>Marketing requirements must be identified during analysis.</li><li>Test that banners, cookies or other links work as expected.</li><li>Technical research to feed into analysis & design.</li><li>Test across a variety of identified browsers.</li></ul>
<ul><li>Visitors don't complete visit (reported in MIS).</li><li>Complaints to call centre.</li><li>Visitors don't return.</li><li>Visitors warn others against visiting the site.</li></ul>	<ul><li>Technical error forced transaction to end.</li></ul>	<ul><li>Review architecture during design.</li><li>Test during system & integration testing.</li><li>Test MIS processes to ensure that such errors are captured, reported and analysed.</li></ul>
<ul><li>Visitors don't return to site.</li><li>Complaints to call centre.</li><li>Visitors abandon transactions (reported in MIS).</li><li>Variation of actual vs. target business volumes.</li></ul>	<ul><li>Functionality does not match customer expectation.</li><li>Look & feel of the site did not match visitor expectation. Website doesn't supply the information/ transaction expected.</li><li>Poor navigation routes prevent visitors from quickly finding the relevant information or transaction.</li></ul>	<ul><li>Review Requirements & Design.</li><li>Test during system & integration and user acceptance testing.</li><li>Consider use of a pilot implementation to minimise initial exposure.</li><li>Use a range of 'testers' from novice to experienced including real customers.</li></ul>
<ul><li>Visitors don't return to site.</li><li>Complaints to call centre.</li><li>Visitors abandon transactions (reported in MIS).</li><li>Variation of actual vs. target business volumes.</li></ul>	<ul><li>Pricing information is incorrect.</li><li>Terms of transaction are unacceptable to the customer. Method of transaction is unacceptable, e.g. the customer does not wish to disclose credit card or bank details online.</li></ul>	<ul><li>QA during analysis and design.</li><li>Ensure test data is correctly constructed to simulate pricing scenario.</li><li>Define, instigate and test audit and monitoring processes.</li><li>Ensure that appropriate market research has been incorporated during analysis & design.</li></ul>

Possible Symptoms	Potential Causes	QA/Test Remedy
▪ Business decisions are taken without any reference being made to MIS. ▪ Incorrect business decisions are taken based upon MIS. ▪ Nobody knows that there is any MIS. ▪ People only get MIS if they happen to ask for it.	▪ MIS is sent to the wrong people. ▪ Presenting incorrect data or incomplete information. ▪ Data presentation is too complex. ▪ MIS is not provided in a timely fashion. ▪ Skills/experience are not in place to interpret the MIS. ▪ MIS is not being collected, reported or analysed.	▪ Incorporate MIS into the success criteria for any business case. ▪ Ensure that MIS requirements, skills and supporting processes are defined during analysis & design. ▪ Test MIS processes during development. ▪ Apply MIS to the development website and act upon it during the project e.g. Examine the MIS relating to object presentation to ensure objects are efficiently presented to the customer with key objects presented first.

Failure to manage the risks arising from each cause can have an adverse business impact across profit targets, cost reduction, customer retention, market share and brand reputation. Each of the symptoms or causes listed above have been experienced on real life e-commerce projects. All are predictable and to some extent avoidable if time is set aside to understand the risk scenario and plan QA and testing against it.

An important aid to QA and testing is the use of automated test tools. These are particularly useful for:

- The creation of re-usable test scripts to save in excess of 20% of traditional testing effort. It also enables testing to simulate larger numbers of users simultaneously inputting a range of complex, high-value or high-volume transactions without requiring the physical presence of many testers.
- Script capture/replay to recreate error/defect scenarios. This is particularly useful to capture the activities of user testers who may have difficulty in expressing the precise sequence of events leading up to an error.
- Load simulation and stress testing. Simulation of the loading and presentation of objects an offer an early insight into the customer perspective of the website. It also offers the opportunity to simulate peaks of usage.

Automated test tools should be used with care. They do not provide the answer to everything and they need to be applied where they are likely to be most effective.

This is not a comprehensive list of all of the potential risks that an e-commerce project or business may face. However, is should now be clear that QA and testing can be used as part of the broader risk management portfolio on e-commerce projects. It will not eliminate all risks or defects but it will provide the opportunity to minimise the frequency with which major business risks can strike in the e-business world.

4 Summary

This article has shown that much of the QA and testing knowledge or techniques employed to test client-server technology can be used to manage risk on e-commerce projects. However, the immediacy of experience that e-commerce confers does change the emphasis and nature of risks. For instance; poor performance that could remain hidden away from user view under batch processing or that could be exposed to a controlled audience in traditional client-server applications, can suddenly have an unlimited audience and increased potential for damage on the World Wide Web.

It should now be clear that using a careful assessment of potential risks and the identification of activities for the management thereof would produce specific requirements for QA and testing on e-commerce projects. QA and testing should not just be confined to the code, data and transactional capabilities of the web application. It must also be applied to the business requirements, supporting processes and business models that are to be used.

It will not be possible to QA and test in mitigation of all risks. Prioritisation of identified and assessed risks must be used to provide focus for the application of QA and testing to ensure that appropriate effective test coverage is achieved.

Establishing Quality Procedures for Incremental Software Development

ANDREAS KRAMP
Dresdner Bank AG (Germany)

CO-AUTHORS: TESSA DÖRING, STEPHAN FRIEDRICH
Dresdner Bank AG (Germany)

Abstract: With its 'oskar' project (online strategic position keeping and reporting), Dresdner Bank has created an accounting platform that is capable of handling multiple clients, and can thus be marketed to third parties outside the Dresdner Bank Group. Conceived along the lines of an industrial production process, *oskar* was created as an 'information factory'. In order to meet the bank's time-to-market targets, as set out in its e-business strategy, this Java-based proprietary development required a new approach in terms of quality management. The *oskar* project opted for an integration of quality management into the project structure from the very start. In addition to being involved in organising the framework for the development project – by shaping the model approach and development architecture – this also included the establishment of an acceptance procedure designed to expose any weaknesses in the results of individual project phases at an early stage, thus furthering a continuous improvement process. Transparency of objectives and approach within the scope of the acceptance procedure as well as active co-operation by quality management staff in the individual teams were major success factors for establishing such a process. The introduction of integrated quality management drives the transformation from a 'pure', product-oriented acceptance approach adopted in traditional software development procedures towards active process integration.

Keywords: Quality management, software development, software acceptance

1 Introduction

Dresdner Bank AG was faced with the challenge of replacing a 30-year-old accounting system. Its old accounting platform was a proprietary, Cobol-based development that had been subject to constant amendments over the past 30 years. Replacing an accounting system – the very core of a bank – could only be carried out in one fell swoop. Within the framework of its e-commerce strategy, Dresdner Bank decided to develop this core operative system from scratch, with the objective of creating a state-of-the-art, real-time accounting system for major banks, as a scalable insourcing platform designed to handle multiple clients. A further requirement was a high level of flexibility and the capability to adapt to the introduction of new processes – a crucial ingredient for short time-to-market periods. This task was put into practice within the scope of the *oskar* project (online strategic position keeping and reporting). The product was developed in the style of an 'information factory': processing cash transaction data as a commodity – just like in an industrial production process. Using modular assembly lines, production is highly automated and standardised. The outputs are cost-efficient real-time entry facilities and the provision of near-time transaction information, resembling a platform strategy for both purchasers and suppliers [WARG01]. Dresdner Bank integrated quality management into the process flow for the realisation of this major project. Having been established as a sub-project within the *oskar* project structure, the quality management team was assigned the task of defining quality objectives in co-operation with project managers, establishing quality assurance measures and supporting the individual sub-projects in achieving the quality targets. One of quality management's targets within the scope of the overall project is to establish an acceptance procedure which ensures that quality is 'built' into the process flow already during the development process.

To allow early client access to the product, the project decided to split the construction process for *oskar* into a series of independent releases. Following the iterative, incremental software development approach, each release was in turn sub-divided into numerous iterations. The first chapter of this article outlines the prerequisites of the project to set up the process of software development. Integration of the role of quality management in the process flow has been a major aspect. Based on the experience of drawing up the first increment, quality management initiated procedural changes and adjustments to the acceptance process, which are detailed in the subsequent chapters.

2 Establishing a QM Procedure

In order to set up QM procedures in a major project, various prerequisites must be dealt with. Suitable approaches and methods for *oskar* were chosen from a selection of model approaches and software architectural models; "blending the best", these were then integrated in the project in the form of guidelines. Active co-operation of the quality management team has been required to develop and co-ordinate the contents of these guidelines and standards. At the same time, this has permitted the QM team to generate ideas for subsequent acceptance procedures and to create frameworks to ensure that quality management is properly integrated in the process flow. The most important requirements which have to be met during the development process prior to defining and establishing an acceptance procedure are specified in this document. Furthermore, the role of quality management in defining the process is explained.

2.1 Defining the Phases of the Development Procedure

2.1.1 Analytical and Design Phase

The analytical and design phase of *oskar* was performed on a UML (unified modelling language) basis aided by the Rational Rose tool. A procedural guideline planning analysis was set up for this phase, with the objective of providing support to the analysts in developing the target concept. The individual result types of this phase have been detailed in these procedural guidelines. Furthermore, examples and templates were used to indicate ways of achieving individual project results. These guidelines were complemented by naming conventions and guidelines for the use of the Rational Rose tool and the project's own repository. In addition, the necessary requirements for the start of the phases were described and the *oskar* approach differentiated to the theoretical approach.

2.1.2 Implementation Phase

An incremental, iterative software development procedure was chosen for the implementation of *oskar*. Each increment represents an independent product that can be installed on its own. Programming took place in Java, using the 'Visual Age for Java' (VAJ) development environment. Development testing was carried out using the 'JUnit' tool. The software was developed for a mainframe target environment (IBM OS/390 using a CICS transaction monitor and DB2 relational database). An implementation guideline describing the general approach for the development test was established for this phase. These guidelines include Java programming conventions, guidelines for program documentation and guidelines for the use of the repository incorporated in VAJ.

2.1.3 Test Phase

Due to the testing approach adopted by the bank, the *oskar* test phase was split into three stages: functional testing, application testing and connectivity/integration testing. Test manuals containing existing extensive procedural descriptions were prepared for all stages. The functional testing phase was supported by tools and a process model developed by SQS AG, with the specific parameters for *oskar* set out in a testing guideline.

2.2 Definition of Quality Management Integrated in the Process Flow

As a significant condition for establishing a project-integrated QM process, the role of quality management within the project was also defined from the outset. Within the scope of the overall *oskar* project, the roles of the quality management project are to establish quality assurance measures and to provide the necessary support for these measures. It is important to note that the quality management project does not assume the role of a 'project policeman', but rather of an authority on quality planning, quality control and quality checking. The *oskar* quality management system was documented in a QA guideline. This outlines a comprehensive set of objectives in terms of both procedural and product quality and sets the scene for the execution of integrated quality assurance, including a description of methods to carry out constructive and analytical quality assurance measures.

The *oskar* QM team combines staff with technological and methodical expertise from software development and with a banking background. They form a team which is integrated in the project structure as a cross-sectional activity. In addition to active process support and acceptance of results, its tasks include coaching the project teams and conducting reviews.

The role of quality management in the individual project stages comprises the selection and determination of result types. In co-operation with those assuming responsibility for the respective products at a later stage, the first results from each stage were used by quality management to evaluate whether the result types were useful for auditing within the bank or for external auditing purposes. This inspection has had an impact on the degree of detail used for the descriptions contained in procedural guidelines for the analytical and design phase. Workshops supported by project-related examples were organised and conducted by quality management, and have lead to a uniform understanding of and approach towards the project during this phase. Integrated quality management tasks also include selecting review partners with suitable technical and banking expertise to audit these analytical and design results. Quality management generally incorporates future review partners as early as in the definition of the analytical and design phase to ensure that gaps in the result types are recognised and improved. A further important quality management task comprises the definition of the completion criteria for the individual result types which are described in the procedural guidelines. To ensure close interaction with individual project teams, QM team members also work in other teams, assuming responsibility for the respective results achieved. For instance, the QM team compiled a chapter of the implementation guidelines for the development test. The definition of the implementation phase also focused, for example, on determining the software documentation deemed necessary by quality management. This also involved selecting and customising tools for the static analysis of the programming guidelines stipulated in the implementation guidelines. These examples should illustrate that in laying down the procedural guidelines, the QM team has already focused on establishing an appropriate acceptance procedure.

2.3 Co-operation with Other Project-Integrated Tasks

Co-operation with additional integrated sub-projects is essential for establishing quality management integrated in the process flow. Co-operation with project controlling as well as the standards, architecture and methods project is outlined here.

Permanent interaction with project management and project controlling is important for integrated quality management as a means of gaining acceptance. *oskar* has been conceived in a production process that unites established planning approaches used for major projects. Using a top-down planning approach, release plans are created which are then broken down to project and sub-project levels. Production instalments, which are defined as 'milestones', represent the lowest level of this process. The definitions of these milestones are used as a prerequisite for progress controls, which are also carried out on higher project levels such as sub-projects and projects ('bottom-up approach'). A cross-section of both approaches is used by project controlling for the purpose of operative project management. The completion of one of the milestones within the *oskar* project generally implies successful implementation of established QA measures and internal acceptance by the QM team.

Quality management's role in this procedure is to co-operate with those responsible and with project controlling on the definition of individual projects, sub-projects and production instalments. Support ranges from reviewing project plans to delimiting the milestone definitions and reviewing dependencies which are necessary to reach the individual milestones. Quality management actively contributes to release planning by taking into account compliance with project objectives and by planning expenditures for quality assurance measures for milestones. Further tasks where quality management co-operates with project controlling are the definition of a change management process and determining and evaluating project risks. Close co-operation with project controlling is facilitated by separating the responsibilities: Project controlling is responsible for monitoring and management of project planning and the production process in terms of deadlines, expenditures, budget and resources. Quality management is responsible for the functional acceptance of production instalments, sub-projects and releases in terms of content and for planning and monitoring the quality assurance measures which need to be implemented.

A separate team was set up within the project *oskar* to define the standards, architecture and methods necessary for the project process. The experts of this team draw up a large proportion of the previously mentioned procedural guidelines and help coach project members to implement these internal project rules. This team also closely interacts with quality management. Preliminary experience with the standards and methods created has been gained from assigning staff-coaching duties to the QM team members and the project-integrated review of result types generated from the development process. Experience from these activities has been used by the standards, architecture and methods team to further improve and update the *oskar* model approach. Quality management experts also assumed responsibility for individual results such as creating the change management approach.

3   Experience with Integrated Quality Management

The creation of the requirements outlined for establishing a QM procedure within the *oskar* project was followed by the exciting phase of establishing integrated quality management for the software development process. With the onset of creating the initial iteration and starting the work in the individual phases, the QM team has been able to stay abreast of the current project status by way of project-integrated reviews of work results and by contributing to the definition of result types. The following issues are important in this context:

- Are there gaps or potential for improvement in the project's model approach?
- How are staff coping with the tasks described in the model approach?
- Are the training and coaching measures for the individual sectors adequate?
- How are the individual planning stages harmonised?
- Are the planned quality assurance measures appropriate and can they be implemented successfully?
- Are the result types compiled in terms of uniform depth and scope?
- Can the acceptors of the project result types work with the preliminary versions?

Answering these questions results in a re-assessment of the frameworks, guidelines, result types and planning data initially defined at the start of the project. In addition to the willingness by the project team to conduct such a re-assessment, defining the time point at which this information should be evaluated and analysed is of significant importance. For the *oskar* project, this re-assessment was carried out following the creation of the first increment. The input of these quality management analyses, in conjunction with experience gathered by other project teams, is used to decide on and implement changes and adjustments to the process. A few examples are given below:

- The number and quality of change requests exchanged between the analysis and design team and implementation resulted in a restructuring of the development process. The responsibilities for individual result types were revised and a decision reached on merging the teams into a single development team.
- Permanent revision of analytical and design results resulted in higher expenditures for the test team due to the rework of test items and test cases. Separating

the analytical model based on functional requirements from the technically oriented development model resulted in an improvement of the requirements for functional test case specification. The recruitment of additional banking experts in the development teams also improved the quality of analytical results.

- Creating an expanded cluster test that used the test cases prepared by the test team into consideration was decided and implemented. Consequently, preference was given to functional test activities during the development phase, and as a result the functional features could be tested at an early stage.

- A description of the development process was required to complement established project guidelines, to clearly describe the assignment of responsibilities to individual roles within the development process and to provide an overview of the result types in the individual phases.

4 Acceptance Procedure

From a quality management perspective, it should be possible to review technical feasibility and cost-benefit aspects during initial project phases. Performance, operative security and feasibility in terms of maintenance are important quality features in this context. Therefore, a QM procedure for accepting the results from the software development procedure was defined. The definition time point was fixed prior to the beginning of the second iteration. Experience gained from the first iteration – as described in the previous chapter – represented a significant input for this process. The definition of the acceptance procedure, which is described below, in turn depended on the existence of a complete model approach that had been tested by the project team and documentation of the software development procedure.

4.1 Objective and Content of the Acceptance Process

The objective of the acceptance process is the early verification and acceptance of results from individual tasks of the development process. The focus is on recognising potential for improvement in individual result types and checking interfaces between individual production stages. This acceptance process is not geared towards acceptance of a total product or the release of a software product. They are defined in a separate process which is not the subject of this article.

4.2 Integration in the Software Development Production Process

The workflow to be defined should be integrated in the software development process. Acceptance of result types by quality management must be transparent to everyone involved and responsible. The interaction between quality management's work products and the production process is illustrated in Diagram 1.

Sets of requirements which apply throughout the production process are defined, starting with the planning of individual iterations. The production process comprises the definition of requirements, analysis, design, implementation and testing. A further phase is the connectivity/integration test which, prior to going 'live' in production, is run on one of the bank's simulated production computers. All phases deliver various result types which have been defined and determined in the form of guidelines in the project's model approach. Quality management chose the following results, from the aggregate of result types, as test items:

- **Analytical model**
  Business entity model

- **Application documentation**
  Complete description of functional features required to achieve the milestones.

- **Development model**
  Describes the lower level of classes, methods and attributes which must be implemented.

- **Development documentation**
  Describes the design and aspects relevant to implementation.

- **Java code**
  Java code and procedures; software documentation extracted using Javadoc.

- **Development test**
  Documentation (generated with Javadoc) of test cases and testing using Junit.

- **Description of test cases**
  Description of test cases that are relevant for the functional features.

On the basis of references, these result types are checked by experts within the QM process. The QM team recruits experts from individual development and test teams. Guidelines included in the model approach and templates are made available as reference material. Acceptance protocols for chosen groups of result types are drawn up to represent result types from this acceptance process. The test items are checked for the following features:

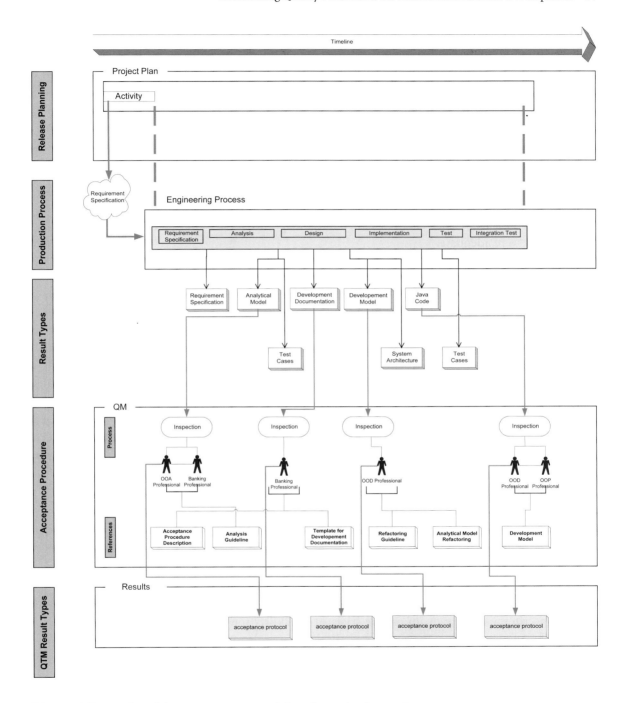

Diagram 1: Integration of the acceptance process into software development

- Compliance with the guidelines and standards for the relevant result type including compliance with the provisions arising from the development process and planned QA measures;
- absence of contradictions within each result type;
- consistency of each result type;
- consistency across result types; and
- expressive and meaningful language (for documents).

Functional correctness, performance and other required QA features are not checked by the QM team but rather by those responsible in the respective development process. However, the QM team does check whether these inspections have been carried out and that they were adequate.

4.3   Sequence of the Acceptance Process

The acceptance process is based on the *oskar* development process, taking the completed, use case-based target analysis as a starting point, in conjunction with the functional project concept developed on that basis. Consistency to other result types is checked by comparing results achieved at a later stage in the development process against the corresponding result types determined in advance. Hence it is necessary that all result types are available at the time of acceptance. Preference can be given to a review and partial acceptance of individual result types as long as the result types necessary for the consistency check are available. The sequence of the acceptance procedure of result types is illustrated in Diagram 2. The defined result types in the individual phases are determined by those responsible within the development process. The results from the development procedure are inspected by quality management staff on the basis of inspection criteria and using defined guidelines and standards. These inspections can lead to acceptance of the result types for this iteration or may call for amendments and renewed acceptance.

4.4   Inspection Criteria for Result Types

Inspection criteria are drawn up on the basis of checklists for the individual result types. Following acceptance, the completed checklists are also used to document the respective individual inspections. The degree of relevance of inspection criteria for acceptance is differentiated according to the criteria ("must have", "important", "nice to have"). The following extracts from the inspection criteria have been included to illustrate on which criteria the quality manager's decision is based:

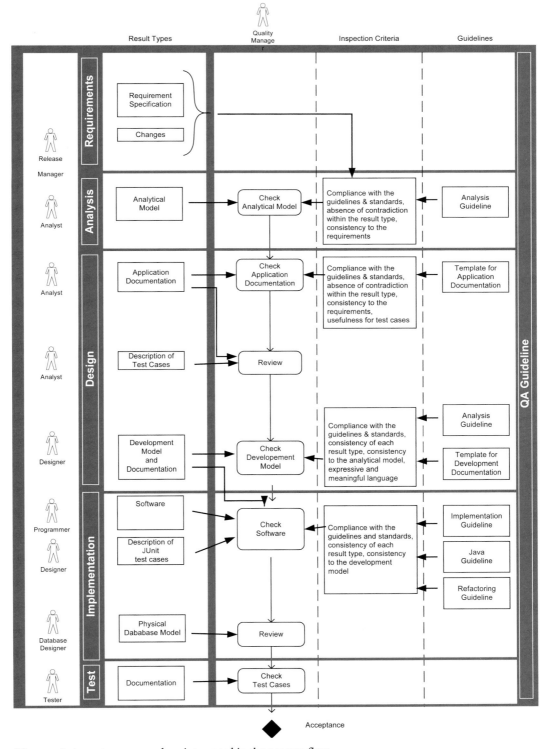

Diagram 2: Acceptance procedure integrated in the process flow

4.4.1   Inspection Criteria for the Development Model

Artefact	Criteria	Fulfilled [YES] [NO]	Acceptance relevance [MUST HAVE] [IMPORTANT] [NICE TO HAVE]	Note
General relationships				
	Are there any multiplicities?		MUST HAVE	
	Were the relationships between the business entities modelled (in line with requirements)?		MUST HAVE	
Classes				
	Have all identified stati been implemented in the affected class (as attributes)?		MUST HAVE	
	Do all methods exist which are required to access <u>relevant</u> attributes?		IMPORTANT	
	Does each class have at least one attribute which is not a key or at least one operation?		NICE TO HAVE	
Attributes				
	Does the attribute describe a class feature? Or is it actually a feature of another class (single best home)?		MUST HAVE	
Methods				
	Does the operation perform exactly one task (multiple tasks, when described, are often linked using 'and')?		IMPORTANT	

4.4.2   Inspection Criteria for the Application Documentation (Excerpt)

Artefact	Criteria	Fulfilled [YES] NO]	Acceptance relevance [MUST HAVE] [IMPORTANT] [NICE TO HAVE]	Remarks
	Class model: Do all business entities exist which are required for this task?		MUST HAVE	
	Class model: Have all entities been correctly and adequately described from a functional perspective?		IMPORTANT	
	Class model: Do the necessary status diagrams exist, and are they correct?		NICE TO HAVE	

Designing Processes for User-oriented Quality Engineering

MICHAEL MEYER, ASTRID DEHNEL, ELMAR FICHTL
T-Systems Nova GmbH, Berkom (Germany)

Abstract:. Developing products and services fitting the customers' needs are the main target and challenge at the same time for current projects managers.

The complexity of the products and services demanded by customers is steadily increasing, while the allowed time to market and the approved development budgets are at an all-time low.

In this situation, the application of structured software-development processes, the usage of modern design and development techniques and the application of up-to-date testing processes may work. But what if the client not only calls for a working product, but also for the development of successful products?

Here, the application of traditional test techniques most likely will leave some relevant questions relating to acceptability, usability, quality of service and profitability unanswered. Therefore, a new approach must be considered.

Therefore, we have introduced user-oriented quality engineering and other related topics into our process structure.

By applying this new approach within development projects efficiency increases, costs are reduced and the end-user acceptance and satisfaction with the product or service increases, since the needs of the customer and the market are met.

Keywords: Process management, process design, user-oriented quality engineering, testing, online services, acceptability, usability, quality of service

1   Introduction

Berkom, the application-oriented innovation center of T-Systems Nova, offers services and solutions in the area of speech, media, security, e-business and interactive solutions. In addition, Berkom provides technical consulting and support. Primary customers are medium and large-sized organisations as well as service providers from almost all sectors, with a focus on telecommunication, public organisations and government.

In this area, the technological progress and the world-wide opening of markets for international competitors forces service providers to increase the features of their products and services. This leads directly to an enormous increase of product complexity. At the same time, the increasing competition and deregulation of formerly regulated markets sets limits for product prices – and therefore development costs - and also reduces the acceptable time to market.

To address large international markets on a high level of quality, the service providers have little scope left for unique selling points. Therefore, the only way to offer differing products is to better adapt the product to the needs of the end customer. But increasing the quality and complexity of the product in general increases the time for development and costs at the same time.

Faced with this unfortunate structure, a project was started to address and solve these problems, or at least find a good compromise. Since all the requirements to be addressed are linked to each other, a process redesign was started.

2   Role, Significance and Design of Processes

At the moment, the manufacturers of innovative, interactive products and services in the area of telecommunication are under considerable pressure to develop better products in ever shorter periods of time. At the same time, the customers are less and less in a position to invest more for the development of new features due to the constraints of greater competition. Moreover, especially in the high-quality area, the possibilities are reduced to stand out against other competitors by means of technically unique product features. Therefore, to manufacture successful products, i.e. to be successful on the market, demands that the requirements of the future buyers and users are already integrated in very early phases of development. This integration can only be successful and economical if it is integrated in the company processes applied in practice.

On the basis of these motives, the approach of user-centred quality engineering has been developed at Berkom to ensure the integration of the user and their requirements in the development processes. By including and integrating this in the development process, know-how could be firmly incorporated in the structures of the development projects.

2.1 Starting Basis

When the project for the integration of user-centred quality engineering in the development processes was started, a process-oriented management system certified according to DIN EN ISO 9001 was already in place.

Within the scope of this management system, a development process was developed which is outlined in Figure 1.

Figure 1: Development Process

Within the scope of this development process, all requirements for development projects are described and flexibly documented in form of an Internet presentation.

The process structure is divided into three levels which are described firstly on the process level, secondly on the level of partial processes and thirdly, as the most detailed description, on the activity level. By means of these activities, the steps are described which are necessary in the development process for fulfilling the tasks or the possible steps according to the type. They represent the central theme.

They are described by means of the following essential aspects:

- Short description of the activity
- Description of the activity
- Possible methods to be applied and available tools
- Criteria for the realisation
- Criteria for the result
- Participating roles and their responsibility
- Documents and results to be evaluated (inputs)
- Results reached when realising the activities (outputs)

The following figure gives an overview of the overall structure of the process model.

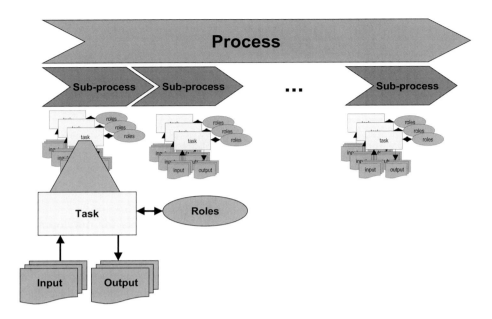

Figure 2: Structure of the Process Model

The overall process concept consists of a set of processes such as for example the described development process, but it also includes a purchase process or a human resource management process, each of whose description satisfies the structure illustrated above.

2.2 Roles

Within the scope of the development process, the different stakeholders of the product or service development have to be considered. The corresponding roles in the process are classified. On the one hand, the roles concern the management of the development project (customer, project manager, sub-contractor etc.) but, on the other hand, they also concern the different production roles (developer, tester, and so on). Moreover, the following customer-related roles are distinguished which are especially important within the scope of user-centred quality engineering:

- The role of the **customer** initiating the development project. This is for example the product manager of a product line who wants to establish a new service.
- The role of the **end-customer** who is a member of the target group for which the service has been developed and who demands the service as a buyer on the market. At the same time, he can also be the user of the service. Especially in the business-to-business area, this role is very important.

- The role of the **user**, who finally uses the service. This can be for example the buyer's child using learning software or the customer of the service operator who subscribes to a service and uses it. In the standard consumer business, the role of the customer and the user is represented in one person.

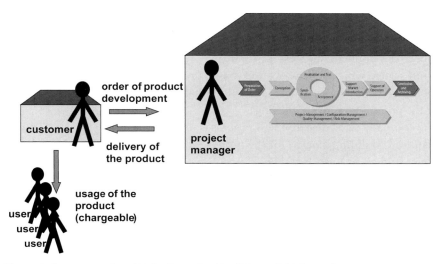

Figure 3: Customer-related Roles Described by Using a B2B Scenario

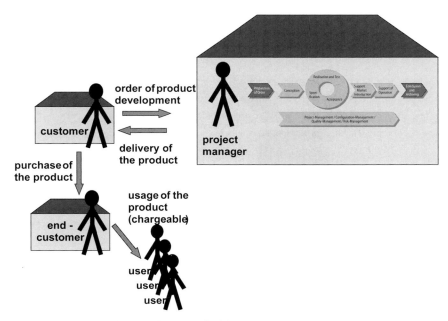

Figure 4: Customer-related Roles Described by Using a B2C Scenario

2.3 Flexible Application of the Processes in Practice

This development process incorporated in the company-wide process model is used by projects on the basis of a specific customising. The activities of the overall development process required are selected on the basis of the concrete project's objectives and its basic circumstances. The project-specific activities are then documented in an individual project development process. In order to act quickly and economically, this adaptation process is supported by internal consultants. The project-specific documentation of the adapted project development process is conducted with the aid of a database-based documentation system which generates a web-based process presentation for the project. The time needed is minimal, since there is no additional documentation effort other than customising the process (simply by clicking).

Hereby, the company-wide development process is understood as a "Lego box", out of which the required "building blocks" for the project (activities, results, partial processes, processes, roles and so on) can be taken. If necessary, new or missing building blocks can be added and building blocks which are not required can be left out.

Moreover, the project-specific development process can again be adapted (simplified or extended) to meet modified requirements at any time. The provision of such processes as pre-tailored versions of the development process, e.g. for special development approaches or for small projects as a simplified basis, is also offered.

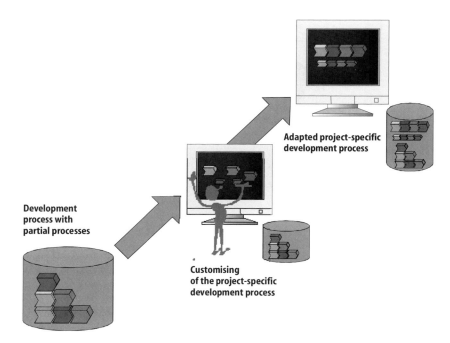

Adapted project-specific development process

Development process with partial processes

Customising of the project-specific development process

Figure 5: Customising the Development Process

A simple navigation within the overall process model is of special importance. Thanks to the database-based implementation, a role-related view of the process is just as possible as a result-based view or other forms of presentation and navigation in supporting the current user of the process model.

One of the most important quality criteria for the use of the process is it to design it as simply and economically as possible. Therefore, each document referred to in the process model is described by means of a template and filed in the Intranet. These templates are automatically linked with the process description and are also available for the user in his adapted project-specific development process. Additionally, information on past experiences can be found in practice-related examples.

3 User-centred Quality Engineering: A Customer-Oriented Approach Including Acceptability, Usability and Quality-of-Service Analysis

3.1 Motivation

With its flexibility and adaptability, the process model described in the previous chapter is the formal basis for different development projects and thus makes it possible to develop efficiently a new, innovative product.

The use of professional services guarantees the high quality of the work and the product. However, other aspects are important for the success on the market, for which only the end-customer or the user can provide information. In a fast-developing market with many similar offerings, it is absolutely necessary that the product fulfils the requirements of the user. The logical consequence is to integrate the user requirements and thus also the potential users in this process world.

Because only what users really like – they will buy. Therefore, the aim of user-centred quality engineering is:

- to know what users want
- to know what users need
- to avoid expensive redesigns

In summary: to design user-friendly and well-accepted products and services.

3.2 Usability, Acceptability and Quality Assessment

The concept of user-centred quality engineering considers three user or customer-relevant aspects:

Usability
Usability concentrates on the use of products and services in an ergonomic sense. Usability engineering allows an optimised design of products and services from a usability point of view. Style guides and CI/CD regulations as well as usability guidelines (e.g. from ISO) for the design of software and hardware provide the necessary conditions.
In summary, usability engineering and testing guarantee an easy-to-use and best look-and-feel tested in user tests or expert evaluations.

Acceptance
A set of product-specific, user-specific and environment-specific factors influence the acceptance. In the business-to-business market there are also enterprise-specific determinants such as organisation and qualification of staff, among others.
  Product-specific factors are those which can be influenced before, during or after product development. Functions of the product, its usability, design and additional features, but also the cost and the price are included in these factors. Product-specific factors are determined among others by user and environment-specific factors. Some user-specific factors are for example the user's readiness to take risks, the added value and the affinity for technology. The environment-specific factors include innovation

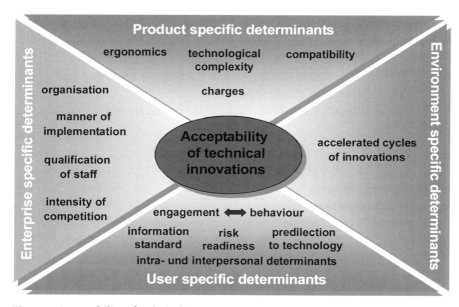

Figure 6: Acceptability of technical innovations

cycles and advertising. The objective is to optimise the product-specific features which can be influenced corresponding to the user and environment-specific factors. In summary, acceptability covers the users' sense of the whole product and their willingness to use the product including the relationships between influencing factors evaluated with potential end-customers of a target group.

Quality-of-Service Analysis

Quality considerations also concentrate on the user. Here, it is for example the question of the end-to-end quality of an IP telephony connection as perceived by the user. Objective QoS parameters in the IP network can be an indicator for the quality, but they leave open how much of it the user really perceives or in how far further influences on quality have to be considered by for example terminals. In summary, quality-of-service analysis is the evaluation of the user-perceived transmission quality of speech, audio, video, and audio-visual through user tests or instrumental methods.

   Upon closer examination of these three aspects, it becomes clear that they are closely coupled and that each aspect includes a comprehensive set of methods and questions. Thus, usability and transmission quality are finally also important factors influencing the acceptance. Therefore, a close coupling of these three aspects makes sense and is important.

3.3 Integrated Process-Accompanying Approach

A joint consideration of the three aspects integrated in the processes of a product, from the idea of the product to the finished product, is the core of user-centred quality engineering that supports product and marketing management and development processes. Acceptability, usability and quality-of-service analysis contribute to the entire development cycle of a product or service:

Figure 7: A Development Cycle

The development cycle is here divided into four phases and is still very theoretical:

Product Idea

In this stage, there are first product ideas or the incentive to generate them with end-customers. First, new product ideas can be discussed with potential end-customers under different viewpoints. Questions concerning the acceptance and further design of the idea, tops and flops of possible functions and features, quality requirements and user needs or possible target groups are interesting as well. Thus, important information regarding further specifications and possibly a first feeling for the market can be obtained.

There is a further possibility to create product ideas by means of generative methods. It is also possible to develop concrete use concepts together with the end-customers or the users.

Product Development

By accompanying the product in the conceptual phase, requirements of the future users or the market can be included in the development process. Support can be given until the product is finished by means of usability reviews, acceptance tests or quality of service examinations of partial implementations, pre-products or prototypes.

Product Initiation

Before the product is introduced on the market, it is necessary to test the product regarding its suitability for the market. Here, apart from evaluating the product and its features, potentials for improvement can be identified and ideas for a successful marketing can be derived. Examinations at this time can also be used to restrict or characterise the target group for the product or the service.

Product on Market

As soon as a product has been placed on the market, the customary use and the user satisfaction with the product and its features are especially interesting.

The main target here is analysis of the product on the market and to find suggestions for improvement as well as the basis for decisions regarding how to further proceed with the product.

4   Integration of User-Centred Quality Engineering and Quality Criteria for Processes

In order to integrate user-centred quality engineering in the development processes easily and economically, a three-stage approach was chosen:

- Analysis
- Integration in the processes and their application
- Review.

4.1 Analysis

To obtain an overview of the use of the existing process structure and to optimise the introduction of new user-centred quality engineering topics into the processes, the first stage of analysing the current process structures and their use was carried out. The objective was to identify approaches for integrating the measures regarding user-centred quality engineering. As a result, the described "building blocks" or elements for a user-centred quality engineering described above were integrated into the development process with their description (roles, documents etc) as partial processes or activities. Because internal Bootstrap assessments have been used in the company since the management system was built, it was decided to carry out this analysis also on the basis of a Bootstrap assessment.

4.1.1   Bootstrap Analysis

To obtain representative results projects were chosen that focussed on the topics

- Web-based or online service projects,
- covering the support of our customer, end-customer and user, e.g. by means of user surveys dealing with usability, acceptability and quality-of-service surveys,
- of different sizes and duration,
- initiated by our main customers.

To focus the Bootstrap analysis on the relevant questions, the following processes were chosen from the Bootstrap Process Structure (Figure 8):

- Project management (as a general topic to understand the project and to find out how the project is managed)
- Quality management (to learn how the quality of the products and project processes is managed)
- Quality assurance (to discover how the project assures the quality of their products and the QA methods used, etc.)
- Customer Need Management (to learn how the customer and user demands and expectations are understood and managed with special focus on integration of the customer/user into the lifecycle)
- Process design (to find out how projects deal with their processes)

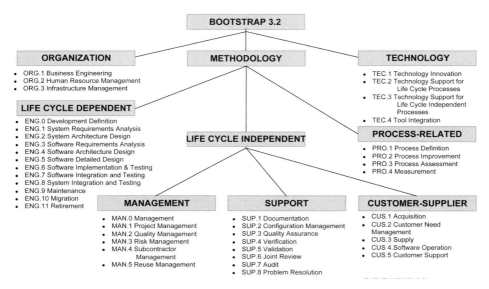

Figure 8: The Bootstrap Structure

4.1.2   Quality Criteria for Process Integration

Collecting the main, common findings of the assessment reports we learned from the problems or suggestions of our project managers and derived the relevant quality criteria for the introduction of user-centred quality engineering into the process structure.

Flexibility and customisability

- Since the process had to fit various projects of very different sizes, the additional features had to be introduced in a way that the processes are easy to use, easy to customise and therefore applicable to all relevant project types and sizes.

Supporting the project managers and project staff (guideline)

- The project managers called for more complete process descriptions and explanations of the relevant activities and required results as a supporting basis for their work.
- All types of internal services can be used to simplify project work and organisation (e.g. test support, internal consulting, operations support, creation of business cases, market research, quality-of-service analysis, usability analysis, etc). In addition to including these different techniques and services, the planning and preparation requirements should also be included in the early stages of the project processes.

Completeness with respect to different QA techniques and internal services

- Different, optional types of quality assurance techniques and the internal quality assurance service providers must be included and mentioned within the process structure. This ensures that requirements of internal service providers are adhered to at the right time thus increasing productivity, since mistakes and misunderstandings are avoided.

In addition to these more project-based quality criteria, the following criteria were added to keep our company and customer demands in view:

- open design and good supportability to keep our processes open to new, upcoming topics,
- reduction of development costs and shortening of time to market,
- increase of the managed complexity and quality of products and services,
- and, last but not least, increase of customer satisfaction with our services.

With this list of quality criteria, new processes were designed.

4.2 Integration in the Processes

In the following, the integration in current processes is described with respect to the quality criteria mentioned above. With the help of an example, the possible process steps and activities and those applied in practice are also explained.

This example describes the development of a Unified Messaging Service, which can uniformly administer news of every kind (telephone conversations, e-mails, Fax, SMS etc.), convert them into other formats and transfer them to any terminal such as a fixed-line telephone, PC or mobile phone.

Typical end-customers for such a service are its operators, e.g. a company buying the product/service from the customer. Every end-customer (employee) of this company can be a user of this service. Here, the acceptance of the end-customer depends on the acceptance of the user using such a service or not using it because it is poorly designed.

When integrating user-centred quality engineering into the process world, the quality requirements for processes described in the previous chapter should be considered. Here, the flexibility and customisability of the processes are especially important. Corresponding to the respective project requirements, a flexible and adaptable system has to be available, which leaves enough scope for the project manager without relieving him from the most important quality requirements.

Here, the approach is an integration of measures for user-centred quality engineering in the current process steps. Obligatory measures and optional measures are distinguished.

As an accompanying process, user-centred quality engineering spans over the entire development process. Here, the product as well as the measures for user-centred quality engineering are designed or specified in the phases of order preparation, conception and specification.

The designed and specified measures for user-centred quality engineering are taken, however, reaching over several phases, starting in the conception phase of the product via specification to operational support.

4.2.1   Preparation of Order

While preparing the order, the project manager works out the basic conditions with the customer. Here, a close co-ordination with the customer of the quality criteria which are followed within the scope of the project-related quality management and derived QA measures is important. This also includes the measures of user-centred quality engineering. As far as user-centred quality engineering is concerned, the project manager is even obliged to discuss this topic with the customer and thus possibly integrate the end-customer or the user in the project development. If necessary, the experts are integrated in the preparation of order as consultants on this topic.

In parallel to order preparation, the development process is customised. Here, it is important that the objectives of the project are supported as optimally as possible by means of the development process selected.

Explanation using an example
In the UMS example described above, it became obvious that within the scope of establishing the quality criteria and the derived QA measures, the customer needed user-oriented quality engineering and that there was also a need in the project.

That meant that the experts responsible for user-oriented quality management had to be addressed at an early stage and be integrated in the project work. Within the scope of a joint analysis in the project team, it became quickly obvious that this service included many aspects concerning the matters usability, acceptance and quality of service analysis and that the customer as well as the project team had to consider them in their project work.

Quality-of-service analysis
In order to put the customer requirements for the user-oriented QA in concrete form, a co-ordination meeting with the customer was arranged with the help of the project manager. In this co-ordination meeting, the advantages and starting points for user-oriented quality management were introduced and discussed. The objective was to win

the customer over for this (new) method and while preparing the order to integrate a requirement analysis for measures for user-oriented quality management.

On the basis of these concrete arrangements, the costs were estimated with the project manager on the basis of a first rough conception of user-centred quality engineering and integrated into the offer.

4.2.2   Conception

After the project initiation, project planning and all further planning documents have to be put in concrete form and the project-specific development process required for the achievement of the project objective has to be adapted if necessary. In the conception phase of the project, it is necessary to detail the technical requirements of the customer which are established only on a very general level for the offer, to work out the technical solution (conception of the service) and to document it in parallel in the specification.

As far as user-centred quality engineering is important for the project, the requirements from the user's point of view concerning usability, acceptance and quality-of-service analysis aspects have to be described at this point. These requirements usually are also documented in the specification. Moreover, the measures taken to fulfil and examine the requirements are subject matter of a first examination concept. This concept can be available as a separate document or else as a part of the specification.

Explanation using an example
After having placed the order, the planned development process for the project had to be adapted first. Here, the development process roughly available from the phase of offer was examined in a discussion with the project quality manager and the project manager, and a project-specific web-based development process documentation was generated.

Here, the relevant aspects, i.e. expected results and required activities within the scope of user-centred quality engineering were also identified and included in the revised project planning as well as the development process. They are shortly explained in the following:

From the user's point of view, the following requirements were defined and included in the specification:

Usability requirements
The known usability criteria ([DIN] ISO 9241) for the design of speech-based dialogues such as e.g. the menu depths and breadths but also criteria for suitability of tasks, learnability etc.

Adherence to CI/CD guidelines

Acceptance requirements
Values for user satisfaction according to an index established from information about importance and satisfaction of individual service features
Share of users of a sample defined on the basis of information given by the customer evaluating the service as good and very good
Rate for success concerning the solution of given tasks

QoS-requirements
Requirements for the speech recognition rate, the speaker recognition rate (for authentication), the speech synthesis (TTS) and other things

Moreover, the required measures for user-centred quality engineering were identified and integrated in the specification, a first measure already having been planned within the conception phase.

Here, it was the question of an acceptance test in the form of discussion groups with users who should provide information about the following subjects:

- Use scenarios,
- Identification of user requirements
- Generation of ideas / functions of the service,
- Identification of quality criteria and evaluation of quality criteria according to their significance

This information supported the formulation of requirements when preparing the specification.

4.2.3   Specification

Regarding the measures within the scope of a user-centred quality engineering, the individual examinations of usability, acceptance and quality-of-service analysis are described here. If a separate document with an examination concept is available, this one is improved, otherwise it can also be integrated in the specification document
Moreover, it is possible to already include the user or customer within the scope of the specification and to carry out examinations within the scope of a user-centred quality engineering. Here, methods such as e.g. Focus Groups are suitable in order to generate ideas for design, and in order to establish and give priority to user requirements or to answer similar questions.

Explanation by using an example

In our example, the examinations were already carried out in the conception phase. Therefore, it was possible at this point to support the designers through consulting and provision of results reached in this examination when preparing the specification. Moreover, meetings with the customer took place where the examination concepts of user-centred quality engineering generated were discussed within the scope of the specification.

Within the scope of usability engineering there was close co-operation between the developers concerning design of dialogues and call flow. Here, suggestions for an optimal design of speech dialogues were made.

4.2.4   Realisation & Test

Within the scope of the product realisation, measures for user-centred quality engineering can give important indicators for the selection of product components and solutions, and thus they can contribute to an early product optimisation from the customer's point of view. Here, prototypes or partial realisations for example are evaluated or different components are compared in order to use the best from the user's point of view. These measures are taken independently of other testing activities such as functional tests, system integration tests, load tests and so on within the scope of the project-related quality management.

Explanation using an example

In the current service available, products for speaker verification and speech recognition regarding their quality with customers were tested. Here, tests with potential users were made in a speech quality laboratory.

Within the scope of usability, the first dialogues were evaluated by experts and a set of categorised and prioritised potentials for improvement could be derived.
Since the means as well as time were limited acceptance examinations with the users were not carried out in this phase of the process.

4.2.5   Acceptance

Here, measures for user-centred quality engineering are not important.

4.2.6   Support for Market Introduction

The market introduction, for example with a pilot operation, should be accompanied by measures of user-centred quality engineering in order to test the service's suitability for the market. Here, usability, acceptance and quality-of-service analysis provides indicators for potential improvements. If errors are being found when guiding the users within the accompanying acceptance examination, these should be examined further in additional usability tests. Measures suggested and highly prioritised in the examination reports have then to be identified before the final market introduction. Moreover, important information about the support of marketing and distribution such as tops and flops is collected.

Explanation using an example
This phase is one of the most important for the acceptance. Now, it is necessary to evaluate the market suitability of the developed service. The criteria have already been defined in the specification but can be formulated more precisely with the participation of all.

In the example, a pilot test with 100 users was carried out. Apart from the evaluation of the service and its features, these users received a comprehensive view of the functions provided by the real system. When questioned, the users identified strengths and weaknesses of the system as well as areas for improvement. In addition, the users were asked for their ideas on pricing or the maximum price for the use of the product. These results and the requirements were then included in the specification.

On the basis of the results reached in the examination, the product could be technically further optimised before the market introduction by extending the "Alias" term in the speech recognition (e.g. 'OK' additionally to 'Yes' and 'Correct') and thus it could be better adapted to the usual set of terms future users are used to. In addition, information about the support of the product marketing (e.g. advertising of the product) could be derived.

4.2.7   Operational Support

During operation, questions about frequency of use and user satisfaction (customer satisfaction at the operator) are interesting. This information is the basis for decisions on how to proceed further with the product. Thus, a decision on "Abmanagen" or for a further release can be made. For the latter, potentials for improvements such as user interviews and evaluation of statistical data such as logging data of the service are identified within the scope of user-centred quality engineering measures.

Explanation using an example
In our example, the service did not provide the expected number of users after several months in operation.

We were asked to find the possible reasons such as the interim introduction of a competition product (e.g. of another ISP) or initially a too rough definition of the target group for which the product was developed and consequently misdirected marketing measures, etc.

Therefore, in order to examine the reasons for the too small number of users, interviews were conducted with help of a questionnaire with a comprehensive, representative sample of the total population. The questionnaire contained questions concerning the general reputation of the product and the description of the users within the sample of the interviewees regarding the modification of the definition of a concrete target group for the product. It referred as well as to the comparison with the competition product.

It became obvious that the product was not well-known enough; moreover, a modification of the target group definition proved to be necessary. Suggestions for further marketing measures could be worked out.

After weaknesses had become obvious when comparing the product with the competition product, the results of the examination could serve as a basis for the planning and preparation of a new release.

4.2.8   Conclusion and Archiving

Within the scope of the project conclusion, the experiences gained in the course of the project from the point of view of user-centred quality engineering have to be evaluated, and relevant results, data and so on have to be archived according to data protection regulations.

4.3 Experience

On the basis of the results of several projects which were realised using application and integration of user-centred quality engineering in the development process, we can say:

- The flexible and modular structure of the development process enables the use of the described methodologies for different kinds and sizes of projects. On the one hand, we have learned that small projects work best on the basis of pre-fabricated 'ready-to-go' solutions, requiring only a small or no adaptation to the needs of the project. For bigger projects, on the other hand, the flexible and complete approach provides the possibility to increase efficiency and profitability of the development approach as well as to act in a faster and more controlled way. The customer benefits from higher quality.

- With the help of a good explication and complete integration of optionally possible activities in the development process with project-specific adaptation, the use of user-oriented QA could be extended and deepened. A first analysis showed that above all the active selection or non-selection of the required modules from the development process involved an additional QA of the planning. After that, our internal support departments also benefited from easier co-ordination and fewer difficulties at interfaces within the development process.

- The integrated approach of usability, acceptability and quality-of-service assessments, summarised in user-centred quality engineering, enables a broad cost and time-efficient quality assurance from the users' viewpoint. In comparison to a separated application of usability, acceptability and quality-of-service assessments, the integrated approach exploits synergy effects. This results in a reduction of time and costs by simultaneously increasing the quality of the analysis results.

- Last but not least, we would like to mention the possibly most powerful feedback of the first projects: the customer is more successful thanks to the results, because the products and services are better tailored to the needs of the target groups. Important areas of improvement and serious defects of the product or service were found in time before the introduction on the market so that necessary steps could still be taken before commercialisation.

5 Summary

In summary, we can say that on the basis of our flexible, modular approach of a project-specific adaptation of the development process, the integration of the user-quality engineering approach was successful and could be designed economically.

On the basis of the development process, we succeeded in designing a manageable process and fulfilling the quality requirements.

By flexibly customising the development process and the objective-oriented selection of suitable activities of user-centred quality engineering, the project manager is able to select the ones actually required out of a complete offer of possible activities. Through this conscious decision, an additional check for completeness is guaranteed ensuring that the central theme remains the same and all relevant matters are paid attention to.

The productivity and efficiency of the projects were increased and the required time of development was reduced.

The use of user-centred quality engineering in our projects led to a higher customer satisfaction with us. First inquiries show that the success of products and services on the market and the user satisfaction (an acceptance rate of up to 97% of the target group) are increasing.

Using Extreme Programming to Manage High-Risk Projects Successfully

Martin Lippert, Heinz Züllighoven

it - Workplace Solutions GmbH & University of Hamburg (Germany)

Abstract: Today, software development and its process management is a demanding task. The development company must reach the project goals on time and in budget. On the other hand, requirements change daily, developers are not domain experts and customers want to maintain close control of the project. Web application development has increased this challenge as new project-management issues have to be met. Extreme Programming (XP), a lightweight development process, is designed to meet the challenge. We have used XP successfully in a number of projects and attained the goals mentioned above. Using XP enabled us to deliver software on time and in budget, while supporting close communication between the (potential) customer and the development team as requirements changed daily. One to two releases per customer per week (two per day at the peak) indicate the flexibility and risk-minimising capabilities of the process. This allowed optimal control and planning of the projects by the development company. We illustrate our experiences using one particular time-critical project.

Keywords: Extreme programming, project management, agile processes, risk minimisation

1 Flexible Processes for High-Risk Projects

Everyone of the software community is talking about Extreme Programming (XP, see [BECK99], but few people actually apply it in their projects. Most developers, managers and project leaders see XP as a process without a plan, without documentation and, most important, without control. They look on XP as the tribal rites of a group of hackers. A more serious view accepts XP as suitable for very small application programs where there is no need for major planning or specification efforts. Critics point to unfamiliar things like "lack of up-front design" or "pair programming", viewing them as contradictory to the principles of software engineering. There seems to be a general consensus that XP will never work for large systems and high-risk projects where one needs to be in control of what is going on.

We will try to unriddle some of the myths about XP and show that it does not mean working without plans, design or control. These fundamentals are simply used and implemented differently. And, as with every methodology or technique, XP ideas must be adapted to meet the user's specific needs.

We have used XP in a number of successful projects and will demonstrate how to face the risks of today's software development projects. We have delivered high-quality software to our customers in cycles within weeks. This is crucial for web applications. And we were in control of the projects and able to react to changing requirements on a daily basis. Problems that caused other projects to fail or run out of funds hardly affected us at all.

To attain these goals, we adapted Extreme Programming to our needs and combined it with other project-planning techniques. Today, we have elaborated our planning techniques to enable us to achieve optimal control and planning for high-risk projects within a flexible process.

1.1 Risk

Development projects often involve a lot of risk. Reducing and managing risks is one of the major challenges of project management. But what is the nature of these risks? What are the main problems causing risks? Based on a number of high-risk projects, we have collected the following list of risk causes in software projects:

- Often, the team has to develop a software system for an application domain they are not familiar with. Such application domains are usually complex and hard to understand. The chance of making mistakes due to misunderstandings is high.

- New technologies are emerging every day. Frequently, they must be used for a software project, though the developers have little or no experience with their use. Sometimes it is the combination of new and untried technologies that is troublesome, but in most cases the impact of these new technologies is unclear to both the developers and the client. Thus the risk of having to replace an unmanageable technology late on in a project is high.

- User requirements change daily. The reasons are manifold: the client learns more about the possibilities of the new system during the development process; the client's organisation changes; and the customer nearly always has new ideas after seeing the first part of the system running.

These are some of the causes. There may be more risks arising in a development project, but the above list should do for the moment. The crucial question we face is: How can we reduce major risks?

Analysing the list of causes helped us to draw up some ideas and guidelines. These we have successfully used in a number of projects to reduce risks. Here, then, is our list of "first-aid" measures to tackle project risks:

- Deliver small, usable systems as early as possible. Get feedback from the users by trying out the small system. A short "author-critic cycle" helps avoid building unsuitable or unusable systems. And it reduces the risk of dissatisfied customers (who are not normally willing to pay for poor work).

- Present the future development of the system as a sequence of small, comprehensive iterations and discuss them with your customers. Plan only the next small release in detail and explain it. It is essential to react swiftly to changes.

- Provide for a flexible development process – crucial in most settings – but make sure that you will be able to plan and control it. Remember that resources and money are limited, even in new-economy companies.

Obviously, traditional software engineering methodologies and processes are unable to meet these requirements. The key question is: What kind of processes do we need to attain these goals?

1.2 Extreme Programming

Extreme Programming is an example of an agile process. Agile processes are based on a set of principles [AGIL01]:

- Our highest priority is to satisfy the customer through early and continuous delivery of valuable software.

- Welcome changing requirements, even late on in development. Agile processes harness change to the customer's competitive advantage.

- Deliver working software frequently, every couple of weeks or couple of months, with a preference for the shorter time scale.

- Business experts and developers must work together daily throughout the project.

- Build projects around motivated individuals. Give them the environment and support they need, and trust them to get the job done.

- The most efficient and effective way of conveying information to and within a development team is face-to-face conversation.

- Working software is the primary measure of progress.

- Agile processes promote sustainable development. The sponsors, developers and users should be able to maintain a constant pace indefinitely.

- Continuous attention to technical excellence and good design enhances agility.

- Simplicity – the art of maximising the amount of work that doesn't need doing – is essential.

- The best architectures, requirements and designs emerge from self-organising teams.
- At regular intervals, the team reflects on how to become more effective, then tunes and adjusts its behaviour accordingly.

Extreme Programming itself is based on four values: Simplicity, Communication, Feedback and Courage. They are all used in combination with one another, allowing us to form a development team that is able to deal with risks. Using the twelve techniques contained in the Extreme Programming concept [BECK99], we can create a development process that is geared to low risk.

But why is XP a feasible solution? An important feature of the XP idea is the value of feedback. If a team gets feedback early on, project management can react to that feedback and steer the project in the right direction. In order to get early feedback, the team must develop valuable software within a short period of time. This does not mean six months or more: we are talking about release cycles of one month or less. With very short release cycles, we get feedback from the customer and become aware of problems and misunderstandings very early on. This is invaluable.

However, it is not easy to create a workable release every two weeks. The small-releases technique can only work in conjunction with the other features: continuous integration, re-factoring, testing, simple design, pair programming, a 40-hour week, coding conventions, on-site customer, collective ownership, metaphors and the planning game. All these techniques help to build a system of interconnected elements. Using these techniques in combination is not a simple job for "hackers" that can be done at will. A team needs a lot of discipline to learn the XP way of software development. But once they have the concepts, they will be a powerful team. They will produce high-quality software at high speed on time and on budget. And customers can change their requirements every day. What else do we want?

This short section on XP can only serve as a quick overview. We do not attempt to describe every technique in detail in this article. It is largely devoted to the planning and steering aspects of XP. Changing requirements every day sounds great, but it suggests not being able to plan anything. Let us take a closer look, then, at how we can plan a project and how we can stay in firm control of the costs. Then we will see how we can adapt XP to meet our needs.

2 Steering XP Projects

The planning and steering aspect of pure XP is fairly simple. We will summarise the main points in the following sections. They should demonstrate how realistic and iterative project planning can be done.

2.1 The Planning Game

Based on so-called story cards, the development team and the customer can plan their project together. The customer writes stories about what the system should do. These stories are not detailed specifications of the system. Figure 1 shows some examples taken from [BECK00]. They provide informal information. Therefore they are backed up with one of the most important elements of XP: the dialogue between the customer and the developers. The developers' first job is to understand the stories. The second step is to assess each story and to give the customer an estimate of how much they can get done within the next iteration. The customer then prioritises the stories, deciding what is to be built first and what is to be implemented in a later iteration.

User stories are written on cards. That is why we call them story cards. It is very convenient to have them written on cards when discussing them in the planning of the next iteration.

Sort available flights by convenience
When you're showing the flights, sort them by convenience: time of journey, number of changes, closeness to desired departure

---

Print immigration paperwork
Print paperwork required to leave and arrive at a planet – only for the easier planets (e.g., not Vogon)

Figure 1: Example user stories. They can be enhanced with fields for date, planned iteration, estimation, etc.[1]

This planning game not only *sounds* simple and straightforward, it *is* simple and straightforward. The most demanding task in this game is assessing the stories. Based on their experience, the developers should give the customer an idea of how much can be done in the next iteration. This is not a trivial task. But the developers don't have to assess the whole system as they do in traditional projects with bulky requirement documents. They only have to deal with a small part of the future system. And they have the chance to ask the customer when something is unclear. Sometimes the stories are too long. The customers must then split them into smaller parts, the developers assessing each part individually. Developers learn from assessments they have made in

---

[1] We use these examples from the XP planning book to give you an impression of what user stories are like. The stories we used for the project (see below) were somewhat more detailed, but unfortunately we are not allowed to publish them.

the past. They can look at a similar story they have implemented in the past to see what will be a realistic time span. Using this kind of assessment helps the team to be increasingly precise in estimating projects. After a few planning-game cycles, the time and resource plan will be fairly accurate. This is usually the case after a few weeks if the release cycles are short enough. (More about story assessment can be found in [BECK00]).

2.2 Small and Frequent Releases

We have already said that early feedback is essential to reduce risks in a software project. And we have also discussed how to get early feedback from the customer. The key is to deliver small releases of valuable software to the customer at the end of nearly every period of short iterations. Each iteration might take one week and a first release should be delivered after two weeks of development. This is a good basis for continuous feedback.

At first, this might sound strange. You might say that this kind of release cycle would be wonderful to obtain early feedback, but a release after two or four weeks? Never! This objection is justified if you think in terms of current project settings with separate software components that are implemented by independent programmers or individual sub-teams. Given this kind of division of labour, software integration is a major and time-consuming task. So how can we make small releases possible without subjecting the software team to round-the-clock stress? The answer is clear: continuous integration.

The idea of continuous integration is to make small changes to the system and integrate these as often as possible, at least once a day. This provides an excellent basis for the team to share code and benefit from one another's development activities.

And then there is the testing strategy. You write the test first, and then the new program feature. If you are not that rigorous, you at least do extensive unit testing.

In combination with the frequent testing, the small-releases strategy is easy to pursue, so easy that it does require thinking about, because if you make small changes to the system and continuous integration is combined with unit testing, you at least have the previous integration as a running system. Then you might deliver this version as a release to your customer. Why not? Maybe it does not contain all the features you would like to present to the customer, but if there are fixed dates for the release, you will have a running system that is as close as possible to the customer's requirements. Your customer will see that the system can do something valuable. Often, this is much better than delaying a release merely in order to achieve the complete set of features.

2.3   Project Planning

We have discussed small releases and risk reduction with early feedback. This is important and forms the foundation for project planning. Without this sound foundation, no planning will be possible.

The simple XP planning game can be used not only to plan the next one or two iterations, but also for planning the major steps of a project. The participants then play the planning game on a larger scale, making a rough plan for the entire project. This is sufficient for smaller or less complex projects. If our projects are on a major scale, we would like to reify the whole planning process by adding artifacts (see also [LIPP01-a], [LIPP01-b]).

Martin Fowler and Kent Beck propose a simplified version of a release plan to do the rough long-term planning (see [BECK00]). We have extended this idea. The large-scale planning process described in the next section has proved useful in various projects over the past ten years and fits in well with the planning ideas of XP.

2.3.1   Kernel System with Extensions and Special Systems

We always begin by clarifying which part of the system is to be implemented in the project. In many cases, we come to the conclusion that an application system with the proposed functionality does not need to be built in a single project cycle. We then break down the target system into subsystems. We call this concept a *kernel system* with *extensions* and *special systems*.

In this way, we can decompose a complex system into parts that are meaningful for the application domain and can be developed at different times. In most cases, the *kernel system* has to be implemented first. It provides the basic services that are needed by nearly all the other parts of the application. In domain terms, the kernel system meets urgent requirements. As the kernel system itself is often still too big to be built "at one go", we break it down into *extensions*. These extensions are defined in terms of logical dependencies between the system components from the domain perspective. The components on which all other components depend are the first to be built. Figure 2 shows a kernel system – designed to be built in five extensions – of process automation software for hot rolling mills. The software components of Extension 1 are needed for the components to be built in Extension 2, i.e. the Primary Data Handler builds on the Telegram Handler. The component for Model Computation to be developed in Extension 4 cannot be developed without the Extension-3 components Measured Value Processing, Model Control and Material Tracking.

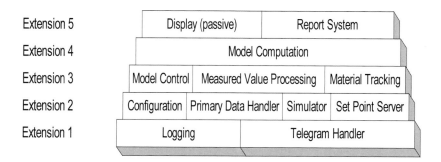

Figure 2: Example of a kernel system with extensions

For the kernel system and extensions concept, it is important that the system is decomposed along domain lines and in a user-comprehensible manner. This enables users and specialist departments in the application domain to be involved in the planning process and to adjust to this planning horizon. We select the extensions such that they can be delivered to the users (or at least some of the future users) as executable versions or components. An extension should, at the very least, always be implemented as a prototype that can be evaluated. This is very important, because an operative system or prototype which can be evaluated usually has a strong impact on the application domain. It gives both users and developers the necessary experience to decide what functionality the subsequent extensions should actually contain. So, the initial specification of kernel system and extensions serves as a kind of commonly accepted blueprint for the overall project, while each extension adds more insight into how this system should be built in detail.

Special systems can be added to the kernel system. These should be designed to interface with the kernel system, but should otherwise be independent of one another. This also enables them to be developed concurrently in sub-projects. In the case of special systems, it is often worth looking for finished, off-the-shelf solutions.

2.3.2   Stages and Reference Lines

If we are planning a large-scale project in iterations, we must often take into account external schedules and domain constraints. This leads to a rough planning in what we call *project stages*, which, in turn, are planned individually, in terms of XP, using *reference lines*.

A *stage* defines a – from the domain perspective – relevant state of the project at a specific point in time. A project stage is reached when the substantive goal is realised and a executable system version, i.e. a prototype, an extension or a component is ready. Stages thus become synchronisation points for developers and users. The necessity of integrating executable systems in the project planning at manageably short intervals

Table 2: Integrations per week

Week	Number of Integrations	Ø Integrations per day
1st week	24	4.8
2nd week	19	3.8
3rd week	25	5
4th week	43	8.6
5th week	45	9
6th week	93	18.6
7th week	91	18.2
8th week	105	21
9th week	67	13.4
10th week	115	23
11th week	77	15.4
12th week (only 3 days)	44	14.7
Total	748	12.9

This kind of development provided us with a running system every day. And that was not the only benefit. Each release also meant feedback from our customer and a platform for continuous planning. This is an important key to reducing risk within a software project (cf. Section 1.1).

The process benefited in another way, too: by using this kind of iterative development, the users were able to change priorities whenever they wanted. We will take a closer look at this in the next sections.

3.2 Internal Daily Planning

The main planning was done for every new release. Thus, the scheduling of development activities was conducted for one week at a time. Our customer presented his priorities for the next release, which we then used to adjust our plans. Sometimes it was not just the priorities the customer wanted to change. Over the twelve weeks, the product requirements changed, but at the same time they became clearer. We observed a very common phenomenon: every new product feature in a new release raised new questions.

These questions led to new feature requests, new story cards or changes to implemented functionality. These results of mutual learning and communication are not merely consequences of the iterative process. If development is not done in short release cycles, all these problems typically surface at the end of the project, causing major problems with the customer. Our short release cycles enabled us to deal with these problems, which are common to every development project.

But what about project planning? Is planning possible with all these moving targets?

Yes, it is. But you need to plan from a different perspective. We used daily activity planning for the project, which involved a stand-up meeting every morning (see [JEFF00]). At the stand-up meeting, each developer explained what he/she had done the day before and what he/she planned to do that day. Then we updated the daily schedule on the whiteboard.

Figure 3 gives an idea of what a schedule on the whiteboard looks like. Each row is for one team member, each column for one development day. Daily cells contain the numbers of the story cards to be processed by a team member. Project previews for the following week were also possible using this daily schedule.

We deliberately chose a whiteboard for daily scheduling of activities, instead of an Excel spreadsheet or other planning software. One of the most important aspects of daily planning is communication within the team. This can be improved by using a whiteboard that everyone can see and point to. A software product would be inconvenient at planning meetings because everyone would have to sit in front of a computer screen.

Of course, the project manager can transfer the whiteboard image to project-planning software or a simple spreadsheet in order to present the plan to top management.

In addition to the activities, each release day was marked on the whiteboard with an "R". Below the daily plan, we drew a small table showing the story-card estimates and the time taken to implement story cards. By working with story cards and the daily planning schedule, we were able to respond very quickly to wrong estimates.

How did we respond? First, the project manager checks whether the other story cards are on time. If some cards are likely to be done in less time, resources are shifted to enable the late story card to be finished within the iteration. If not, the manager notifies the customer. They discuss the situation frankly and decide what to do. The options are clear: the customer has at his disposal all the story cards that are still unfinished and

Figure 3: Daily planning on the white board

can thus rearrange priorities for the current release. Our customer realised very early on in the project that a wise choice on the available design options was vital to the success of the project. So the story cards for the next release were chosen with great care. Once the customer had made the decision, the developers could be sure they would deliver the most valuable system possible to the customer with the next release.

This is the way to respond to changed requirements and wrong estimates. And, we found, it is another key to reducing project risks.

3.3   Estimates and Forecasts

One of the main tasks of project management is dealing with estimates and forecasts. We did initial planning based on the prototype and estimated that we could build the system within twelve weeks. Obviously, these estimates were rough for all participants. But how could we get better estimates and ensure planning safety?

Every time we worked on a story card, we learned more about the efficiency and capabilities of the team. We wrote down the time needed for each story card every day. This helped improve our ability to estimate. Kent Beck and Martin Fowler call this the Yesterday's Weather technique (see [BECK00]).

Within the project, we had to assess about 30 story cards with a wide range of issues. Table 3 shows how the estimates evolved: the first 26 finished story cards with the estimates, reduced to four releases within the twelve-week period. The next column shows the real size needed to finish the set of stories. The last column is the most important. It shows the difference between the estimated and real sizes of the stories. As can be seen, we had a difference of about 10% at the end of the project and a fairly good development over the twelve- week period.

Table 3: Estimates and real values.

Release	No. of story cards finished	Estimated size	Real finished size	Difference between estimated and real values
2001-01-08	5	20	25	+25%
2001-02-01	8	39	43.5	+10%
2001-02-22	17	109	124.5	+14%
2001-03-13	26	169	156.25	-8%

This helps to provide the customer with more accurate feedback on changes to requirements or priorities. And we demonstrated that we were able to improve the estimates within this fairly short project, achieving a fairly acceptable size. Using this kind of estimate enabled us to make minor project corrections smoothly. Kent Beck demonstrates this idea of project steering using the car-driving metaphor (see [BECK99]). Many small corrections are better then a few big ones.

3.4   Lessons Learned

What are the main lessons we learned using this software development approach for professional high-risk projects?

- *The steering capabilities of this approach are excellent.* We were in control of the project throughout the entire development process. Projects risks were reduced to a very acceptable level.

- *The process is easy to communicate and handle.* After initial scepticism, our customer responded very positively to the flexible process and the fairly good project estimates. The team was able to respond quite smoothly and quickly to changes without extra cost.

- *The process has to be adapted to the individual project settings.* It is not a ready-to-use process with an "instruction manual". Users must learn how to adapt it to their specific needs.

- *Unit testing is essential*: The general Extreme Programming description recommends test-first programming. It guides the developer to simpler interfaces and provides major support for constructive quality assurance. We made the mistake of not incorporating this element of XP as an essential in our daily programming. We had unit tests, but not enough of them. This caused problems that could have been avoided with a better set of unit tests.

4   Summary and Perspective

Nearly all major software projects are high-risk. Many of them are not completed successfully. We used the techniques known from Extreme Programming and adapted them to our project settings. This paper presented and discussed some additional techniques to improve the planning capabilities of XP.

In addition to the essentials for dealing with high-risk projects, we presented some material based on projects we successfully completed using this approach.

Our experience with this approach has been very positive and we are currently using similar techniques – with success – for a number of other projects.

Adapting the Test Process for Web Applications – Strategies from Practice

Dirk Huberty
SQS AG (Germany)

Abstract: This article describes the quality characteristics that are relevant for web applications as well as the test objectives that can be derived from those characteristics. First, those architectural characteristics specific to web applications which have an influence on quality assurance are briefly explained. Practical approaches for the testing of web applications are then introduced, based on a generalised, but well-tried approach for testing software applications. The article closes with a description of experience gained with testing tools, test automation and test organisation.

Keywords: Internet, quality objectives, software test process, test, Web applications

1 Introduction

The Internet offers companies and their customers a multitude of possibilities for providing and purchasing services and goods. In addition, the Internet has the potential to change work processes through the decentralisation of workplaces on the one hand and the utilisation of distributed resources and know-how in global projects on the other hand.

Commercial use of the Internet is complex. This can begin with the offering of information for customers free of charge, for example in order to advertise a product or demonstrate competency in selected topics, whereby individual support can strengthen customer loyalty. Shop solutions offer content or products for a fee, with the access to content or products taking place via Internet and the delivery through email, snail mail or courier. Another category is the Internet-based access to software systems that implement a service. For example, a customer can access the online banking system of his bank through the Internet using the HBCI standard (Home Banking Computer Interface).

Commercial offerings compete at present almost exclusively through the form and clarity of their product presentation and the simple usage of the Internet solution. The absence of classical sales aspects such as customer consulting and extensive customer dialog must be compensated by a corresponding presentation of the Internet offering. For the consumer who purchases a book through the Internet, the quality of offerings and their presentation in the Internet are factors which determine his decision, especially when book prices are almost fixed and the terms for delivery are also more or less the same. Comparable decision criteria also apply to hiring a car if the customer selects the car rental on the basis of the information content and user-friendliness of the Internet application.

Internet customers are generally not known for their customer loyalty. Quality therefore becomes an aspect which can make or break the success of an Internet offering.

2   Internet Architecture and Infrastructure

The term Internet refers to a de-centrally organised network in which local computers and networks are directly or indirectly connected with one another. The commuication layer is comprised of TCP/IP (Transmission Control Protocol/Internet Protocol) and the network addresses of the computers, the so-called IP addresses. The exchange of data takes place in the form of data packages which are sent over the backbones and exchanged via CIX (Commercial Internet Exchange) between the backbones. The route of the individual data packages between sender and receiver is not known beforehand, but rather determined at run time. In this way, if one route breaks down an alternative line of communication can be chosen. The Internet thus offers a communication infrastructure for the exchange of information between partners having equal rights.

It is thus becomes possible that all computers in one network can communicate with all computers in other networks. The Internet is not built on the basis of any special hardware, but rather is primarily software based. The existence of any network or data connection is sufficient for the communication between computers.

Internet access can take place over a dedicated or switched line. Dedicated lines are primarily used by larger corporations whose internal networks thus receive a direct connection to the Internet. In addition, further possibilities of access can be provided for third parties. The private user dials into the Internet over his analogue telephone line via modem or over his digital telephone network via ISDN using a provider. There are basically two types of providers: the online services as Internet Service Providers (ISP) and the Internet Access Providers. The online services, e.g. AOL or T-Online, also provide services and forums on the basis of proprietary standards, in addition to Internet access. A special access software is required to use these services. Internet access providers offer no content or services of their own, but rather only make access to the Internet available without proprietary extensions.

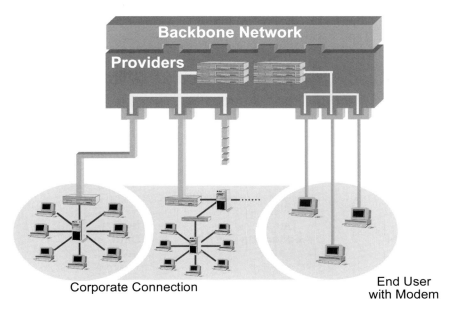

Figure 1: Internet Infrastructure

In principle, the structure of the Internet corresponds to a three-tier client-server architecture with TCP/IP as standardised transfer protocol.

The communication on the basis of requests permits a high variability with respect to the location and number of computers connected to the network. A connection resulting from a request by a client which is answered by a server is subsequently discontinued, whereby it is common for the communication in the Internet that neither the client nor the server note the status of the connection. If the communication extends over several requests, then all relevant data must be sent anew (invisible to the user) in each subsequent transmission (redundant data transmission). One possibility to avoid redundancy in data transmission is the use of so-called cookies. Put simply, cookies are electronic "Post-its" kept in the background of a client that reveal the status of the connection to the server.

Cookies present a potential danger however, because the electronic Post-its access the local computer in an update modus, and this update modus can be misused. Therefore many users refuse to accept cookies.

System with application server and back-end system for data storage

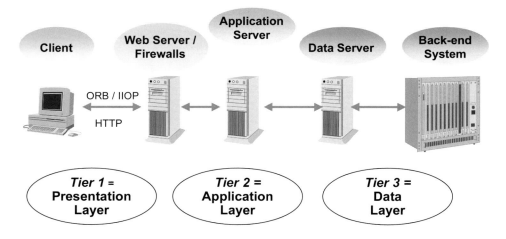

Figure 2: Three-Tier Architecture of the Internet

Applications in the Internet can be classified with respect to their functionality in the following way:

- Client applications for the use of services
  - Operating system-independent applications in a browser environment, e.g. a home-banking application as Java applet
  - Operating system-dependent applications such as a Windows™-based micro-payment application
- Server applications that provide services (application servers, web servers)
- Server applications with security tasks, so-called firewalls that protect internal networks and data

In the early stages of the Internet command line-oriented services were in the foreground of interest. Representatives of this group are telnet, which enables interactive access to other computers, and ftp, the standard protocol for accessing data on remote computers. Mail for the transmission of messages and news for the exchange of information on blackboards both served as communication services. The breakthrough for the Internet, however, did not occur until the introduction of graphical user interfaces with extended functionality and the integration of existing services in the form of the World Wide Web (WWW).

Browsers from different vendors, the best-known are Internet Explorer from Microsoft and Navigator from Netscape, are the general clients in the Internet client-server architecture. On the basis of the Hypertext Transfer Protocol (HTTP), the browser requests a hypertext document (home page) with a specific address from the web server. The requested file is sent to the browser and the connection is then closed. Besides pure text files based on the Hypertext Markup Language (HTML), other types of data such as Java applets, audio, video and images can also be transmitted.

As far as quality assurance (QA) for Internet applications is concerned, particular test objectives result from the depicted infrastructure, the variability of the hardware and the short innovation cycles of the software and the software architecture. A differentiation of these test objectives according to the "classical" structure of test levels is possible, with the exception of the QA measures for publishing applications. In addition to new aspects in quality assurance, the importance of the individual quality objectives already defined for application software also changes.

3   Quality Objectives for Internet Applications

Quality objectives or requirements for Internet applications go beyond those for "classical" or conventional software development. Although comparable requirements for functional accurateness still hold true, special requirements or challenges result from the potential usage of an Internet application by any user. Especially high demands are placed on the user-friendliness (usability) as well the performance and reliability of the applications. The openness and free availability of Internet applications also lead to fundamental problems for quality assurance: often the sociological structure of the future user group cannot be foreseen. A further aspect which cannot be definitely determined before the introduction of a new application or services is the frequency, type and number of expected accesses. The definition of the expected behaviour of an application in the area of performance and reliability thus becomes more complicated. The effects of an insufficient estimation of the expected user load can be the crash of the entire system or a lack of application availability immediately following introduction. On the positive side it can be said that in comparison to "classical" applications the functionality of Internet applications is often considerably less in scope.

In summary, the following quality aspects for Internet or web applications can be emphasised:

- **User-friendliness**
  Many Internet applications are targeted towards a very heterogeneous group of users. The intention of a bookseller with his shop application is to be open and accessible to every user able and willing to spend money. This also means that only few general statements can be made with any certainty about the user's expectations, his education, his computer knowledge and many other factors relevant for the design of screens and business processes. The result of this is the quality requirement

that the look and feel of the Internet application be as intuitive and generally understandable as possible. In contrast to classical application development, it cannot be assumed for Internet applications that idiosyncratic or otherwise unusual features in the functionality or the interface can be compensated by user training, manuals or help texts. The importance of this quality requirement therefore becomes correspondingly greater.

- **Performance and reliability**
  Due to the heterogeneous user community and the influence of unpredictable events such as current media reports, predictions of the expected number of users that might concurrently use an Internet application become especially difficult. The press or announcements in the Internet can unleash a stampede of users on certain websites or web applications. Quality requirements with respect to performance and reliability must therefore be given greater emphasis so that Internet applications can handle an assumed number of concurrent users and can also react in an acceptable manner to a much greater number.

- **Multi-platform installability**
  The provision of an application in the Internet for different system platforms is made easier by the use of standardised protocols. At the same time though, there are new challenges in the software area (e.g. operating system, browser, user settings). The hardware and software configurations of users in the Internet can only be controlled in exceptional cases. The spectrum ranges from computer "amateurs" who use a pre-configured browser with standard settings on their PC to computer "experts" who use an uncommon, perhaps even self-developed, browser with many user-defined settings. A quality objective is therefore the operability of the application in all pre-defined target environments of potential users. Installation control tests must therefore be carried out in the different system configurations. Representatives of this type of application are banking applications in which the user prepares his transactions offline and only goes in online modus in order to transmit his transaction data. Experience has shown that specifics of the user environment often lead to unexpected system behaviour. When such system reactions occur, the user always places the blame on the software supplier.

- **Accessability**
  The type of user access to the Internet is also diverse. A firewall is usually integrated into the system architecture of users who access the Internet from their workplace. Private users often use dial-up access via modem and a local provider. Altogether this results in quality requirements concerning user access to an application. Every potential user of the Internet application should be able to use his preferred type of access.

- **Security**
  The danger exists that unauthorised users access information and Internet applications in an improper manner. The quality objective here is to provide all products and services only to the authorised user. At the same time, all unauthorised users must be denied access.

- **Up-to-dateness**
  The quality objective of up-to-dateness can be seen from both a contextual and a technical point of view. In the Internet, the user expects up-to-date content of an application and a modern and at all times up-to-date presentation of that content. Due to the short innovation cycles for technology and content – one speaks of seven Internet years per calendar year - a continual update of Internet applications is necessary. Links which today lead the user to associated companies or complementary products might be a dead end tomorrow. User interfaces which today appear "dynamic" and "cosmopolitan" might look "frumpy" tomorrow.

Each of these aspects can entail different activities and objectives for QA in Internet projects. As a result of the extremely short development cycles in the Internet area, these tasks and activities must be solved in a pragmatic way. Even though in general the functional scope of Internet applications is less than in conventional development projects, this is essentially more than compensated by the multitude of technical challenges in the automation of testing.

4   Classical Test Levels

In software quality assurance the principle of "divide and conquer" has asserted itself just as in software development. In software development there is the differentiation between the development of individual classes or modules, the integration of the classes and modules into an application as well as the integration of the application with neighbouring applications, for example via interfaces or common data.

Each of the different development and integration phases necessitates appropriate quality objectives or a different perspective. As an appropriate response to the different objectives in the process as a whole, the entire QA process is divided into different test levels. The different QA objectives, responsibilities, methods and tools are assigned to these test levels. Figure 3 shows one possible partitioning of the test objectives into test levels as practised in many enterprises today.

In the first test level, the documentation test, the accurateness of specifications and design decisions are examined. The focus is on functional and technical design documentation, for example the results of an object-oriented analysis or design. The design documentation is subjected to a test in the form of a review with the participation of developers and domain experts.

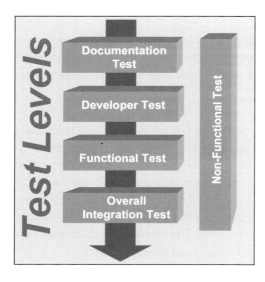

- **Documentation Review with User Department**

- **White-Box Test by Developers**

- **Black-Box Test by User Department**

- **Grey Box Test by User Department, Developers, Technical Experts**

Figure 3: Test Levels

In the developer test the developer or a tester from the development team tests the correct implementation (coding) of the specifications. During functional testing the accurateness of the implemented functions are tested from a user's point of view. Functional testing can be further divided into functional system testing, which focuses on the individual functions of an application, and functional integration testing (application testing or integration testing in the small), which tests the correct integration of the individual functions within an application. Sometimes an overall integration test (integration test in the large) is also carried out in which the correct integration of the application with other complete systems is verified. Non-functional testing takes place in parallel to these test levels, concentrating on non-functional quality characteristics such as performance, fault tolerance, reliability, usability and installability. Extensive descriptions of QA methods and procedures can be found in the testing literature (see e.g. [MYER79, BEIZ90, SCHU92]).

5 Testing Internet Applications

Within the classical test levels, which are still valid for Internet applications, there are new test objectives that result from the specific features of Internet architectures and requirements.

5.1 Differences in Documentation and Developer Testing

The objectives of documentation and developer testing remain unchanged. The methods used in these test levels must merely be adapted to the new, usually object-oriented design and development methods.

The special testing requirements of Internet applications implemented in Java should be taken into account already during the planning phase. The Java principle "Write once – run everywhere" in its current status of development can still cause problems. Experience has shown that different Java development kits (JDK) are often used. The danger of this is that the Java byte code can produce different results in different target systems. The integration of the JDKs in current browser versions is also problematic. It usually takes six months until a new JDK is implemented in current browser versions. Even the same release of a JDK on all computers does not guarantee that a Java application will behave the same on all platforms. Therefore the maxim "Write once – test everywhere" holds true for testing Java applications.

Building Internet applications with the help of Java applets or Java applications is only one aspect of Internet programming. Script languages such as JavaScript and VB Script (Visual Basic Script) also play an important role in web-based applications. Both have borrowed syntactically and semantically from their big brothers Java and Visual Basic, but still retain differences which are relevant for testing. Both script languages lack typing and are interpreted, not compiled. Type information is only known at run time. Type errors such as referencing non-existent methods of an object can therefore not be discovered until the application is executed. Simple syntax errors are no longer automatically uncovered through compilation.

The coverage of all program statements is a quality objective to be aimed at for web applications based on script languages. There is therefore the demand that every syntax error be found that can lead to a script error and consequently to a termination of the application. Unfortunately there are scarcely tools available which automatically measure the statement coverage for these script languages. Because the paradigm of object-oriented programming underlies both script languages, the established methods for testing object-oriented applications are also recommended (see e.g. [BIND00, MEYE99]).

5.2 Differences in Functional Testing

The task of testing the accurateness of functions is expanded by additional influencing factors such as diverse browsers and browser settings. The heterogeneous hardware configurations as well as the different possibilities of Internet access and consequently application use must already be taken into account when testing the individual user functions. These additional factors place increased demands on the methodical approach and qualifications of testers. In addition, individual tests should be repeated in diverse environments in order to discover differing behaviour, for example in different browsers.

Further relevant factors are the cache behaviour of the browsers, security settings and the activation of functionality such as JavaScript or the support of ActiveX components. This is an important area in practice because many environment properties which actually should not influence the application do indeed have an effect. Examples are the inadequate representation of objects using a certain screen resolution, failure of the application when using a certain browser and problems executing Java scripts on certain operating systems, just to name a few.

A decision matrix can help when analysing the factors to tested. The parameters in the matrix are the values to be covered in testing (browsers X, Y and Z; operating systems A, B and C; and further influencing factors) and the estimated risk for a combination of values. In essence, the risk for any combination of values can be calculated as the product of the probability that a failure will occur and the costs associated with that failure. The result is a matrix with weighted pairs of values which can be used as a basis for decisions on test case specification and the repeated execution of tests. Functional test cases, for example, are repeatedly executed on different platforms of the Internet application with different browsers. This places increased demands on test automation. Flexible test tools lend a helping hand here. Many capture-playback tools now allow a test to be recorded using one browser (e.g. Internet Explorer) and replayed in other browsers (e.g. various versions of Netscape Navigator).

5.3 Differences in Overall Integration Testing

In the overall integration test the use of the application beyond its boundaries is tested. At this point in time, the entire application (presentation, application and data layers) is available, and the connections and references within the application are also a subjected to QA activities. Upon integration of the application into the Internet environment it is also possible to examine external references, whereby the technical and functional correctness of these links should be assured.

Due to the fact that the Internet is a public, de-centrally administered network, the testing objective security becomes a new QA activity. Security checks of the setup, the technical implementation and the process organisation of the security systems (e.g. firewalls) are new challenges. Special security requirements apply to payment and home banking as well as many other Internet applications. These requirements are implemented for example with the help of encryption and signature mechanisms, which can make test planning and automation more difficult.

When building a test environment, data encryption should be taken into account as far as possible through integration of the corresponding components and creation of protocol files in a readable format. A conventional server test through the protocol layer with encrypted data transmission is of little help, because there is no or only a very costly possibility to intervene. One solution is to adapt the client application so that the test data can be edited as readable messages. Such an approach has been implemented in the HBCI TestSuite [MEYE01-b].

5.4 Differences in Non-Functional Testing

Load and performance tests for Internet applications are highly recommended due to the potentially very high number of users [CASP99]. A load test checks whether system behaviour remains stable when subjected to a defined base load, a permanent load and to load peaks. In addition to system stability, the examination of an application's performance according to specifications is also a test objective. Many tools support performance testing [FEWS99]. Tight delivery deadlines necessitate a pragmatic approach. The performance of the presentation layer (e.g. in the browser), the network connections, the web server, the application server and the database back-end system should be tested separately (see [ANDE99]).

Further non-functional requirements are relevant for web applications, e.g. security, user-friendliness and the adherence to design guidelines. The user-friendliness of an application is tested in a usability test. Because the user interfaces in the fast-moving Internet change so frequently, pragmatic methods are needed. During test preparation, checklists for the QA of graphical user interfaces (GUI) can be assembled based on general style guides or corporate guidelines. The tester then works through the checklists during test execution.

An extension of this rather formal method of usability testing is the definition of scenarios or user tasks that are executed by the tester. Measures for quality improvement can then be derived from the observation of test execution.

It is preferable that GUI experts prepare the GUI test. Additional testers can then help with execution. These testers should represent a statistical cross section of the future user community. Test results are evaluated according to a dual procedure. First, testers are observed in order to determine whether they encounter any handling problems while working through the scenarios. Then, questionnaires are used to guarantee a standardised feedback from the testers. The questions are an aid to determine whether the interface supports the work processes adequately and whether the structure and design of the application corresponds to expectations.

Loading times for individual web pages are longer in comparison to conventional applications. Often information is presented with a time delay. Therefore the questions should also clarify whether the user receives all information he requires for a task at one place or whether he has to navigate through several pages. The balance between an overabundance of information and the distribution of information over several pages is one of the key quality aspects that determine the user-friendliness of a web application.

5.5 Publishing

The formal and organisational separation of the test objectives into different test levels expedites the quality assurance process for complex applications. However, these test objectives can be combined for publishing applications. The term publishing application comprises corporate presentations as well as other publications in the Internet. In addition to examining the content, the representation of content in different browsers is tested. Performance and handling aspects are also tested. The integration of "external" services such as mail is a subject of quality assurance. Testing the content and accessibility of links - especially in the case of maintenance – should also be taken into account and automated, because periodical maintenance is essential.

6 Test Tools and Test Automation

In general, test tools for Internet applications have developed at the same rate as the Internet itself. Detailed statements about specific tools are only briefly relevant. Evaluation results that are more than four months old should therefore not be used when selecting suitable test tools. A renewed research and evaluation of tools then becomes necessary.

There is an array of capture-playback tools for graphical user interfaces. In Internet applications very many and different techniques are used to implement the control elements of the GUI (DHTML behaviour, Active-X controls, Java applets, etc.). Therefore an intensive evaluation of whether a given tool also supports the techniques used is necessary. When using capture-playback tools it is important that the effort needed for the creation and maintenance of scripts remains in a justifiable proportion to the effort required for manual testing. It is also important to remember that the automation of test activities is no substitute for a methodical approach. Test automation should also be based on a solid approach (see [DUST99, FEWS99]).

Practical experience has shown that test execution should be carried out through external Internet connections already at an early stage (in functional testing). That way, any problems in the technical design of the application which are caused by integrated third-party systems that cannot be influenced (firewalls, providers, etc.) are also discovered early.

7 Differences in Test Organisation

At least 30 % to 40 % of the total project effort should be set aside for testing and as such explicitly included in the project planning. For Internet applications it is a good idea to estimate test effort more generously due to the complexity of the technical environment. The same tests must be repeated in different environments, often though in the face of scarce resources. The decision on the prioritisation of QA measures in a project should therefore be based on a risk analysis.

The complexity of the test environments must be considered already during the specification of QA measures. The availability of different browsers and types of Internet access via various providers should be taken into consideration in the planning phase. These and other demands on the technical test environment are a decisive aspect for the organisational test planning. External test service providers who offer standardised access tests and test environment components can shorten the project duration. This also shortens the all-decisive time to market.

8 Summary

The Internet poses new challenges for software quality assurance and quality management. The familiar test levels remain but are supplemented by new test objectives, supported by corresponding methods and tools. With Internet technology new hardware and software components must be integrated into the test environment. The multifaceted requirements in the area of test preparation, test execution, the setup and organisation of test environments and the relevance of new test objectives must be considered early in the organisation of testing.

Due to continual technological change which is certain to continue in the future, the flexible adaptation of test methods and test tools remains a permanent task, especially for the Internet quality assurer and tester.

Part III

Testing from the User´s Perspective

Business–Oriented Testing in E-Commerce

THOMAS FEHLMANN

Euro Project Office AG (Switzerland)

Abstract: Time–to–market pressure and the ever–underestimated difficulty to get business requirements understood by Web designers, software engineers, and business people themselves do always constitute threats for serious Web testing. However, with the advent of B2B and B2G applications in the Web, thorough Web testing has become much more than a matter of customer satisfaction only. Erratic behaviour of a Web–based system is not only a threat to the Web site itself, it apparently has become one for the business behind it.

Testing concepts must be adapted to the needs of today's emerging Web economy. The goal of Web testing is to verify trustworthiness in all interactions. It requires the analysis of user and system interaction scenarios. This article is about how to derive a test strategy based on the nature of the Web interaction. We present a framework of Web testing, using a variety of testing techniques such as prototyping, usability tests, functionality tests, marketplace compliance, and law compliance tests.

The rules in the emerging Web business are changing fast. The traditional waterfall model for software testing does not work very well in the Web environment. Thus, we use dynamic models that combine the test methods with the rules and needs of the business transactions. We demonstrate this approach for a sample Web–based hotel reservation system.

Keywords: Internet testing, web testing, e-commerce, e–com trust, Internet-based applications, quality function deployment.

1 Software Testing and E-Commerce

1.1 Testing in E-Commerce

Testing means comparing the observed, "true" behaviour with the expected or specified behaviour of a system. In E-Commerce, the system providing the Web–based service includes business processes, network communications, various software components and data base engines. Web testing therefore includes testing of business processes (with hotline and physical intervention, if applicable), but it also includes system testing as well as testing of different client-side and server-side software components. It is further necessary to integrate aspects like availability, accessibility, and information rendering into the Web test strategy, since it would be shortsighted to concentrate only on how the system presents information needed to execute business processes. Rather we must test how the services finally reach the target customer if we do not want to miss the true behaviour of the Web–based service from the customer's viewpoint.

Formal specifications to test against are difficult to get. They are not always available. User expectations are even harder to understand. Sometimes, it is not even clear who the target users are.

In short, Web testing is a far step more complicated than traditional software testing. In addition, there is much more at stake: Tomorrow's markets.

1.2 A Model for an E-Commerce System

To understand what happens on a commercial Web site, we use a model for the transactions that characterise a commercial Web site. It consists of the following seven basic steps:

a. Attract. The prospective customer is attracted through a link, by a portal, by some feature, or other available information that is highly valuable for him.

b. Inform. The adjacent information provides the necessary knowledge to base a buying decision on it.

c. Select. The customer selects the exact features of the items, based on the available information mostly from this E-Commerce site.

d. Contract. The customer chooses to enter a contractual agreement with the seller on purchase of goods or services offered.

e. Deliver. The supplier takes the necessary measures to ensure timely delivery according to the contracted terms.

f. Billing. The supplier bills the customer according to the contracted terms.

g. Retention. The supplier acts appropriately to make sure the customer retrieves his Web site in time for new business transactions.

This model suits all sorts of Web transactions, such as C2C, B2C, B2B, G2C as well as G2G[1].It includes the sales process on the Web (step a – d), the fulfilment processes (step e & f), and the customer retention process (step g).

---

[1] G means Government; B means Business, C means Customer or Citizen, depending on the context.

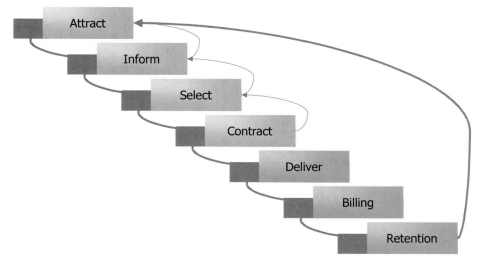

Figure 1: A Model of Web Business

1.2.1 Sales Process on the Web

Test criteria for the sales processes on the Web include

- Do we address the target customers?
- Do we look attractive for the target customers?
- Do we provide the kind of information they need?
- Are we speaking the language they understand and appreciate?
- Is our Web site available and fast enough for our customers?
- Is the focus on service?
- Is there anything that may divert the customer from doing business with us?

This kind of criteria we best test with an early prototype, using focus groups of customers to get their voice understood.

Other criteria for the sales processes on the Web relate to contractual and legal risks:

- Is the information we provide correct and conclusive?
- Is the information the customer needs for selection complete?
- What if access to information is not available (e.g. for technical reasons)?
- Do the selection mechanisms reflect the customer's choice possibilities?
- Are the terms and conditions clearly stated?

- Is the customer explicitly asked for consent?
- Do the legally relevant transactions survive system unavailability (e.g. breakdown of network communications)?
- Are technical restraints (e.g. browser incompatibilities) detected that may impact legally relevant transactions?
- Are contractual terms mutually understood?

All these criteria have both technical aspects as well as cultural and lingual aspects. While static quality assurance (e.g. formal reviews) may suffice to deal with the static content of your E-Commerce site, software tests are necessary to assess the dynamic aspects. We need system tests to assess behaviour under stress (performance, breakdown of a component), thus we use a full range of test tools already at this point.

1.2.2 Fulfilment Processes on the Web

Billing is a very complicated step on an E-Commerce site in Europe, because there are so many different payment methods and processes[2]. Test criteria include

- Delivery by downloads: Reliability and Recovery
- Physical delivery:
    - Reliability of delivery confirmation
    - Reliability of delivery status tracking
    - Exception handling
    - Handling of guaranteed delivery
    - Handling of damage incurred on transportation
    - Handling of delayed delivery
- Delivery split and part delivery (if not all parts are available)
- Order consolidation (for instance to deliver two orders at once)
- Link between bill and delivery (When is the amount due?)
- Credit Card handling
- Secure Transfer
- Solvency Check (depends much from the selected payment method)
- Identification and Authorisation
- Address validation
- Fraudulent use detection
- Local regulations

---

[2] A recent count showed about 54 different payment variants in EU countries.

Testing these fulfilment processes usually requires a combination between business process validation and software test. This is necessary on very different levels.

1.2.3 Customer Retention

Will the customer find his way back? There are many ideas on the Web on how to retain customer loyalty. They may lead to the following tests:

- Does the customer successfully sign on an interest list?
- Can we validate his address?
- Handling of address changes
- Correct recording of customer's preferences
- Verification or validation of customer's profile
- Do we successfully identify the market segment he fits into?
- Can we guess what our customer will buy next?

Again, tests will be a mix of business process tests with software tests.

2   Interaction Scenarios & Testing Techniques

2.1 Scenario Overview

The tests needed for a Web–based system are located on various *topic levels*. We have based our development model on the well-known *V-model*, extended to an additional upper topic level. This upper topic level represents the needs of the Web users.

Each level on the Web Development Model corresponds to one of the topics [FEHL00-b] addressed in a Web project. We address the following four topics for a Web–based system: Customer's Needs, Business Processes, Web–based System Architecture, and Web Software Components. The Web Architecture consists of Web design & ICT integration and defines how our Web–based system will offer its services. On each level, we have deliveries and tests that specify the behaviour of the deliverables. Following the eXtreme Programming paradigm [BECK99], we specify the behaviour of the system and its components by the tests the system is supposed to pass. This is applicable on each of the four topic levels.

It is possible that one single level splits into several planes, still on the same level, but with different subtopics. This may happen for instance if custom coding becomes a goal in itself and the Web Software Components level has a standard component part and a custom component part that requires custom programming including coding. In addition, different design approaches may co-exist for data base services and information rendering.

There is indeed a significant difference between the V–model as we know it from standard software development, and the Web Development Model. As we will see, testing is the first development task on each of the development planes, and the last task as well. Testing on each of the planes occurs many times during the first tests and the last tests. Testing is almost an ongoing task, however, we *plan* for each of those tasks[3].

The development model for Web–based systems consists of four levels; as follows:

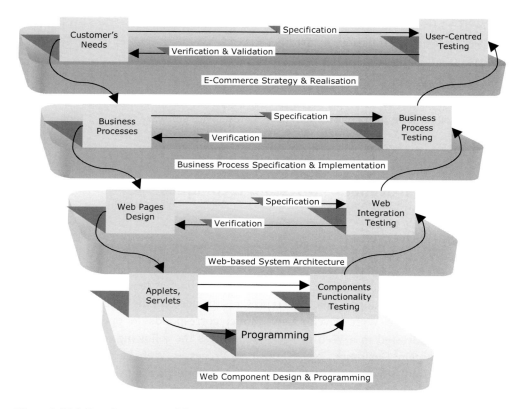

Figure 2: Web Development Model

---

[3] Tests that are not planned will never be executed (wisdom of the Eternal Project Manager).

2.2 User–Centred Testing

The Top Level is "E-Commerce Strategy & Realisation". Test on that level is the first to commence with the initial requirements for the Web–based service.

2.2.1 Prototyping

We recommend to execute all user interaction tests at least twice, and maybe many times in between: At the very beginning of construction of the Web-based service, to document and validate the specifications, and at the end, as the final acceptance test. While acceptance testing executes on the final system, the first tests require a prototype. Prototypes allow at an early stage to emulate the behaviour of a system, even if the system as such does not yet exist.

The difficulty with prototyping in E-Commerce is that testers behave differently as long as they know they are testers. For instance, they do trust a site because they know the site's operator being their employer. Therefore, they are very unlikely to detect such aspects that may lead to a bad image of the site towards prospective customers. They may generate extended traffic as long as they spend their employer's money and not their own. Thus it is not enough to build a prototype, hire testers and collect their opinion. Prototyping does work only if we assess the usefulness of a tested feature for the target customer, e.g. by using *metrics* to identify the value that the Web–based service can provide to customers. Such value may be saving of time, less handling cost, faster availability, or expert advice in selecting the best configuration. Such metrics define the *user profile* for this particular task. Thus, a profile is can be seen as a metric. We therefore have to set up user profiles for the target customers that are supposed to use our Web–based service.

We can also test trust, if we use double-blind testing scenarios. That is, we define two groups of testers, show them our prototype and a reference site and let them evaluate characteristic aspects for trust. To find such characteristic aspects, we use the techniques of *Combinatory Metrics* that we explain in section 3.2: Business Metrics. The two groups get each two sites, our prototype and another well-known E-Commerce site, to evaluate for their trustworthiness, but we will tell only one group that this is the task, the other will be asked for their opinion concerning usability of the sites. Both will answer the same questionnaire, but from different viewpoints. The two groups must not communicate.

2.2.2 Acceptance Testing

The result of building the prototype is a set of test cases that defines the acceptance tests. We will rerun them many times throughout the various development phases for the E-Commerce site. However, the final step is the formal acceptance test by executing all documented acceptance test cases on the finished target system. This "Last Run" closes the development phases and initiates the maintenance phase of the E-Commerce project.

We strongly recommend automating the acceptance test cases at least for that last run. For efficiency, if automation becomes available much earlier in the project, however, we will see that the acceptance test cases will be rerun again and again during the life cycle of the E-Commerce Web–based service.

2.3 Business Process Testing

2.3.1 Requirements Engineering and Testing

We define the test cases for the business processes our Web–based system shall perform. Business processes consist of input, output, and of transactions in between. They become test cases when we supply test input, specify expected output and the cost and cycle times targets.

We explain the process for specifying the requirements and the corresponding tests by presenting the form that we use (Figure 3). The upper part presents the external input, output and enquiries that we need to execute the business process. In our simplified payment process example below, we have two external inputs (customer and amount due, from the Web interface), one output (the bill for the customer's records), two external interface files (phone book and accounting). The payment process manages four internal data stores (customer information, their accounts, account receivables, and a customer relations log file). Arrows indicate data flow. The form automatically calculates the size of the software needed to implement this process in unadjusted function points (FP).

The "Process Manager" is the owner of the payment process. He draws the process and specifies which tests he wants the Web–based service to pass. Together with the analyst, and based on the prototype, he also helps to determine what kind of data is needed to run the process (i.e. the DETs and RETs, [IFPU00]), and provides test data and test conditions (e.g. breakdown of communication during data transfer).

2.3.2 Web Application Testing

Business Process testing starts later than user-centred testing but constitutes a repeated activity during Web development. Compared to the rapid change of business offers, the business processes are more stable. It is therefore essential that whenever new offers (i.e. not just a change of price or item, but of pricing or bundling strategy) go life, all business processes undergo an automated regression test to ensure that they still run properly.

Based on the requirements, it is now straightforward to calculate error density. Because we had Function Points already in the requirements, we easily find out how many defects we can remove within a given time and effort frame. Thus, we know with how many defects our system has to start with, and therefore we can right-size hotline staffing using statistical methods. As a result, we can care for our customers even if we have to start with a still immature system to support our Web–based service.

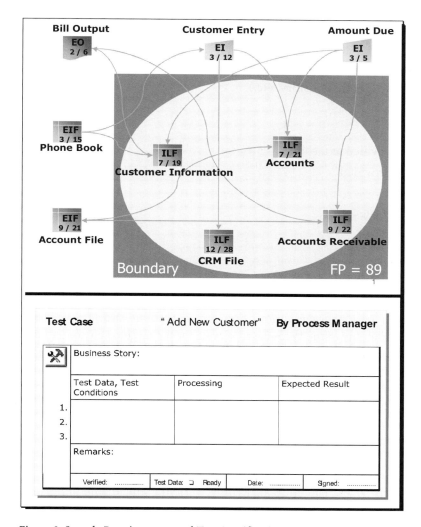

Figure 3: Sample Requirements and Test Specification Form

2.4 Web Integration Testing

The topic level is about how the various components of the Web–based systems architecture work together. Typical topics include

- Portal functionality – integrating various services on the Web
- Information retrieval, data base access
- Parameter passing from one part of the Web–based system into another

- Navigation completeness
- Context dependencies
- Information display
- Context sensitivity (profiles, history, etc.)
- Browser support
- Platform support
- Mail addresses provided as a contact
- Phone numbers provided
- Links outbound
- Automatic URL checks
- Links inbound
- Search engines

There are many country-dependencies such as phone integration and translation issues, which need testing. Legal statements also do vary depending on the country.

Compatibility issues arise between various browser generations and Java versions. We must optimise availability of the Web–based service for the targeted customer base. Extended backward compatibility may be an issue if you address an audience of teachers, public servants, or people in the health services, but makes no sense if you address a young affluent community – you better care for the latest gadget here.

We use the same procedure as mentioned above in the case of business processes and specify the tests that our system must pass. Function Points are of less importance on this level because of the heavy use of component integration rather than custom programming. The effort of writing the interfaces is not only dependent on the interface functionality alone, but also on the component's design. Furthermore, it is yet unclear how to size static Web pages. The effort of writing, verifying and maintaining such pages depends on content, not on information size.

Thus, we face many technical risks on this level and better care for complementing our Web testing effort with suitable risk management, see for example [MELI98].

3   Dynamic Testing According to Business Needs

We have seen that the preparation of tests for a Web–based system involves considerably more effort than conventional testing. It is worthy of note that in the beginning of Web business, managers did believe that the Web is a particularly cheap sales channel, knowing indeed already, that the complexity and challenge of traditional software projects had for long already been continuously underestimated. We think that this is a misconception. The Web is not a cheap sales channel, but one that allows providing much better service than any other does. This is because the Web allows simultaneous access to the very best offers and the information needed to evaluate them.

Nevertheless, it is a long way to go until we can be sure to make the best use of the new media. Until then, we have to live with the rapid change that this new market embraces. Spending significant investments for Web testing is reasonable only if we can reuse our test investments while our Web–based service evolves. This is where Combinatory Metrics starts playing a crucial role for the Web business.

3.1 Combinatory Metrics

3.1.1 Measuring Goals and Objectives

Combinatory Metrics is an extension of Comprehensive Quality Function Deployment (QFD). For introductions into various application of QFD, see [AKAO90], [FEHL00-a], [FEHL00-b], [MELI98], [HERZ97].

We use Combinatory Metrics when we cannot measure directly. Although we can provide cost & revenue projections, we find it difficult to measure the goals and objectives our Web–based service must satisfy to reach the financial targets. This is because complete specifications cannot exist. For all practical purposes, specifications of goals and objectives are incomplete and only partially suited to measure the likelihood of future success.

However, as shown by Engeler [4], infinite combinatory models approximate such systems that we cannot specify completely. In project management practice and product development, Quality Function Deployment (QFD) [AKAO90], [COHE95], [MAZU93], [MIZU94], [SHIL00], [ZULT92] constitutes such an infinite combinatory model for quality that today is widely in use.

3.1.2 Elements of QFD

QFD allows for two basic operations:

a.   It describes how a solution approach contributes to solve a problem. Traditionally, the problem has been stated as how to satisfy customers' needs; the solution to it being the optimum choice of solution components that constitute the solution approach. The tool used is the well-known correlation matrix, commonly referred to as the "House of Qualities[4]".

---

[4] Strictly speaking, the "House of Qualities" is the first of a sequence of correlation matrices that describe the quality deployment for a given project, product, or service.

We call the items being correlated to each other, such as solution approaches and the problem under question, *Deployment Topics*. The target Deployment Topics we call *Goal Topics* (the left–hand side of the correlation matrix), the means describing the solution approach we call *Solution Topics* (bottom of the matrix).

We refer to these links between the *Deployment Topics* described by such correlation matrices as *Cause–Effect Combinators*[5].

The cause–effect relation itself we describe by an approximated value that is suitable to the topics combined. If human perception is involved, the most appropriate rating scale is "1" for low, "3" for medium, and "9" for high impact. Although we can have precision as needed, this scale is the most popular [AKAO90], [SHIL00].

The following is a sample Cause–Effect Combinator used for the Hotel Reservation System explained below:

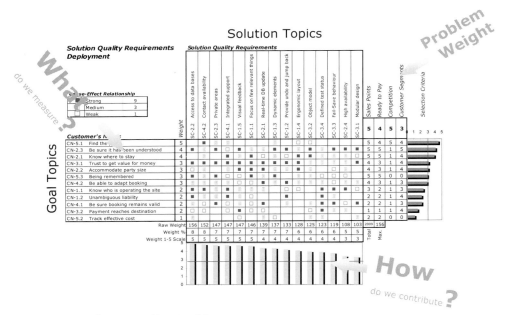

Figure 4: A Sample Cause–Effect Combinator

b. Furthermore, QFD describes how two Cause–Effect Combinators $F * G$ may be applied to each other. The Solution Topics that are the cause for the Goal Topics of the Cause–Effect Combinator F become in turn the Solution Topics in Cause–Effect Combinator G. We thus can daisy chain our cause–effect combinators and

---

[5] Cause–Effect Combinators are sometimes referred to as Cause–Effect Analysis. However, there exist many approaches to cause–effect analysis and not many of those share the capability of being combinators.

thus get profiles for the solution topics down the line. We refer to such combination chains as *Comprehensive QFD*.

These profiles weight the different solution topics with respect to the goal topics. We therefore get a metric for the solution topics that tell us their relative importance with respect to the customer's needs. When the solution topics become the goal topics for the next step down the line, then the resulting profile still references the customer's needs as its anchor point. Such a succession of profiles connected by cause–effect diagrams we call Combinatory Metrics.

We cannot measure Combinatory Metrics directly, so their accuracy depends on the correctness and completeness of the cause–effect analysis, as well as on the existence of "anchor points". Anchor points are topic levels that we can measure directly[6].

To take good advantage of Combinatory Metrics, it is important to measure available topics as exactly and effectively as possible. The better we e.g. know Customer's Needs, the better our Web–based service can meet them. Measuring them is in general not easy, but using our Web–site we have many possibilities to gather data about our customers and using these for better understanding of the views and values of the customer.

3.2 Business Metrics

The left-hand side of the Web Development Metrics (Figure 5) shows three deployments in sequence between the four topic levels Customer's Needs, Business Processes, Web–based System Architecture, and Web Software Components. These three deployments combine the solution topics with the goal topic "Customer's Needs". The combinations thus yield a profile for each topic level that tells us how much each of them contributes to the goal topic. This metric links all business topics to Customer's Needs and therefore to business results.

However, after we just stated that Web testing is expensive, are we now going to propagate yet another expensive tool? It is obvious that analysing cause and effect and drawing matrices as in Figure 4 is a time- and effort-consuming task.

Let us first note that cause–effects relations do not change much over time. We may add or disregard topic items, but as long as cause–effect combinations are involved, they remain. Thus constructing a combinator is not a significant investment, certainly not if compared with Web Testing.

However, the importance of the topics, and the topic items itself, change quite frequently. Thus, once we have understood the combinators, playing with different sets of topics and different values given to them is the fun part of it. We can follow changing customer's needs as they get increasingly into adopting E-Commerce, and adjust pri-

---

[6] For instance, New Lanchester Theory links Combinatory Metrics to market share data, see [FEHL00-a].

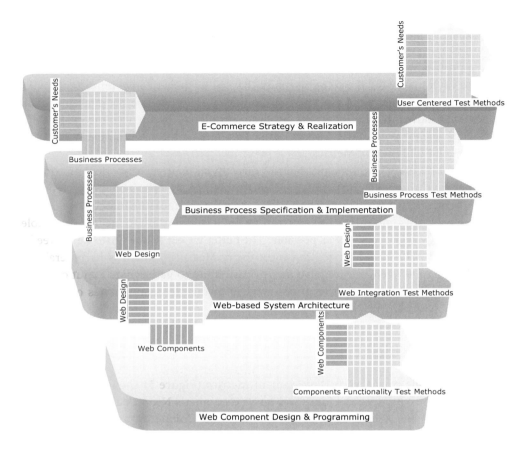

Figure 5: Web Development Metrics

orities on all topic levels accordingly. Thus, we have metrics at hand that tell us where to focus further development and change efforts.

Using these metrics, it is possible to direct development of the Web–based service towards better business results. Because the matrices describe cause–effect relationships, we can directly influence business results by adding certain features to our Web–base service that yield maximum effect towards satisfying customer's needs even better. Investments and development decisions depend therefore both on our understanding of customer's needs. With such an optimisation strategy, we can expand our E-Commerce towards a higher market share.

3.3 Test Coverage Combinators

We again use the same technique to understand how well the tests we have conceived cover the features that are important for the customer. The cause–effect relation now indicates if a particular test case is capable to uncover a defect within our approach to the goal topic. These combinators describe the test coverage, but not as percentage of lines of code touched by testing, not even of Function Points, but rather in relation to Customer's Needs. We therefore have a means to immediately detect where changes in the environment, or within our Web–based service, did affect the trustworthiness of our system. We also can select test cases according to their capability to detect as many defects as possible. Thus, we can spend the test money on those features that matter most for the business.

3.4 Example: Hotel Reservation System

In this case study, we outline the testing strategy for a hotel reservation system[7] that allows for checking available rooms, online booking, down–payment, and online check–out. The Web users may access the system from anywhere on the Internet, including the Internet terminals in their hotel room, or at the reception desk. As a means for customer retention, the customers can post images and other memories of their stay on a personalised customer profile page, linking the site to their own home page or favourite link collection.

As an example for how to deal with the moving target, we have added two more customer's needs that have not been known when the first release of the hotel reservation system went online. It became apparent that the users did not trust the provider of the Web–based service; thus, we later added these needs to the list of Customer's Needs. The List of Customer's Needs is shown in Figure 6: We assume that the profile for the Customer's Needs is the result of market studies and customer enquiries.

Customer's Needs			Explanations	0 1 2 3 4 5
CN-1 Trust	CN-1.1	Know who is operating the site	The need to know who is operating the Web business.	
	CN-1.2	Unambiguous liability	Know how to act in case of incidents or fraud	
CN-2 Booking	CN-2.1	Know where to stay	The need to identify the place where the hotel is.	
	CN-2.2	Accommodate party size	Availability of suitable rooms for all the party.	
	CN-2.3	Be sure it has been understood	Unambiguousity across language and cultural borders.	
CN-3 Pricing	CN-3.1	Trust to get value for money	Have the opportunity to compare price levels.	
	CN-3.2	Payment reaches destination	Know where to pay and where the payment goes.	
CN-4 Traveling	CN-4.1	Be sure booking remains valid	... and you don't arrive at midnight and won't find a bed.	
	CN-4.2	Be able to adapt booking	Flexibility of travel plans change.	
CN-5 Stay	CN-5.1	Find the place	Actually retrieve the hotel upon arrival.	
	CN-5.2	Track effective cost	Get a detailed bill that identifyes cost items.	
	CN-5.3	Being remembered	Have the feeling to be highly estimated as a guest.	

Figure 6: Customer's Needs in a Web–based Hotel Reservation System

---

[7] This is a fake system to demonstrate our experiences with Web–based systems. Not related with www.hrs.de.

3.4.1 Customer's Needs Deployment into Business Processes

Based on that anchor point, we know from our expertise which business processes affect customer's needs:

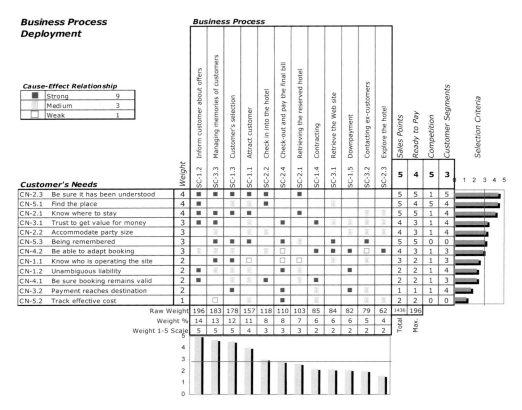

Figure 7: Deployment of Business Processes

This combinator gives a strong precedence for these three processes:

a. SC-1.2: Inform customer about offers.
b. SC-3.3: Managing memories of customers.
c. SC-1.3: Customer's selection.

The next business process that is almost as important is

d. SC-1.1: Attract customer.

This is already quite an interesting insight, possibly enough to re-think the focus of our Web marketing.

3.4.2 Deployment of Business Processes into the Systems Architecture

We describe the system architecture by the use case design, from which we show a simplified sample in the combinator below.

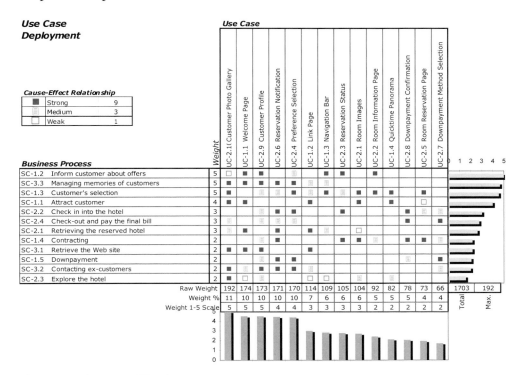

Figure 8: Deployment of Use Cases

We find precedence for the following use cases:

a. UC-2.10: Customer Photo Gallery
b. UC-1.1: Welcome Page
c. UC-2.9: Customer Profile
d. UC-2.6: Reservation Notification
e. UC-2.4: Preference Selection

3.4.3 Test Coverage Metrics for the Web Components

The result of the coverage matrix (not shown) was that the most important tests were on billing components (not surprising) and on the upload service, used for uploading pictures for the photo gallery. The team had not anticipated this because they thought the picture gallery was rather a marketing gag than something serious. However, seen from the customer's perspective, the reliability of the picture upload is taken easily as an indication of how reliable all the remaining features on the Web site really are.

And even more interesting: This upload – feature rated significantly lower before we took the two trust – related customer's needs into consideration. It turned up because of the shift in the marketplace, not because we detected any new cause – effect relationship.

3.4.4 Test Coverage Metrics for the Systems Architecture

We can check how well our system tests cover the system architecture. To do this, we use again the technique of combinatory metrics. The cause–effect relation between tests and the use cases is our estimation of how many defects the test is able to detect in each use case. We rate this ability again with numbers between "1" and "9" and prepare test coverage combinators as follows (Figure 9).

The metrics detect if our test cases cover the use cases according to their relevance to the customer's needs. To demonstrate, we compare the weight profiles of the use cases (light profile) with the coverage profile of the test cases (dark profile).

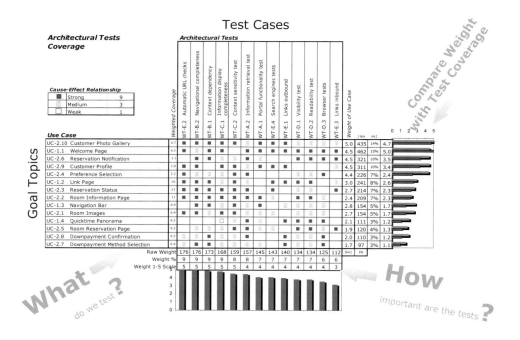

Figure 9: Test Coverage for the Web–based Systems Architecture

We see from the profile (right side of the matrix) that we do not have equally well covered the following use cases:

- UC-2.6: Reservation Notification
- UC-2.9: Customer Profile
- UC-2.4: Preference Selection

as we did with the UC-2.10: Customer Photo Gallery and the UC-1.1: Welcome Page.

This indicates that we may either miss some of the defects, or waste some testing effort on the first two use cases in the matrix.

When selecting test cases, such conflicts may not always be avoidable, but we can detect them.

3.4.5 Test Coverage Metrics for the Business Processes

For the Business Processes, we consider the following tests:

		Test Case Identifier		Short Description
AT-A	**Forms functionality**	BT-A.1	Information completeness	Static review and dynamic semi-automated test if everything is visible.
		BT-A.2	Field validation	Automated test for all fields.
		BT-A.3	Internationalization	Regression tests with change of language.
AT-B	**Acknowledgement**	BT-B.1	Confirmation pages	Correctness of confirmations. Automated API test.
		BT-B.2	Workflow notification	Correctness of workflow. Automated API test.
AT-C	**Business contacts**	BT-C.1	CRM track and exception handling	Browser screen scripts with various exceptions.
		BT-C.2	E-mails received and answered	Business process test; no software involved (except e-mail).
		BT-C.3	Phone numbers work internationally	Conducted once with help of international partners.
		BT-C.4	Process owners in charge	Repeated QMS audit; business test.
		BT-C.5	Customer Information correctness	Focus Group customer data is checked with customer for correctness.
AT-D	**Compliance**	BT-D.1	Law compliance test	Static review and dynamic semi-automated test if everything is visible.
		BT-D.2	Marketplace compliance test	Business inquiry rerun after each new release.
		BT-D.3	Geographic compliance test	Test if hotel locations are understandably correct.

Figure 10: Application Tests for the Business Processes

Test coverage for the business processes is calculated using a combinator similar to Figure 9: Test Coverage for the Web–based Systems Architecture.

3.4.6 Test Coverage Metrics for the Customer's Needs

	Test Case Identifier		Short Description
ACT-A Navigation	UT-A.1	Ergonomic tests	Lab tests that let users process their requests and watches them.
	UT-A.2	User associations	What users associate with each of the items shown (Focus group)
	UT-A.3	Process Navigation	Automated Test; Counts the number of clicks needed for a process.
	UT-A.4	Usage statistics	Automated data collection. Should match the New Lanchester Theory predictions.
ACT-Z Business	UT-B.1	Hits Counter	Automated data collection. Should be the target customers.
	UT-B.2	Order statistics	Automated data collection. Should match the New Lanchester Theory predictions.
ACT-Z Satisfaction	UT-C.1	Expectations inquiry	Short 1-page satisfaction inquiry
	UT-C.2	4 hour memory	Group of testers been asked what they remember after 4 hours
	UT-C.3	36 hour memory	group of testers been asked what they remember after 36 hours

Figure 11: Acceptance Tests for the Web–based Service

We drafted this acceptance test in order to know if we did match customer's needs. Note how much the customer's needs differ in weight, and how the test coverage reflects that difference.

Passing the test, we had tested what really did matter. Note that we had not to introduce new tests for trust here, but to interpret them differently.

As before, test coverage for the acceptance tests is calculated using a similar combinator as in Figure 9: Test Coverage for the Web–based Systems Architecture.

4 Conclusions

Web testing is more complex than traditional software testing. It must include business processes and organisational settings. Thus, cost of testing is an issue. At the same time, the users are much less forgiving than internal employee users for traditional applications. They have a choice to turn away from our Web–based service if it does not satisfy their needs and expectations (and they did so in masses during the first wave of E–Commerce). Since no E–Commerce culture exists yet, expectations and requirements change too frequently to allow for traditional approaches in testing. Specifications to test against are not readily available, and if they are, then they are not technical in nature.

We need new techniques to adapt more flexible and faster to business needs. The technique of Comprehensive QFD Combinators is available for this purpose and people have gathered much experience with it, although not exactly in the testing area. In addition, we know only of a few applications of QFD to Web business so far, but those we know are very successful.

Test Combinators for measuring test coverage are in use in many forms, however, it is not yet common to use them in a dynamic setting. Combinators remain stable, but market needs are not.

Strategic Testing: Focus on the Business

PAUL KEESE
SQS AG (Germany)

Abstract: This article describes a flexible approach for integration testing based on business processes. The approach was successfully implemented in medium, large and very large projects in large organisations of different industries. In this approach the tester defines test cases for the functions of a business process. The test cases are then linked together to form test case sequences. Each test case sequence tests a certain path through a business process. The approach supports various testing strategies for applications in a time-constrained project environment. A testing strategy with business-oriented integration testing as its focal point can quickly deliver a picture of an application's overall quality as well as point out areas where more detailed and intensive testing is needed. The test approach is tool-supported.

Keywords: Integration testing, business processes, test case specification, test management

1 Introduction

In a time of rapid technological change and increasing competition the lifecycle of software applications – as well as the associated time-to-market for new software products – is becoming ever shorter. This makes the lives of not only software developers but also of testers more difficult, because less and less time remains for testing the software before it "goes live." Or if we describe the problem as a challenge: the tester must use the little time he has as efficiently as possible in order to attain the highest level of software quality possible and thus avoid a "meltdown" in production.

In such situations, integration testing based on business processes can be a very powerful and efficient weapon. Integration testing can give an enterprise the assurance that its business processes are adequately supported by newly developed or changed software. This is especially important for critical, i.e. high-income, high-volume, and high-visibility business processes. Integration testing can also quickly deliver an overall picture of the quality of a software system and uncover areas where more intensive testing is necessary.

In order to maximise the benefits of integration testing, a testing approach is called for which is flexible and, if possible, tool-supported. This paper describes an integration testing approach in a step-by-step manner using an example from a commercial software system. A test tool that supports this approach is also outlined.

2 Business Processes and Integration Testing

2.1 Testing Business Processes

In a software project, one or more software applications are modified or newly developed. From the user's point-of-view this means that new software-supported business functions are created or existing functions are changed.

The task of business testing is to verify that the new or modified software performs according to business requirements and specifications. Business-oriented testing can be performed for individual functions – this is commonly referred to as functional testing. For the user though it is essential that he can correctly carry out his business tasks with the software. In other words, it is important to verify that the individual functions in integration with one another correctly support the work – the business processes – of the user.

In order to test the business-oriented integration of newly developed or modified software, the software functions that are created or changed within a project are assigned to the business processes that they support. A business integration test can then be defined and executed on the basis of the relevant business processes (Figure 1).

The definitions for a business process are numerous and vary widely, especially with respect to the scope of a single business process. Here, a *business process* refers to a sequence of work steps that begins with an external input or action (for example, a customer enters the bank and fills out a withdrawal form) and ends with an external

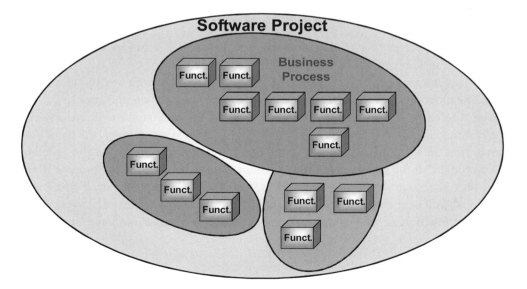

Figure 1: Business Processes in Integration Testing

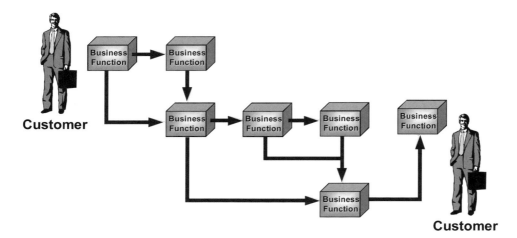

Figure 2: A Business Process

output or action (for example, the customer receives the cash as well as a printed receipt and his account his debited). Each non-manual step of a business process is supported by a business function of a software application (Figure 2).

The processing within a business process is often called *end-to-end processing*, whereby different paths through a business process can be possible, depending on the business situation.

2.2 The Business Process "New Bank Account"

The business process "New Bank Account" will be used to illustrate the integration testing approach as well as possibilities for tool support.

A person enters the bank and wishes to open a bank account with or without a credit card. The functions that are part of this business process are shown in Figure 3.

First, the bank employee runs a credit check for the person through an external credit rating agency. Assuming the person's credit rating is satisfactory, the bank employee first adds the person as a new customer or branches directly to the function "Add account" if the person is already a customer at the bank. If the customer is to receive special account terms or a credit card, then the bank employee must first input additional data before he reports the new credit information to the external agency.

The last function of the business process updates the customer and account master data.

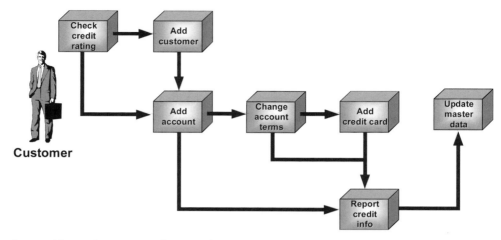

Figure 3: The Business Process "New Bank Account"

With the help of a tool, the tester can specify an integration test for the business process "New Bank Account" with the following steps:

- Create a test scheme for the business process.
- For each function of the business process, create a system function and assign it to the test scheme.
- Create an empty test case sequence for a selected path through the business process.
- Complete the test case sequence by defining a test case for each system function on the business process path and inserting the test case in the test case sequence.

The following objects are involved (Figure 4).

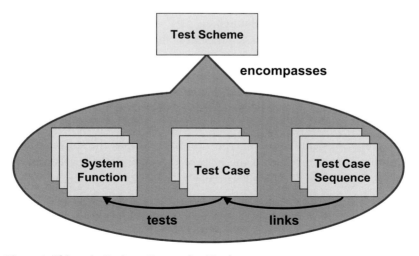

Figure 4: Objects in Business Integration Testing

3   Structuring the Test

3.1   Organisation of Integration Testing

Before actual testing can begin, the overall testing task (e.g. testing of software developed within a project) must first be broken down into smaller, more manageable units (*test items*).

In the approach described here, the tester can organise the test with the help of test schemes. A *test scheme* is a specific plan for testing a given software using pre-defined test activities carried out by assigned persons within a certain timeframe in order to achieve one or more test objectives. Test schemes can be hierarchically structured, whereby each "node" of the test scheme hierarchy can be assigned a specific meaning (test scheme type).

The highest-level test scheme is usually the (test) project. Depending on the size of a project, the project can also be divided into sub-projects. A test project can encompass different test levels, each with its own test objectives. Test levels in this example are "Developers Test", "Function Test", and "Integration Test". Finally the test items for each business process to be tested in integration testing – including the test item "New Bank Account" – are created beneath the test scheme "Integration Test".

3.2   Description of Software to be Tested

The tester describes the "world" to be tested with the help of system functions. *System functions* can be used to structure software from a user's point of view (e.g. business functions) or from a technical standpoint (e.g. technical functions or individual modules). Which software is relevant and how it is best depicted by system functions depends on the types of tests (test schemes) planned.

For integration testing based on business processes, the user-oriented (business) functions needed to execute the business process are of interest. Therefore, the system functions in this case are the user functions in the business processes to be tested. This can also include business functions not developed or modified within the current project but needed for the business process. It is recommended to structure the system functions within a hierarchy. The specific meaning of a "node" in such a hierarchy can be specified by assigning a system function "type". In this example, the software to be executed during testing is structured with the help of three hierarchy levels and the system function types "application" ("Retail Banking"), "product" (e.g. "Credit Info"), and "function" (e.g. "Check credit rating").

3.3 Test Item Definition

The test schemes at the (lowest) most detailed level of the test scheme hierarchy are called "test items". They organise or group the test cases and test case sequences for use in a specific project. Tests are prepared and executed in the context of a test item. The tester should define exactly which system functions are to be tested by each test item. One possible test completion criterion can call for each system function of a certain type to be tested by at least one test item.

The integration test item "New Bank Account" tests all functions of the business process, i.e. the system functions "Check credit rating", "Add customer", "Add account", "Change account terms", "Add credit card", "Report credit info", and "Update master data". In the software that supports such tests – namely SQS-TEST/Professional - these system functions are assigned to the test item by "drag and drop" (Figure 5).

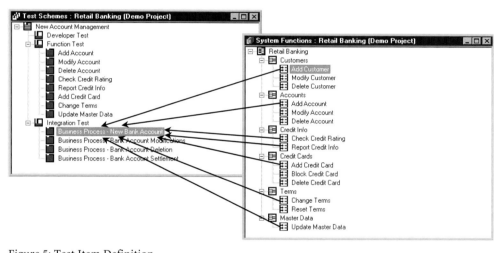

Figure 5: Test Item Definition

4   From Business Process to Test Case Sequence

4.1 Level of Testing Intensity

The integration testing approach described here can be carried out with varying degrees of intensity. For a given testing approach, the completion criteria applied during test specification significantly determine the level of test coverage achieved but also the costs of the test in terms of time and money [KEES01-a]. The test completion criterion suitable for integration testing a given business process is dependent upon the risk of the business process on the one hand and the available resources (time, personnel, budget) on the other hand.

For an integration test on the basis of business processes, different test completion criteria are possible. Of the criteria suggested below, the first criterion requires the least effort but also delivers the lowest level of test coverage; the last criterion can easily be the most costly but can also guarantee a high level of quality.

1. Each business function of the business process has been executed at least once during the test.
2. Each possible path through the business process has been executed at least once during the test.
3. Each possible path has been executed at least "n" times, whereby "n" must be determined beforehand based upon risk and available resources.
4. As an addition to any criterion above: Define test cases for critical functions and execute each test case at least once.

4.2 Building a Test Case Sequence

4.2.1 Business Process Path as Test Case Sequence

When integration testing a business process, the tester always executes a certain path through the process, i.e. a sequence of business functions. The manner in which a given business function is to be executed can be described by a functional test case. The end-to-end specification of an integration test consists therefore of a succession of test cases or a *test case sequence*. The individual test cases in a test case sequence must "fit" together in such a way that the data created or changed by one test case corresponds or at least does not contradict the data needed or expected by the test cases that follow (Figure 6).

One such path through the business process "New Bank Account" is shown below (Figure 7).

In order to define a test case for this path in the test tool SQS-TEST/Professional, we first create an "empty" test case sequence with the name "Standard Account for New Customer". The next step is to fill the test case sequence with "life", that is, define test cases for the functions that lie on the path and then link the test cases together.

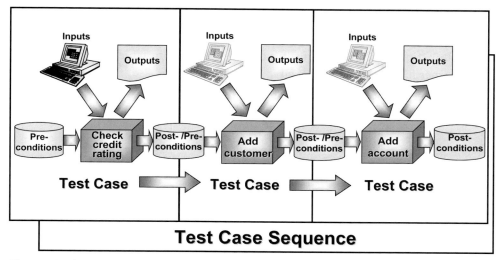

Figure 6: Business Process Path as Test Case Sequence

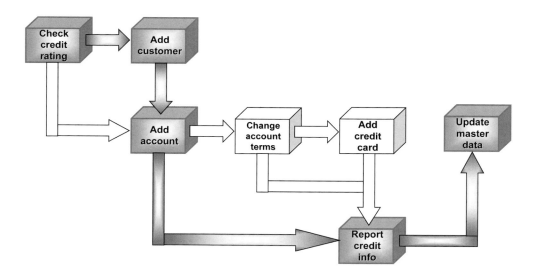

Figure 7: Path "Standard Account for New Customer"

4.2.2 Test Cases for Business Functions

The expected behaviour of a business function can be described with the help of a test case. A *test case* can be defined using the following *components* (Figure 8):

- At the "center" of the test case is the *system function* or functionality to be tested (e.g. "Add customer").

- The functionality has prerequisites or *pre-conditions* in tables and files (e.g. the customer to be added does not already exist in the database).

- Depending on the function under test, online *inputs* or parameters might be necessary (e.g. specific data for a certain type of customer must be entered in a screen).

- The processing of pre-conditions and inputs leads to a new state in tables and files or *post-conditions* (e.g. the customer now exists in the database). Post-conditions describe expected results of the test case.

- In addition, the functionality can produce results that are not relevant for further processing or *outputs* (e.g. a customer receipt). Outputs are likewise part of a test case's expected results.

The level of detail that is suitable for a test case depends among other things on the testing level. While functional testing usually focuses on the detailed business logic of a function, integration testing is more concerned with status changes of the objects involved.

The first system function on the path "Standard Account for New Customer" is "Check credit rating". A test case is defined with the help of the attributes explained above and then assigned to the system function "Check credit rating". Finally, the test case is inserted into the test case sequence as the first *step* of the sequence.

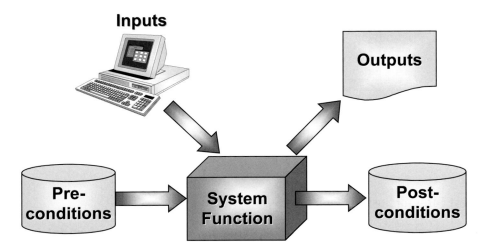

Figure 8: Components of a Test Case

4.2.3 Completing the Test Case Sequence

In order to complete the test case sequence "Standard Account for New Customer", the tester must:

- determine the next system function on the path according to the definition of the business process,
- create a test case for the system function or select an existing test case, and
- insert the test case as the next step in the test case sequence

until the end of the business process path is reached (Figure 9).

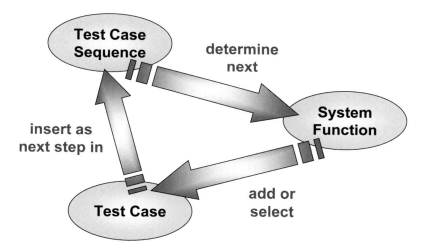

Figure 9: Completing the Test Case Sequence

Once the test case sequence is complete, the tester can define the test data to be used during execution. While a test case is normally descriptive and general, *test data definition* is quantitative and specific. During test data definition, the tester documents concrete values to be entered during testing (e.g. the customer data as inputs) as well as detailed expected results (as values for post-conditions and outputs).

5 Planning Test Execution

5.1 Organisation of Test Execution

In general it is possible to execute individual test case sequences in parallel. The assignment and exclusive use of customer and account numbers can normally ensure that the test case sequences do not interfere with each other.

If batch processing is also part of the integration test (as is frequently the case in many banks), then it also becomes necessary to plan the execution of the test case sequences with respect to the batch processing. Batch programs normally process the data of all test case sequences. In such cases, a centralised test execution plan becomes unavoidable in order to ensure that the test case sequences can be executed in parallel.

In a test execution plan or *test calendar*, test execution is divided up into logical units or *test days*. The test calendar defines when online inputs are possible as well as when a pre-determined type of batch processing is scheduled (e.g. end-of-day, end-of-month etc.). The execution of each test case sequence must be planned within the framework of the test calendar. Once all test case sequences have reached a synchronisation point during testing, batch processing is started. Upon the completion of batch processing, the online execution of each sequence can be continued (Figure 10).

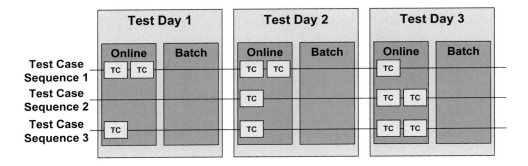

Figure 10: Execution of Test Case Sequences within Test Calender

5.2 Planning Test Case Sequences for Execution

In order to plan the execution of a test case sequence, its individual steps must be synchronised with the test calendar. In SQS-TEST/Professional the tester assigns a test day of a pre-defined, project-specific test calendar to each step of the test case sequence. The test case sequence "Standard Account for New Customer" requires only end-of-day batch processing and can therefore be executed on any day of the test calendar. Planning considerations can also call for executing the test case sequence on the second or third test day, for example, in order to distribute the test load more evenly and thus optimally utilise testing resources (workplaces, testers etc.).

SQS-TEST/Professional produces a documentation of the test specification in the form of a *test script* which can be used for manual test execution and the evaluation of test results (Figure 11).

Tester:	Keais, Paul		
Test Date:	**Test Day 1**		

Test Case Sequence: New Bank Account - Standard Account for New Customer

Description:	New customer applies for standard account (no individualized terms) without a credit card.	
Number of Steps:	5	
Risk:	Medium	
Author:	Keais, Paul	
Quality Assurer:	Smith, Patti	
Checker:	Euro, Dolly	
Preparation Status:	In Progress	New Preparation Status:
Execution Status:	Not Executed	New Execution Status:
Defect Status:	Not Evaluated	New Defect Status:
Precondition:	Online processing possible; External connection to external credit info provider available	

				ok	not ok
Step:	1				
System Function:	Check Credit Rating				
Test Case:	Credit rating check for individual				
Precondition:	Person is in credit rating database	**Precondition Data:**		[ ]	[ ]
Input:		**Input Data:**	Müller, Alfred, born on 5/12/1989	[ ]	[ ]
Postcondition:	Credit query date and result are saved to database	**Postcondition Data:**	Query date = current date	[ ]	[ ]
Output:	Credit rating is displayed on screen	**Output Data:**	Person has no credit rating entries	[ ]	[ ]

Figure 11: Excerpt from Test Script

6   Testing Strategies for Strategic Testing

The integration testing approach outlined above supports different testing strategies for critical applications in a time-constrained project environment. One such strategy is *bottom-up testing*. In bottom-up testing, integration testing builds upon functional testing. Test cases are first specified and executed for individual functions in a function test. Selected functional test cases are then available for re-use in the follow-up integration test where they are linked with one another to test the various business flows.

A superior testing strategy for extremely time-critical testing situations is *top-down testing* because it focuses on the business first. Top-down testing begins with integration testing for the most critical business processes. Based on the results of integration testing, management can make informed decisions on whether a go-live deadline can be met with acceptable business risk. Integration testing can also point to areas of weakness where more detailed functional testing is necessary, for example critical functions with an unacceptable error rate within their respective business processes. For these functions, additional test cases can be defined and executed in a function test while integration testing continues (Figure 12).

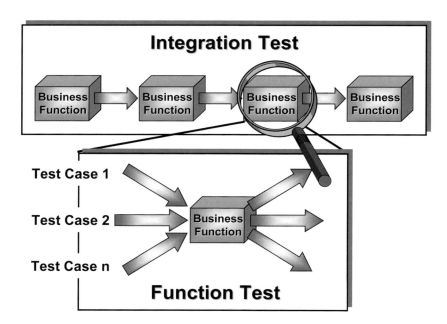

Figure 12: Top-down Testing

7   Experience from Large Projects

The challenges for testers outlined above are relevant in all testing projects. However, in many cases large projects provide a better insight into the problems at hand, because of the greater magnitude of such problems in these projects. A recent study [KEES01-b] analysed three large software projects. The first project was in the finance industry. The task here was to re-implement a software application into an existing portfolio of applications. The second project was a Year-2000 migration project in which every software application of a large bank had to be tested. Finally, the third project developed a payment settlement system for a public transport company. The application was integrated with 14 other applications. The analysis showed that that these projects had a common set of issues that required management attention. The key issues identified were:

- Structuring the test to reduce complexity
- Assuring the completeness of test coverage
- Co-ordinating test execution for optimal throughput
- Gathering aggregated information on testing progress for project management

Each project struggled some time before they had set up an infrastructure of documents, communication channels, agreements and conventions for defining, managing, and communicating the actual goals of the test and the current test status. In all cases, test management identified the above issues as critical, and upon being solved, as the key success factors of their test projects.

8   Tool Support

From the example projects above it is clear that tool support for testing is not only desirable but necessary. In many cases, straightforward approaches such as the use of Excel or Access have been tried. However, experience has shown that these standard tools have technical limitations, for example regarding multiple users, reporting, and maintenance of the testing data collected.

A different approach is the Business Integration Test component of the tool suite SQS-TEST/Professional. This tool is dedicated to the task of integration testing and supports all the key issues identified here.

Independent of the tool selected for supporting integration testing, experience has shown that starting an integration test without a tool approach cannot be recommended. Beginning without a tool in a large integration testing project will commonly lead to different tools and utilities being developed in different areas of the project, thus preventing an optimal solution for the project on the whole.

9 Summary

The approach to integration testing described above has been proven in numerous projects. Its most important components are:

- Organise the test project into test levels and manageable test items
- Structure the software relevant for the chosen types of testing
- Define which software is to be tested by which test item
- Determine the suitable level of testing intensity for each test item dependent upon business risk and available resources
- Define or re-use test cases for the software assigned to a test item and build test cases sequences to test different business flows
- Organise test execution with the help of a test calendar and plan the individual steps of a test case sequence within this framework

From the management perspective, experience has shown that projects have a common set of problems that require management attention. The key issues identified are:

- Structuring the test to reduce complexity
- Assuring the completeness of test coverage
- Co-ordinating test execution for optimal throughput
- Gathering aggregated information on testing progress for project management

The approach described here addresses all these topics and is supported by a dedicated software application. Generally it is recommended to examine these issues and choose an appropriate software support for managing them at the beginning of a testing project.

- a study on outstanding change requests and probably an increase in their priority;
- an improved information service to the users on changed functionality to provide them with more knowledge on how to operate the system;
- a re-evaluation of the training material with user representatives;
- a SUMI test was to be carried out on a regular basis (every two/three months) to track the user satisfaction during implementation of the PDMS.

Currently the follow-up is in progress and no new SUMI test has yet taken place. Consequently, nothing can be said regarding the improvement of usability. However, by means of the SUMI test, usability has become a topic within the PDMS project that gets the attention (time and effort) it apparently needs.

4.3 Project 3: Intranet Site

4.3.1 Approach

By means of MUMMS, the specialised multimedia version of SUMI, the usability of an intranet site prototype of a large bank was evaluated. The intranet site was set up by the test services department to become better known and to present themselves to potential customers. Since during the test only a prototype version of the intranet site was available some pages were not yet accessible. A special sub-scale was introduced for MUMMS, with the objective of measuring the users' multimedia "feeling":

- *Excitement*: extent to which end users feel that they are "drawn into" the world of the multimedia application.

In total, ten users (testers) were involved in the MUMMS evaluation. The set of users can be characterised in the following ways:

- not involved during the development of the intranet site
- potential customers
- four users with Internet experience
- six users without Internet experience
- varying age and background (job title).

4.3.2 Results

The table below shows the overall scores for the various MUMMS sub-scales:

Table 4: Overall MUMMS score table

	Affect	Control	Efficiency	Helpfulness	Learnability	Excitement
average score	69	74	62	67	67	68
median	71	77	67	69	67	72
standard deviation	9	12	11	8	6	12

The various scores were moderately high. However, there seems to be a divergence of opinion on the control and excitement scales. Some low scores pull down the control and efficiency scales (see next table). Two users from the sample gave exceptionally low average scores. They were analysed in detail but no explanation was found.

Table 5: MUMMS scores per user

	A	C	E	H	L	E	Average
User 1	71	81	67	71	74	77	73
User 2	74	74	74	71	67	71	72
User 3	81	84	67	67	74	74	74
User 4	54	51	54	57	64	44	54
User 5	71	74	43	58	55	76	63
User 6	64	84	67	81	67	69	72
User 7	51	81	74	54	74	64	66
User 8	71	81	64	74	71	81	73
User 9	77	81	76	84	77	74	78
User 10	64	47	51	57	57	44	53

As stated the usability of the intranet site was rated moderately high from the users' perspective, although there seemed to be a lot of divergence in the various user opinions. Some more detailed conclusions were:

- *Attractiveness*
  The attractiveness score is high (almost 70%). However some users (4, 7 and 10) have a relatively low score. Especially the statements "this MM system is entertaining and fun to use" and "using this MM system is exiting" are rated in different

ways. It seems some additional MM features should be added to further improve the attractiveness for all users.

- *Control*
  A very high score was given for control in general. Again two users can be identified as outliers (4 and 10) scoring only around 50%, the other scores are around 80%. Problems, if any, in this area could be traced back to the structure of the site.
- *Efficiency*
  The average score on efficiency is the lowest, although still above average. Users need more time than expected to carry out their task, e.g. to find the right information.

On the basis of the MUMMS evaluation it was decided to improve the structure of the intranet site and to add a number of features before releasing the site to the users. Currently an update of the intranet site is being carried out. A MUMMS re-evaluation has been planned to quantify the impact of the improvement regarding usability.

5   Applicability of SUMI

On the basis of tests carried out in practice, a number of conclusions can be drawn regarding the applicability of SUMI and MUMMS:

- It is easy to use and involves few costs. This applies both to the evaluator and the customer. On average a SUMI test can be carried in approximately three days; this includes the time needed for a limited context analysis and reporting.
- During testing the emphasis is on finding defects, this often results in only negative quality indications, e.g. the number of defects found. SUMI however, provides an objective opinion that can also be a positive quality indicator, e.g. a SUMI score of 70 or more.
- The usability score is split into various aspects, making a thorough, more-detailed evaluation possible (using the various output data).
- SUMI provides, after detailed analysis and discussion, directions for improvement and directions for further investigation. SUMI can also be used as a risk analysis method to determine whether more detailed usability testing is necessary.

However, some disadvantages can also be mentioned:

- A running version of the system to be tested must be available; this implies that SUMI can only be carried out at a relatively late stage of the project.

- A high number of users (minimum of ten) with the same background are needed to fill out the questionnaire. Quite often the implementation or test doesn't involve ten or more users belonging to the same user group.

- The accuracy and level of detail of the findings are limited (this can partly be solved by adding a small number of open questions to the SUMI questionnaire). In practice a SUMI evaluation is often carried out in co-operation with a heuristic evaluation. The latter can in such a case provide a thorough interpretation of the SUMI score and concrete direction for improvement.

6 Conclusions

A system's end users are *the* experts in using the system to achieve their goals. Therefore, their voices should be listened to when the system is being evaluated. SUMI does precisely that: it allows quantification of the end users' experience with the software and it encourages the tester to focus on issues that the end users have difficulty with. A heuristics evaluation (preferably with user involvement) is also important, but it inevitably considers the system as a collection of software entities.

A questionnaire such as SUMI represents the end result of a lot of research effort. The tester gets the result of this effort instantly when SUMI is used: the high validity and reliability rates reported for SUMI are to a large measure due to the rigorous and systematic approach adopted in constructing the questionnaire and to the emphasis on industry-based testing during development. However, as with all tools, it is possible to use SUMI both well and badly. Care taken in establishing the context of use, characterising the end user population and understanding the tasks for which the system will be used supports sensitive testing and yields valid and useful results in the end.

Heuristic evaluation and SUMI are testing techniques that can be applied to start usability testing or when limited resources for usability testing are available. Of course it is always a risk management decision, if usability is *the* most critical success factor, more thorough techniques such as full usability test should be applied. However, looking at current industrial usability practices, a large take-up of the discussed low-cost usability testing techniques would provide a great improvement for most projects and organisations, ultimately leading to more usable and more user-friendly systems. User interfaces account for almost 50% of the code in modern software. In contrast, one should consider how much is currently being spent on usability testing in the project at hand.

Quality Aspects of Bots

Michael Vetter

ComValue Internet Consulting (Germany)

Abstract: Bots are a fascinating species. Although they are generally considered to be a product of artificial intelligence (AI) research, they are sort of artificially block-headed, simply displaying human understanding while not possessing a single glimpse of reasoning. However, the available technical means of software robotics provide amazing applicational solutions to us today.

A bot's nature varies according to its developer's skill. And by the developer we do not understand the software engineer, i.e. the one who programmed the software engine or the bot software shell, but basically the knowledge engineer, i.e. the author who creates the bot's conversational scope, its recognition patterns and the range of knowledge topics as well.

Some further soft facts add up to this. Communicational results can only be quantified on the user's side. If during a session the user acts according to a bot's inherent communicational model, this bot has to be considered successful. Admittedly that is not quite true since the user may not know anything about optimising the internal communicational threads on the bot's side. The Turing Test would not be meaningful in that respect since its test setting is solely designed to verify from the user's point of view whether he or she is communicating to a bot.

Keywords: Bot, avatar, software quality, software testing

1 What is a Bot?

"Bot" is a common abbreviation of software robot and denotes a type of software that resides on the Internet, is basically capable of chatting and is sometimes equipped with further potentials like carrying out orders, giving advice, or searching for topics. Such bots do not have much in common with the robots of industrial production, as in vehicle construction. Albeit "bot" has emerged as a colloquial wording among AI maniacs, it is not well defined and may denote almost any type of software service: a search engine, a Web crawler following hyperlinks or a script that fills in a phone number into a data field or sneaks through a log-on procedure automatically. But a bot may also be a complex e-commerce application with a natural-language interface, some animated character on the screen that is usually called "avatar" and furthermore access to external databases. Hence a bot, as we use it in this article, is a conversational software application, visible in the form of an animated character (avatar). Bots may also be equipped with a text-to-speech software (TTS) that automatically translates written text into spoken language or some kind of streaming technology that streams prefabricated audio files onto the user's desk.

Many people use "avatar" and "bot" interchangeably, if not totally confusing both concepts. Apparently, the name "avatar" is more widespread than "bot". However, "avatar" specifically denotes a bot's visual representation on the screen and generally neglects the robotic functions behind that. So any talk about avatars should be dealt with cautiously: Do they really mean functional, conversational software robots? Or is it just coined on the appearance of some virtual character à la E-Cyas, Tyra or even Lara Croft?

Apart from "avatar" and "bot" another label, "embodied conversational agent" or ECA, steps into the foreground. ECA denotes quite precisely a bot's basic characteristics. It's some kind of software capable of chatting (conversational), executing on behalf of the user (agent) and it is visible on the screen (embodied). In a nut shell: a bot is sort of a program extended by some kind of pictorial representation. A bot receives any natural-language input, processes it automatically and reflects natural language answers to it. The communicational input from the user to the bot usually is channelled via keyboard. The reverse direction, bot to user, is channelled via screen output. Technically it's feasible today to communicate to a bot via spoken language – user to bot and reverse – supported by speech synthesiser (text to speech) or streamed speech files, speech recognition and even voice authentication.

Bot technology basically approaches the idea of giving mass market Web applications a human feel. Humans talk and do have faces reflecting emotion. On Web sites, a bot may act as a virtual sales person, a virtual consultant, a spokesman or simply as a bearer of sympathy. Bots enrich Web sites with their humanlike phenotype. But bots are more than just talkative chat machines with a face. Bots may execute jobs, access databases, send e-mails and compute numerical data. A bot is a program that acts conversationally, controlled on behalf of the user's will. Some automatic middleman, a virtual agent that a user may speak to and thus instruct. If not, we have the simpler case of a pure "chatterbot," a virtual someone-to-talk-to, willing to exchange more than just a short greeting.

Bots have been chatterbots from their beginning on, if we agree to accept Joseph Weizenbaum's Eliza from 1966 to be the first chapter of bot technology. A chatterbot's principal job is chatting and conversation. This seems to be easy, but in fact it is not. Much effort is necessary to develop a bot that is almost halfway capable of simulating the human interlocutor. Hence producers of software environments for creating bots have gained a high level of specialisation. This holds true to the same extent for a new guild that creates bots utilising these software environments: the knowledge engineers.

2   Rating of Conversational Systems: A Review

Whenever discussion falls on methods for evaluating bots, Alan Turing's name will be dropped inevitably. In 1950, British mathematician Alan M. Turing, in his treatise "Computing Machinery and Intelligence" [TURI50], raised the question whether a machine could perfectly behave as a human interlocutor so that a test person might mistake it for being human. This is the so-called imitational play, today commonly known under the name "Turing Test." The tester talks to an invisible partner (e.g. Turing utilised a telex machine) in order to find out whether his or her counterpart is human or artificial. Turing held that any artificial system that successfully winds its way through such an imitational play might be attributed to be capable of thinking. On the other hand, such a session may only reveal a less than penetrating interrogation on part of the human tester; thus effectively testing not the bot's but the tester's intelligence.

Recently a new version of Turing's imitational play has come into use: the "Loebner Prize" [LOEB01]. Since 1991 Hugh Loebner together with the Cambridge Center for Behavioural Studies annually donates a public reward for the first conversational machine to be indistinguishable from human talk. Up to now this prize has never been awarded. Relative winners of the contest have always been only those participants whose computers surpassed others in their struggle for the best imitation of human conversational behaviour.

University-bound research activities during the 90s have been searching for new methods to evaluate the absolute degree of intelligence of artificial conversational systems that take economic reasoning and practical scenarios into consideration.

The results of Walker et al. [WALK97] as well as Sanders/Scholtz [SAND00] are an example for a scientific approach. Under the acronym PARADISE (PARAdigm for DIalogue System Evaluation), Walker et. al. have been developing a universal system for evaluating conversational agents on the basis of mathematical calculation. Sanders/Scholtz have based their studies on recognising those pivotal factors which are next important when assessing a dialogue system rather than developing a mathematical formula to calculate the efficiency of a dialogue. Basically, Sanders/Scholtz identify the applicational context as an important criterion for a successful approach. Further items in the evaluation process are related to a precise recording of the user's input, the appropriate reaction to it and the perceptibility of the system's feedback. Other criteria aim at the efficiency of the dialogue, while dialogue length and reaction time play a considerable role.

3   Goal Settings and Premises: Our Approach

Any dialogue we carry on, regardless of whether it be with a human counterpart or a machine, is affected by non-lingual factors such as mimic, gesture, pitch of voice, sympathy, antipathy and emotional involvement. One or all of these factors have a great impact on whether we feel comfortable and successful or unpleasant and dissatisfied during a dialogue. Numerous research results have shown [BALL00] how important these aspects are in dialogues, explicitly in those with bots. The findings of Nass et al. [NASS00] have shown that even ethnic characteristics of avatars are important for their acceptability.

Considering all these insights the question for testing or evaluating conversational software robots becomes enormously complex. Standardised test methods almost run out of sight if we take the applicational context into consideration or the user's expectation along with his or her educational level. Hence, for our purposes, technical test settings for the evaluation of bots can play only a minor role. They may identify a system's inherent functions – i.e. how specific topics are being treated, user inputs are recognised and adequate answers are being processed – but test methods pertaining to this will overlook the critical dimensions of communication and emotion which quite often counterbalance the lack of knowledge.

Focus groups along with test persons could be an alternative to technical test methods. First, they could evaluate a bot's emotional impact; second, they could examine in probatory bot sessions the machine's dialogue efficiency and content. But regarding this second aspect, experience has shown that probands unfortunately failed to produce meaningful results. Probatory inputs differ severely in type or intention from those of authentic users who mostly visit a Web site on purpose. Bots that are developed on the basis of test results hence bear the risk of matching only with a fraction of their knowledge bases when switched online.

Development and operation of a bot requires several software components, i.e. usually some kind of developer kit to create the bot's knowledge base and a runtime server version that allows to operation of the dialogue engine on a Web server. A bot's quality depends on the scope of technical features provided by the dialogue engine and on the tool kit's ability to support the knowledge engineer in accessing the dialogue engine's potentials. Ultimately, even a weak bot software might enable you for a good solution and, vice versa, a proficiency-level product may not keep you from disaster.

Most of the criteria that play a decisive role when choosing a software product for developing ECAs cannot be evaluated online, since products differ primarily in how they ease the developer's work. In the following we will therefore concentrate on the front ends to be found on the Web, not on software products for developing bots.

Turing's aforementioned approach is exciting from a scientific point of view. According to Turing an "intelligent" bot would have to be able to respond meaningfully to any kind of questions. But according to our requirements it would not make much

gether with Boolean operators. If the bot finds among its total set of rules or patterns one that matches the user's input, this pattern will be drawn. This pattern is further linked to at least one or possibly a set of alternative answers. The bot puts out this matching answer or, if there are two or more answers, chooses at random or deterministically among them by index. It is useful to cut down a user's input to a "skeleton" pattern data subset, because there are lots of speech or sentence fill-ins (other than subject, predicative and object) and pleonasms that are not necessary (can be neglected) to fully understand a user's input. Hence patterns are basically reduced to the necessary constituents of any communicational content.

5.3 Examples for Pattern Matching

Let us now have a closer look at the internal process of pattern matching. Supposed we communicate with an expert bot who knows a lot about "phoning". In our scenario the knowledge base contains a rule x that bears the atomic pattern "phone"; this rule x shall be linked to an answer y: "Where do you want to phone to?". Consequently, any user input that contains the word "phone" will be caught by rule x:

(a) I want to phone
(b) I do not want to phone
(c) I want to phone to Alaska
(d) Do you want to phone?
(e) I prefer sending e-mails to communicating by phone.

Each of these five user inputs will be equally given answer y: "Where do you want to phone to?" We can see by this single example that rules require refinement to act appropriately to user inputs. Rule (A) shows how to approach refinement. The exclamation mark "!" denotes the exclusion of its successive word:

(A) I & want & phone & !not

This rule matches only input (a) and (c). Further differentiation requires additional patterns. When testing a knowledge base or a conversational software robot, one therefore tries to gain evidence of the rule's grade of refinement. Preferably one should proceed from general to particular. Say one starts with single prompts related to a topic and then gradually increases intricacy. The degree of refinement can be seen from the preciseness of the given answers. In our example the test person would consecutively try the following input:

(a) telephone
(b) phone

(c) want to phone
(d) I want to phone
(e) I wish to phone
(f) I want to do a phone call
(g) I do not want to phone
(h) you want to phone
(i) I want to phone to Alaska
(j) I want to phone from Germany to Alaska
(k) How can I always phone at the lowest rates

5.4 Quality Grades of a Knowledge Base

After we have discussed the quality of rules we will extend our focus and ask for the overall coherence and inner structure of a knowledge base's rules or patterns. If a bot were limited to a certain quantity of rules with a stable set of related answers, it would just be a simple questions-and-answers machine always ready to reply appropriately. In fact, as our example shows, quite obviously a virtual dialogue requires more than that. The input "I wish to phone" is countered by the bot's question "Where do you want to phone to?". This leads to a dynamic plot of dialogue tags that vary according to context and preceding dialogue threads.

5.4.1 Topics, Context and Consecutive Recognition Rules

Test settings may be subject to whether a bot reacts sensitively to context. In general especially bots with a broad range of knowledge should be capable of replying positively to various topics and contexts. Let us assume a user chats with a bot about sports. In the course of the dialogue the user's input could be "This is a very interesting topic". A context-sensitive bot, whose knowledge base has both been carefully loaded with a broad range of topics and also structured by subjects, could answer "I like to chat about sports, too". A bot non-sensitive to this dialogue thread (due to a lack of data) would possibly answer "Wouldn't it be a pity if I were boring?" While in the first example the bot positively responds to the situational context, the second example shows how the user input possibly triggers a recognition rule containing patterns such as "interesting" and "topic", completely disregarding the communicational flow.

Topics and context are structuring constituents of a knowledge base (dialogue model), that may direct a chat for the length of some consecutive dialogue steps. Another way of contextualising a bot's output is the so-called consecutive pattern matching. This makes a predefined reaction to a specific user input possible. In particular this makes sense when a user's input can be foreseen, which is especially the case with binary decision trees. A bot may ask "Are you male?" thus anticipating either "yes" or "no" on the user's side, as subsequent recognition patterns will make a satisfying dialogue possible further on. Even somewhat more complex feedback situations (back channelling) can be solved elegantly this way. If a bot asks "Do you have coffee black or with milk and sugar?" a limited range of possible answers is quite predictable: "Thank you, black.", "Milk, please.", "With sugar, please.", "I take milk and sugar." etc.

Above all a bot should master the transient dialogue threads. If a bot addresses a topic on its own "free will" it's not demanding too much to expect it to be capable of answering a user's perfect reply. Besides, a common applicational field for topics and consecutive recognition patterns are relative pronouns and other reflexive words ("these", "that" etc.). If a bot praises a product it should know which subject is being referred to when the user replies "How much is it?".

5.4.2 Ambiguities and Homonyms

An interesting aspect of bots is how they deal with ambiguities, which quite often arise from proper names and clock time. Varying to context, a bot may depend on asking for further details when the user puts in "eight o'clock". This would be extremely important in case of a transportation company. A back-channelled question "Eight a.m. or p.m.?" should be mandatory. Identical words with different meanings (homonyms) quite often lead to misunderstandings, and that holds true not only for bots. If thesauri and dictionaries of synonyms are integrated, mistakes of that kind are most likely to happen. Which developer will take into consideration that the user's question"Don't you fiddle around with me!" might trigger responses about music instruments?

Whenever a bot is to provide expert knowledge, such mix ups should be fairly rare. If mistakes of that kind do not cease to occur further engineering effort is necessary.

5.5 Scope of a Knowledge Base

A bot's knowledge base consists of recognition patterns that are potentially attributed to different dialogue topics and, in the case of consecutive recognitions, to the preceding answers. Basically we distinguish context-relevant topics from those that are non-relevant to situational dialogue threads. Context-relevant subjects usually arise from a Web site's content. Apart from these content-related subjects, functional items like company facts (contact, investor relations, business report, history etc.), service (FAQs, support etc.), context-relevant content inevitably refers to a bot's operator, his products, services and the company itself. Content that is non-relevant to context usually is considered as small talk. Most of all small talk has nothing or only little in common with a bot's goal settings. A knowledge base's scope is quite difficult to evaluate in online mode. Being well informed about the bot operator, his products and associated topics is a prerequisite, however.

5.6 Systems Integration, Applicational Solutions

A bot is not just a statistical arrangement of any type of dialogue threads to show reel on demand. In fact, a bot may have access to databases and can be integrated into various other applications. This will not necessarily be visible on the front end's side. A bot in charge of professional data mining might reveal some kind of intricate dialogue strategy by asking "certain" questions – but there are no sure indicators. That way a bot might involve users in a charming chat about their hobbies and customs to keep them from zapping the session while the bot proceeds to trigger their willingness to order. Such a "personal" dialogue could also serve to squeeze out user profiles. Potentially any bit of user information that circulates during a man-machine session can be compiled into relevant market research data.

A bot will not only pass on collected data to databases, it may also extract existing data thus refining its dialogue contributions. In general, dynamic data like prices and product details will be retrieved. That way a bot is always up-to-date concerning these items. Principally, a bot can extract any type of data from databases. Whoever wishes to enable registered users to have access to their accounts by bots may do so.

In online mode, the user will seldom know whether retrieved information stems from databases. Anyway, a single virtual sales agent could also be operated by a host of ten editors who manually update prices and product features day by day.

5.7 Memory Functions and other Scripts

Knowledge engineers are apt to enable their bots with memory functions. This amplifies their imitational dialogue aspects and facilitates the need for integrating them into a Web site framework. Bot memory functions are generally based on scripts and can be tested online. This requires to observing the memory-related data being picked up by the bot in the course of a dialogue session.

5.7.1 Scripts for Dialogue Optimisation

A bot appears to be more impressive or human, if it is capable of referring to previous information within the course of the dialogue. Most bots to be found on Web sites are already equipped with differentiated name recognition.

A typical dialogue starts off like this:

Bot: Hello, I am Bot-i-celli. What is your name?
User: (My name is) X.
Bot: I like your name, X.

Information obtained at "x" can be referred to during the complete further dialogue and thus enable the bot to respond to a user by his or her name, provided the localised information has been recognised properly. Let us assume that the user has not mentioned his name but puts in something else instead. These inputs could be:

(a) Martin
(b) Martin Miller
(c) Ramazan
(d) Immanuel Kant
(e) Idiot
(f) That is not your business.
(g) Why do you want to know that?

This potential range of user inputs shows the grade of variability that developers have to be prepared for. It is up to the individual case which input has to be recognised well and which one can be neglected. A perfect script surely should be ready to react appropriately to the variants shown above. An example:

(a) Hello Martin. How are you?
(b) Hello Martin. I prefer to be on first name terms. Last names always slip my mind.
(c) Ramazan? I never heard that name before. Shall I call you Ramazan?
(d) No problem, just go on chatting, no need for exchanging names.
(e) I just prefer to know my counterpart's name, it's much more pleasant.

Scripts may help to identify and memorise specific user input and catch it up on demand. Our dialogue thus could go on that way:

Bot: Hello, I am Bot-i-celli. What is your name?
User: (My name is) X.
Bot: I like your name, X.
User: My name is Y.
Bot: You have already introduced yourself by the name of X. But I can call you Y if you wish.

Other scripts execute mathematical operations. These are operations that are either commanded by the user's will or carried out as hidden processes. Queries like "What is two times two?" or "What is the time?" belong to the open type of script. Scripts enable bots to deliver proper information. Whether this is always desirable in communicative respects is up to the tester. Being asked for the right time the bot could possibly prefer a sophisticated "Have a look on your screen: bottom line, right side." to a correct, yet boring answer. Therefore the absence of scripts is not necessarily a sign of imperfection or a weak developer. Assessing a bot application one must always consider the bot's overall character and decide on which solution would be most beneficiary to the given individual requirements.

Hidden operations are quite often counters. Let us continue our dialogue:

User: My name is Z.
Bot: You have introduced yourself now by a third name. Could you please confine yourself to one of these?

In this case a script has been counting how often the user told his name and reacts correspondingly. This script could also be utilised to register the user's insults up to a certain limit after which the session will be exited automatically. The total number of dialogue steps might also be registered and thus enable the bot to track a dialogue's duration. When the user quits his or her session the bot may then express regret: "What a pity that you have to go right now. We have just come to know each other." or "Lovely that you spent so much time chatting with me."

5.7.2 Scripts for Process Optimisation

It has been shown how dialogues can be made more credible and interesting with the help of scripts. Scripts can also provide value-added functions to a Web site through process optimisation. Bots then relieve users of cumbersome tasks such as filling in forms, ordering newsletters, sending e-mails and much more. Let us switch back to our travel agency example to illustrate this. A common Web site in such a case would surely present a form to be filled in with data like place of departure, destination, other travel-related data and so on. Consecutive queries for further travel links will result in filling in the same form again and again.

The following dialogue illustrates how this could be in the case of a virtual travel agent. Assumed the user is in a dialogue with a bot and has already mentioned both hometown (Frankfurt) and name (Hans).

User: I need a train connection to Berlin.
Bot: You wish to go from Frankfurt, Hans?
User: Yes. Exactly.
Bot: On which day do you wish to travel?
User: Next Friday.
Bot: What time would be fine, Hans?
User: 8.
Bot: A.m. or p.m.?
User: In the evening.
Bot: Like to book a return?
User: When do I get my tickets?

Bot: You will get them within 48 hours by mail.
User: That's great.
Bot: Then we can go ahead with your reservation. I need to know your return date.

This example shows how the bot makes use of its memory functions by filling in Hans' hometown as place of departure. That way the system collects all relevant data and triggers the process of ticket reservation at the user's request. Furthermore we see how a bot interactively responds to the customer. If additional inquiries arise in the course of a dialogue a bot will answer them just in passing by and immediately thereafter return to the center dialogue.

Bots that successfully process communicational threads of that kind must be considered beneficial to a Web site application. For the time being there are but a few applications on the Web that use dialogue-based interaction for process optimisation.

5.8 Communicational Aspects

A bot's quality and therewith its success do not exclusively depend on technical reasons or hard facts like the usage of scripts and the characteristics of its dialogue rules. Much amounts to the communicational strength of a bot, which emanates from its usage of words, its emotional colouring and the way it intervenes in the dialogue thread. Below some aspects for the rating of a bot's communicational qualities are explained.

5.8.1 Tonality

Sticking to the facts is fine – being stylistically impressive is even better. Writing for bots is dialogue directing, dramaturgy, text analysis, grammatical and lexical subtlety – and hard work. Dialogues should be written by professionals. It is important, above all, to create dialogues that are typical of conversation. This pertains to sentence length, the selection of words and the usability of dialogue threads.

Tonality has to be appropriate. As a matter of fact this does not appear to be a strong side of IT staff members. But the young novelist, in turn, should cut himself short according to an old texter's wisdom, since what applies to writing in general, and most equally to journalism, should be strictly obeyed to when writing for the Internet. Shortness is welcome. Reading from a monitor is exhausting. Carrying on a dialogue means interaction, not monologue.

Bots with non-generic character traits – be they positive or negative ones – are significantly more successful than those without. Characteristics basically emanate from tonality: the conversational "melody" a bot gets across to its human counterpart. Tonality must conform to the social background of a target audience and the stylistic language level that it is attuned to. Basically bots refrain the stylistic language characteristics of their target audience. Small talk tags are particles that show excitement like "wow", "Jesus", "unbelievable", regional colouring (dialects, wording) and preferred speech fill-ins like "well", "ah", "you know", "I think".

5.8.2 Personal Interests of Bots

The naming and looks of a bot must conform to user habits as well as to the related products, CI and a bot's overall applicational goal settings. Subtlety and trend awareness are essential if the designing of a bot is to turn out well.

There is a demand for bots of outstanding personality rather than multiple clones of neck-tied Mr. Nice Guy. Bots that are to earn their target audience's applause preferably have to resemble film actors or pop stars rather than realistic call center agents. Not to mention the operator's goal settings (from e-commerce up to entertainment) that a bot quite basically has to fulfil. Only then will mechanisms of identification and adoration gain momentum. Only then will bots represent corporate identity strategies in a credible manner. Only then will bots become the new idols of the Web.

5.8.3 Active and Passive Dialogue Management

A bad bot is a passive bot that is cautious and restricted to only answering user requests and besides that plays a minor role restricted to being always polite. A bot like that will easily lose its thread – since it lacks communicational impact. When asked for too much a bot will swiftly reveal its blind spots. By no means is a bot capable of providing information on any single topic of our encyclopaedic knowledge of the world. A bot's scope of knowledge is positively confined to its applicational goal settings, backed up by some fringe small-talk competence that in a best case scenario, again, is related to the operator's objectives. Whenever practical, a bot therefore should address its communicational topics proactively in order to keep its human counterpart from drifting out of the knowledge base's scope.

A bot's initial remark, when beginning a dialogue session, shows quite obviously how the virtual agent masters its job, i.e. to what extent it can play an active role. Which user response can be expected on this welcome: "Hello, I am Lisa. What can I do for you?" Thousands of session protocols have supplied evidence that beginnings of this kind will inevitably run into trouble. These are the user responses that are most likely to be provoked:

You ought to know yourself.
No idea.
I am beyond help.
I need money.
What is the weather like in Honolulu.

Yet man-machine dialogues may be directed to much more auspicious fields right from the start. This requires, however, a robot system that proactively speaks to the user and calls its applicational objectives right by their names, as in: "Hi. I am Lisa, your telephone agent. What can I tell you about 'flat rate phoning'?" This welcome makes it quite plain to the user what the bot's purpose is. Subsequently the range of requests and inputs to be expected will be significantly reduced.

The same applies to the internal structure (i.e. the further course) of a dialogue. A bot should beware of switching back to a passive role amidst an ongoing dialogue and thus passing over the baton to the dialogue counterpart, as in:

User: How much is a phone call to Alaska?
Bot: A phone call to Alaska is 50 cents per minute.
User: There I know a much cheaper provider, I say.

Some added proactive dialogue direction would be suitable for the bot:

User: How much is a phone call to Alaska.
Bot: A phone call to Alaska is 50 cents per minute. Have you ever thought of pre-selection to cut down your phone expenses?
User: No.
Bot: Than I am going to make you a favourable offer.
etc.

Admittedly there are dialogues that cannot be steered into a desired direction by this method. But the number of satisfying dialogues will increase significantly, if the bot takes up an active role.

5.8.4 Dealing with non-matching input

Despite all these precautions a dialogue may run into trouble, because the bot fails to match the user's input on the first level of recognition rules. Then a second level of "substitute rules" backs up the system. Those who have already been chatting with a bot surely have come across this back-up function in its basic form: "Unfortunately I haven't got you. Please repeat your request in other words." This or a similar response should be banned to the red-book of bot developers! A substitute recognition of this kind is fatal to a bot dialogue ,because the first-level recognition fails most of all due to non-existing knowledge data rather than missing recognition patterns on the first level. At least this assumption applies to those bots that have been thoroughly furnished with professional recognition rules to match all the relevant topics of the knowledge base. Our female virtual telephone agent will demonstrate this:

Bot: Hello, I am Lisa, your virtual telephone agent. What can I do for you?
User: What is the weather like in Honolulu?
Bot: Unfortunately I haven't got you. Please repeat your request in other words.
User: It's hot or chilly in Honolulu?
Bot: Unfortunately I haven't got you. Please repeat your request in other words.
User: It's sunny skies in Honolulu?

However the user struggles for rewording his or her request – Lisa will not understand, because she is not interested in the weather in Honolulu. Therefore its arbitrary to rephrase the input. This could be a remedy:

Bot: Hello, I am Lisa, your virtual telephone agent. What can I do for you?
User: What is the weather like in Honolulu?
Bot: Sorry? Apparently you are here to gather information on flat rate phoning. Have you ever thought of pre-selection to cut down your phone expenses?

Here too, we have to say: There is no cure-all for ill-fated dialogues. However, a bot will perform better with a proactive conversational role pattern whenever it fails to recognise a user's input. In case of doubt it's better to neglect the user's non-matching input and switch over to a new topic that the bot masters.

5.8.5 The Stages of Bot Qualifications

A bot's usefulness and importance basically depend on communicational aspects. Technical features of a bot engine play only a subordinate role. Even a comparatively weak bot engine will produce satisfying results, provided the engine is hooked onto a well-performing knowledge base. Vice versa, a high-performing bot engine is of little use as long as a bot's conversational ability fails to deliver.

The user's degree of involvement serves as a rule of thumb for the quality rating of bots: The more a user is engaged in his or her man-machine dialogue, the easier a bot can arrive at its goal settings. By involvement we understand the emotional impact that affects a user during the dialogue session. This is associated to aspects such as a bot's grade of credibility, its command of language and its visual representation on the screen.

The Functional Stage
The functional stage is the lowest grade of a bot qualification. On this entry layer, bots improve the usability of Web sites by speeding up the user's search for information. Functional bots add value to or even replace the regular navigation bar and take up the function of a sophisticated text-based search tool. Bots that are operated on this functional layer, however, do not affect users. These bots take up the task of search engines. No user will ever show warm-hearted feelings to such a bot-driven functional utility,

but perhaps negative ones – for example when the bot fails to retrieve relevant information.

The Individual Stage

In the individual stage a bot becomes unique. First-layer bot abilities are accomplished by primary concepts to transform a functional bot into a unique creature. These initial concepts deal with a bot's language and emotions as well as its phenotype and the portfolio of topics to be commanded by the individual stage bot. On this layer the bot becomes a bearer of sympathy.

The individual bot is now equipped with character traits that unmistakably make the bot the someone it is. Humans talk with the individual bot not only to access data or trigger first-layer bot functions but also because they enjoy it. Users become slightly affected by the individual bot –ideally this is plain sympathy.

As a result users will gladly return to the Web site, and be it out of sheer curiosity for whether the bot has some latest news for them. And surely they will tell their friends the Web site address where the bot can be found.

The Stage of Personal Representation

A bot whose personality complies to both the entrepreneurial concepts and the brand image of its corporate operator steps forward onto the third layer. This is the stage of personal representation. A representational bot's character traits are up to the key targets of corporate communication and precisely meet the corporate brand image. A bot of this distinct qualification will not only draw upon the user's sympathy for its own sake. Beyond that, a bot, as a corporate representative, is also capable of directing the user's attention to a corporate brand portfolio.

Further Stages

In the future a bot might be considered a like-minded person, whose statements and suggestions may be trusted in, at least to a certain degree. On this uppermost layer of bot qualification a bot might even reach cult status and be absolutely trustworthy for its devotees in whatever respect. It presumably requires a huge effort to create such a virtual idol, and perhaps it will not be seen in the next decades.

6 Summary

In this article we discussed quality aspects of bots on e-commerce Web sites. The criteria for assessing the quality of a bots were elaborated. The procedures for testing, however, were only sketched. This is partly due to a general recommendation regarding bots: The testing procedures should be defined individually for each project, founded on the criteria most relevant for the project. Standardised tests for conversational bots are – this is our conclusion – nearly impossible. Evaluating an individual bot is more like an individual diagnosis based on the described criteria. Nevertheless we would like to conclude with a template for a testing procedure for bots. In principle a test has to be planned and structured as follows:

I.   Develop a test concept
II.   Run the test and log the conversation
III. Evaluate the conversation

When executing the three steps it seems that the process itself is constantly adapted according to the answers received from the system. Thus it is a dynamic procedure the result of which will by definition be subjective and in many cases not reproducible.

The development of the test concept can be founded on issues like what is the tester trying to find out, what are the quality characteristics to be checked and what is the task of the bot. A bot for consultancy needs to provide a conversation on a level different from an entertainment bot. For entertainment the originality of the bot's statements is important whereas for a consultancy bot the statements have to be follow a logical argumentation.

Every conversation with a bot should be logged for later evaluation. The test can be executed in two phases, namely a black-box test and a white-box test based on the concept of the bot.

In the black-box test the bot's concept should not be considered. This is best done without preparation, by jumping directly into a dialogue with the bot and reacting spontaneously upon the bot's answers. In this dialogue the tester has to check whether and how the bot takes the initiative and how the purpose of the bot is made transparent to the tester in the dialogue. A good bot is expected to drive the conversation and to inform his counterpart about his knowledge. If these issues are neglected by the bot the conversation is likely to fail, since in this case the user might start talking about issues not covered by the bot. Then the bot has to take back the initiative by asking something like "I did not understand you, please repeat in other words". Such a question is clearly a documentation of bot failure

The white-box test is executed based on the concept of the bot. Questions are defined for checking the quality aspects of bots and the answers are checked against the quality criteria as sketched above.

Thus it is a mix of black and white-box testing that is used by testers in order to assess the quality of a bot.

Most modern firewall architectures tend to lie somewhere between these two firewall types. One firewall type combines both basic concepts in one machine; the stateful inspection firewall such as Check Point FireWall-1 overcomes the limitation of the previous two approaches by providing full application-layer awareness without breaking the client/server model. With stateful inspection, the packet is intercepted at the network layer, but then the inspect engine takes over. It extracts state-related information required for the security decision from all communication layers and maintains this information in dynamic state tables for evaluating subsequent connection attempts. This provides a solution that is highly secure and offers maximum performance, scalability and extensibility.

No matter how the Internet border is protected, sometimes another layer of security is needed. This can be implemented by a personal firewall that runs on a client. It monitors network activity and protects against unauthorised use of the Internet by programs that manage to get onto LAN computers.

2.2 Authentication

Authentication is the process of determining whether someone accessing an e-business or any other server, is who he or she declared to be. In the Internet world authentication is commonly done through the use of logon IDs and passwords. Knowledge of the logon ID and password is assumed to guarantee that the user is authentic. Each user registers initially using an assigned or self-declared logon ID and password. On each subsequent use, the user must know and use the previously declared logon ID and password. The inherent weakness in this system is that logon IDs and passwords can often be stolen or accidentally revealed.

The use of a security token like a chipcard carrying an encryption key adds security by ownership, while passwords or PINs provide security by knowledge. A third level of security is reached with security by human trait, e.g. fingerprint, facial features or voiceprints.

For Internet business transactions it is desirable to have a more stringent authentication method than mere passwords. Therefore the use of digital certificates issued and verified by a certificate authority as part of a public key infrastructure (PKI) seems to be becoming the standard way to perform authentication on the Internet. These digital certificates can be regarded as an electronic "credit card" that establishes credentials when doing business transactions over the Internet. It typically contains name, a serial number, expiration dates, a copy of the certificate holder's public key (used for encrypting messages and digital signatures) and the digital signatures of the certificate-issuing authority so that a recipient can verify that the certificate is real.

Digital certificates and biometric data such as fingerprints can be stored securely in smart cards. Files on the cards and permissions to these files are all set by the issuer in advance. The only access to the card's memory is through its operating system.

2.3 Encryption

2.3.1 Symmetric Cryptography

Encryption is a method of obscuring information while still being able to be deciphered by the intended reader. When each communication partner uses the same key to encrypt and decrypt the message, this is called symmetric encryption. This secret key system needs a secure channel, distinct to the communication channel, to agree on a key to be used by both parties. In this case key management is a difficult task especially when communicating across long distances and among people who do not know each other. For this reason, public key cryptography and the public key infrastructure (PKI) is the preferred approach on the Internet.

2.3.2 Public Key Cryptography

The public key infrastructure (PKI) enables users of the Internet to securely and privately exchange data and money through the use of a public and a private cryptographic key pair that is obtained through a trusted authority. This is also called asymmetric cryptography, because two communication partners use different (public) keys to encrypt messages they want to exchange.

Today, using brute-force computation one may compute private keys if the public key is known. By increasing the key size (measured in bit length) one achieves higher security – or at least makes it more time-consuming to compute the keys. In future times there may (or may not) be faster algorithms for prime factor decomposition, and public key encryption (as used today) may be totally unsafe.

2.4 Anti-Virus Software

Anti-virus software searches hard drives and floppy disks for any known computer viruses; it can also screen e-mail attachments and remove any viruses that are found. However, to be effective its database needs to be kept up to date with the latest list of virus patterns.

Generally, there are three main classes of computer viruses:

- File infectors attach themselves to program files, usually selected .COM or .EXE files. However, some can infect any program for which executions are requested, including .SYS, .OVL, .PRG, and .MNU files. When the program is loaded, the virus is loaded as well.

- System or boot-record infectors infect executable code found in certain system areas on a disk. They attach to the boot sector on diskettes or the master boot record on hard disks. Whenever the computer is started with the diskette in the drive, the computer starts from the 'A' drive, loads the virus code into memory and gives control to it.

- Macro viruses are among the most common viruses. Macro viruses are written in a macro language. They typically infect documents or templates of Microsoft applications such as Excel and Word, to be precise: what gets infected is the Word document or template (normal.dot). However, every application utilising a powerful macro language is prone to macro viruses.

The best protection against a virus is to use anti-virus software to screen e-mail attachments, check all files periodically and check all new files before installation of new programs. Generally it is recommended to never execute files of uncertain origin.

2.5 Intrusion Detection Systems (IDS)

As already discussed, typically firewalls and authentication systems are implemented to prevent unauthorised access. However, since there is nothing like 100% security, there should be some means to take care of unauthorised access even if firewalls and authentication systems are in place. Intrusion detection is a set of mechanisms to warn of attempted unauthorised access and misuse to an e-business site from the Internet as well as from inside the LAN.

Network-based intrusion detection systems are usually placed between the firewall and the system being secured, for example, monitoring access from the Internet to sensitive data ports of the secured e-business site to determine whether the firewall has been compromised, or whether an unknown mechanism has been used to bypass the security of the firewall to access the network being protected.

Host-based intrusion detection systems monitor system resources giving alarms when certain threshold values are reached which hint on unusual behaviour of the system and thus potential misuse.

Generally one can say that IDS are difficult to develop and to keep up to date, since hacker programs are developed to confuse IDS[1].

2.6 Penetration Testing

Penetration testing is a set of tests, in which an external security consultant or trained internal company employee plays the role of a hacker who then tries to compromise the security of the site. Ideally such a test is carried out without warning to see if the

---

[1] As reported on CNET during a seminar at the CanSecWest Conference in Vancouver during 2001 a hacker revealed a program he created that can camouflage programs (Trojan horse) that malicious hackers use by employing a cloaking technique aimed at foiling the pattern-recognition intelligence used by many intrusion detection systems. The hacker was quoted as saying "Trust me, this will blow away any pattern matching within an IDS."

organisation can detect the penetration attempts. Penetration testing can be designed to simulate an inside attack or an outside attack via the Internet and can be either technical or non-technical (e.g. the tester may try to "social engineer" his or her way into the site).

However, penetration testing has a flaw because usually its only goal is to compromise security. To do this, the tester first identifies known published vulnerabilities, with emphasis on the ones he or she believes are the most damaging and/or least likely to be detected (from the hacker's perspective). Then it checks if these known vulnerabilities exist within the site. Therefore a penetration tester will only find those vulnerabilities that he or she is testing for. It is expensive to keep knowledge of these testers up to date.

To make penetration test useful from a business perspective, the potential loss of corporate value and data should be demonstrated in business terms. The tester should not only report on the technical aspects of what the potential actions of hackers were but also what this could have meant to the business, e.g. " hackers would have had complete control over customer data and the network access to distribute it." This will give management hints on where to invest in security measures.

Sometimes websites are brought to their knees by so-called denial-of-service (DoS) attacks. Such attacks flood a web server with false requests, overwhelming the system and ultimately crashing it. As all requests have false return addresses, the server can't find the actual requester when it tries to send the acknowledgement. A server normally waits before closing such connections and so it becomes overloaded.

Also covert penetration tests should be performed to see if company employees are following security policies. A publicised test only checks whether or not people know how to follow policy, however it's only human nature to behave differently when one is not aware of being watched. For example, let's say that ABC's corporate security policy prohibits end users from revealing their passwords over the telephone. Therefore, if an outside consultant walked up to an end user and asked, "Do you ever reveal your password to anyone you don't know," the answer would usually be no. But it's a different story if the tester calls up a user, pretends he's from the IT department, and asks the user to reveal his or her password so the tester can "confirm" it. Such social engineering penetration techniques are a much more reliable method of determining actual compliance with security policy.

3   Potential Security Risks from e-Business Applications

Companies engaging in e-business today use greater complexities of software and databases than a static website. Most large e-business sites implement n-tier architectures consisting of a front-end web layer, a business-application layer, back-end databases and legacy systems often located on mainframes. Also as the demand and competition between e-business businesses grow, the sophistication of large-scale business application code grows accordingly and ever more frequently. The end result is large amounts of constantly changing, diverse, complex, custom and bespoke code that, if flawed, can result in a security compromise of the site and thus be regarded as the enemy from within regardless of the implementation of firewalls, authentication and encryption.

Also many organisations secure the operating systems on their hosts but leave the applications and database themselves with little protection, leaving the back door wide open.

3.1 Application Programming

Most e-businesses are driven to get their services and products out quickly. In doing this applications are sometimes not designed with security in mind. As well, most programmers are used to developing trusted internal applications that do not need to be "highly secure." Applications can create security holes that can be hard to detect. Therefore, applications need to be designed with security in mind and not as an afterthought.

Some best practices in application programming are:

- Use compiled programs like C++, VB and Java for connection and stored procedure calls and run these on an application server such as Microsoft's MTS or BEA Tuxedo and create server objects in scripts such as VBS, JavaScript or HTML to use the connections.
- Use J2EE, CORBA or COM+ object protocols
- Use database-stored procedures
- Use native database connections instead of ODBC
- Do not hard code user names and passwords in scripts
- Use simple, clean HTLM - no active content such as ActiveX
- Use OS authentication to access DB servers
- Do not use persistent connection
- Develop programming security templates

There are automated analysis tools available called application scanners that scan for known holes in web applications. These can be very helpful in automating or double-checking the human process. These products look for possible vulnerabilities that can be exploited by some of the following attacks:

- Hidden manipulation
- Cookie poisoning
- Backdoors/debug options

- Buffer overflow
- Stealth commanding
- Tampering cross-site scripting/server side includes
- Forceful browsing

3.2 Database Servers

Web applications bypass normal client-server OS and application security making the databases the lowest common denominator for implementing security. Database systems utilise critical pieces of the OS to function so once compromised these services are now available to the attacker. Some best practices for securing a database are:

- Transaction logging and auditing
- No generic or default passwords or user names
- Application-specific passwords or user names
- Encryption of stored procedures, triggers, views and network protocols
- Only install needed services – know what's on you system
- Keep up to date with service releases or patches
- Do not use extended stored procedures
- Limit admin accounts to DBA use only
- Backup system at appropriate levels for recovery

3.3 Trap Doors

Though usually honest and competent, developers and vendors must be monitored closely to ensure that their work is sound. For example, developers and vendors sometimes leave behind trap doors into systems with the purest intentions of using them to help to either:

- Test the code
- Make future modifications or updates

The down side of this approach is that they leave security holes that can then be used by intruders to break in and steal information from database systems. Furthermore, this leaves a system open to a vendor's or own disgruntled ex-employees who decide to embarrass their former employer by wreaking havoc on the systems. It is recommended to guard against trap doors and make it expressly known that these mechanisms must be first documented, removed and tested to see if they still exist before and after go live.

4   Continuous Testing of e-Business Systems

4.1   Continuous Testing – an Overview

A key to avoiding costly attacks due to flawed security measures and business applications is by implementing a test strategy that addresses this issue. This section describes Continuous Testing and the benefits of adopting the use of a Continuous Testing strategy to constantly monitor the e-business site and its behaviour through 'friendly' eyes. As such, traditional testing methods on their own do not necessarily cover all the security risks faced by a project. Internet applications are generally available 24 hours a day, 7 days a week. As the name implies, Continuous Testing effectively tests a site and business application on a continuous and on-going basis. This testing ensures that components of the service that should be secure and non-accessible are in fact disabled. It also gives an early indication of any security loopholes within the service that need to be addressed before the fault causes disruption to customers.

The ability to perform Continuous Testing must be designed into the initial-offering software. As an example, 'dummy' clients could be set up with access to all the functionality offered, with the exception of the ability to actually trade through the application. Another challenge that faces any organisation charged with supporting e-business applications is that users of a site will not report all of the problems that they detect in the service. Certainly a cyber criminal will not. A continuous test suite can take the role of a 'friendly' user who, while carrying out testing activities, reports and alerts the relevant parties to any discrepancies observed in the tests. With a suite that is executed at least once an hour the support team is provided with regular and constant feedback as to the security and stability of the service.

Continuous Testing is a process by which an e-business offering can be accessed on a regular basis, every hour of every day throughout the year to help ensure that the service is constantly available and secure. The goals can be categorised as:

- To ensure that the site and business application has no security loopholes.
- To act as an early-warning system should the site and/or business application security be breached.
- To ensure that the site infrastructure and business application is available and operable to clients around the clock.
- To act as an early-warning system should the application or any of the primary functionality not be available to the users.
- To monitor and track overall availability, security and response times of the service, to help detect trends and to enable more informed planning of any key maintenance to the business application and infrastructure.

- To proactively test all security aspects and functionality of a site to make sure it is behaving as expected.

- To monitor the adherence to Service Level Agreements (SLAs)

- To aggressively test systems – looking for new, newly visible or dangerous security problems that may occur when implementing fixes and software upgrades.

A comprehensive continuous test should cover a wide spectrum of functionality supported by the business application under test. In the purest form this should also include test scenarios that actually update the databases associated with the application. In certain circumstances, however, this may not be possible without taking preparatory measures in the application or infrastructure development process. It is important that real users are protected from any impact that the continuous test suite may have on common data elements.

Negative testing of the business applications is important, trying to do things with the application that are not expected in order to uncover "features" that are in themselves hidden security risks. As the majority of e-business companies offer a round-the-clock service 365 days of the year, Continuous Testing during operational incidents and events is also very important. The business application might perform differently while application or operational support are fixing defects, swapping hardware/networks, running batch, backing up or installing. This again could expose hidden security loopholes. Security and functional testing while the system is being accessed by large numbers of users and large volumes of data is more important, as the site and business application might perform differently while under stress that exposes hidden security loopholes.

4.2 Implementing the Continuous Testing Strategy

Detailed planning for the implementation of the Continuous Testing strategy needs to be undertaken in the very early stages of the development life cycle. As with all test systems, the creation of the continuous test suite follows the standard process of planning, preparation, verification and execution.

As automation will play a substantial role in the execution of the continuous test suite the planning process should start with the production of the test system design. This process better defines how the continuous suite is to be constructed and what tests need to be created and executed. It also identifies how many test suites are be required. Two basic benefits of Continuous Testing are the detection of security defects and the gathering of information, so there may be benefits to be gained in the creation of a number of separate suites. This should be clarified during the design stage. Also, provided the test system design is done correctly, it should be possible to 'reuse' many of the automated tests from system testing.

IT security groups within the organisation, for one or two reasons, may influence the final scope of the continuous suite. Firstly, the suite as described in the Test System Design (TSD) might have an impact across the whole of the service and external related services. For example: the carrying out of trades on stocks and equities, no matter how small, will after a time affect the stock price in the market place. There are a number of actions that can be taken to minimise the impact of this:

- Use predefined user/client IDs for the continuous suite that can be 'filtered out' of the system before any trades are actually committed. This requires building these filters into the application solution and the thorough testing of those to ensure that integrity is maintained.

- Use predefined user/client IDs and stocks and equities within the continuous test suite and include within the application infrastructure dummy databases that only operate for these predefined clients and stocks. Having these built into the infrastructure ensures that the tests accurately reflect the application without impacting the integrity of the true, live data.

- Design the tests for the continuous suite such that when it comes to actually updating any sensitive data the test itself physically quits from the process at a point immediately prior to committing any updates to sensitive data.

An important risk is associated with this strategy: The tests could end up just running against dummy transactions, leaving the real transactions untested. Testers would be happy while users might run into problems not seen by the test transactions. This risk has to be addressed in reviews of the tests.

A second possible inhibitor is the fact that 'testing in production' has, traditionally been regarded as taboo in the industry. It is a possibility, albeit remote, that the execution of a test in the continuous test suite may actually expose a flaw in the application. Such a flaw might cause a significant degradation in the service that impacts 'real' users. The risk of this possibility needs to be offset against the overall advantages of running a continuous test in the live environment that proactively seeks out problems for resolution before the users. To run the continuous test suite manually is not the most efficient use of resources. The suite must be automated, and able to be scheduled. Three options can be considered for the delivery of the Continuous Testing solution.

- To use existing tools and utilities to create a monitoring suite
- To buy-in software specifically designed to monitor website security
- To use a service provider to provide the facilities and means to monitor and report on a site's security

4.3 Continuous Testing Management

The continuous test suite must be reviewed regularly to ensure that it remains fit for purpose. The business application and infrastructure is likely to change following its launch and the breadth of the offerings will expand. The suite needs to be expanded in line with these changes, and for every increment of change that is applied an allowance is required in the project plans to expand the continuous test suite. Also as the business application is used, both the continuous test suite and real users highlight errors and shortcomings. Therefore the suite must be amended to cater for the correction, and subsequent closer monitoring of weak points identified. The suite should be continually reshaped to allow for a more proactive approach to problem resolution by actively using the suite to look for errors. Areas of concern can be tested in depth by upgrades to the suite to address these areas.

As stated above, the test cases and scripts created during system testing should be re-used in the continuous test suite; therefore all the tests in the suite should be subject to test asset management. The test asset manager must bear in mind the continuous test suite as part of his or her working practices in managing test assets and ensuring the maximum benefit is to be gained from all test assets.

5 Summary

E-business is based on the assumption that data integrity is intact and that online systems are always available when needed. Therefore, ensuring the availability of key components is critical to success and protecting a company's brand name. It is challenging to provide secure and resilient e-business systems. In this article we summarised the typical means used for security and gave hints on how continually testing the e-business security measures (authentication, firewalls, encryption, etc), the business application as well as the databases help here.

Testing for security on an e-business site is a dynamic and on-going process. As sites change rapidly and technical infrastructure and networks continue to evolve constantly, security risks evolve as well. Since not only the firewall but also the business application and database might have security problems it is recommended to implement a continuous approach to security testing.

Website Performance Monitoring

DAVID SINGLETON †
Site Confidence (United Kingdom)

Abstract: Most websites are expected to function around the clock, 24 by 7. This can be seen from a purely technical perspective, but should be seen from the user's perspective, i.e. from outside the firewall. The measure of website performance is the answer to the question 'are the web pages viewable by end users'. Where end users are customers, the issue becomes directly related to organisations' ability to offer online purchasing of goods and services.

The Internet is a distributed system, where software, hardware and network facilities must work together to deliver a web page to the customer. There are therefore many points of failure and decisions about how a website is developed and supported and by whom, all of which can make a critical difference to its availability and responsiveness from the customer viewpoint.

Practical experience derived from automated website performance testing shows that 99% uptime is good, not poor performance in today's commercial Internet world. Reasons for failures are explained and many examples of real-world problems are used to illustrate issues covering network design and implementation, hardware and software technology as well as design and management issues in this chapter.

The author, founder and technical director of SiteConfidence, a UK-based web performance company that offers an automated testing service for websites, discusses experiences gained in practical operation and monitoring of websites.

Keywords: Internet testing, home banking, HBCI, Internet-based applications

1 Business Goals

Monitoring the performance of a website '24 by 7' i.e. around the clock has many technical aspects, and these will be analysed in this chapter, but the fundamental point is that it is the **end user's** experience of the website that is important. Consequently, it is a marketing issue just as much as it is a technical issue, and should be seen as critical to the business, not just the IT department.

Assuming the agreed definition that it is the end user or customer experience that is the key measure of a website, how is this to be measured? There are both qualitative aspects and quantitative aspects. Qualitative aspects are commonly measured using techniques such as focus groups, usability testing, user questionnaires and panel-based data gathered by market research companies. This analysis will concentrate on the quantitative aspects.[1]

From a technical viewpoint aspects of the technical infrastructure are often measured. For example: a query should be performed within so many milliseconds, the web server should support 250 simultaneous users and 500 hits per second, the mean time between failure for the hardware should be greater than three years. These are only partial surrogates for considering the end-to-end experience, i.e. the actual use of a website by a human being. From a human viewpoint the site is slow or fast, a page is not available although it was on a previous visit etc.

The other major issue is the question whether absolute or relative measures should be examined. Both are valuable, but relative measures are ultimately more useful because the Internet is a competitive commercial environment. Users are strongly influenced by their expectations, which are defined by their experience of other websites and other channels such as telephone call centres. When the user or customer connects to a website the availability of the site (uptime), the time they must wait to view web pages or complete a transaction (download speed and time to buy) are compared to their experience of other sites or competing channels.

In the UK the average commercial home page is about 75kb in size and takes about 15 seconds to download over a standard 56 kbps dialup connection. Good availability for a website is 99% over a seven-day period. These are as measured by SiteConfidence testing servers from outside the firewall.

2 Technical Goals

The classic goal for a website is to be 'open for business 24 by 7', i.e. always available to the user. The usual way to define this is to talk of '99.x' availability, where x is the key number. Working on the basis that availability is measured from the user's viewpoint, i.e. across the public Internet, we can by simple arithmetic calculate the following:

Table 1: Availability and downtime

Measurement	Downtime (mins) per year	Downtime per week
99%	5,256	101 mins
99.5%	2,628	51
99.9%	525.6	10
99.99%	52.6	1 min
99.999%	5.3	6 seconds

[1] See [NIEL01] or more broadly search the web for usability. Most large market research companies and design agencies offer usability services as part of their web design/development offering.

To have a realistic chance of actually measuring availability at even the 99.9% level it would be necessary to test every five minutes. One well-known monitoring service notes that 'every 15 minutes is optimal'. It is unlikely that it would be worth testing website availability at the 99.999% level (more on what a proper test is later), even if that were desirable. A frequency of every three seconds would be 10.5 million page hits per annum, the total traffic load of a more than moderately busy commercial website in its own right.[2]

There is an important technical difference between types of testing. The key difference is between within the firewall (internal testing) and outside the firewall (external testing). Unless the site is purely an Intranet site, the user experience cannot by tested inside the firewall.[3]

3   Service Level Agreements

Many ISPs, hosting companies and managed services providers offer their customers Service Level Agreements (SLAs). Based on the simple analysis presented in Table 1, any commercial supplier offering even 99.9% availability must have extremely robust and possibly intrusive testing technology in place. A supplier offering what is often known as "Five nines" uptime, i.e. 99.999% reliability, probably does not have a means to measure compliance with that claim.

Assuming that an SLA has been included in a contract and that non-compliance can be measured, the value of any compensation must also be considered. Typically there is a trade-off, the more compensation, the higher the contractual cost. The site owner must calculate the cost of downtime for the site or key commercial parts of the site. Would a refund of a month's hosting fee actually cover the cost of a four-hour business interruption if it occurred during business hours? Alternatively, if the website goes down for 30 minutes at 3 a.m. on the European servers, but the US and Asian servers remain available, does that actually make any real difference to the business?

The fact that a supplier offers an SLA is in itself not sufficient. The details of measurement, enforcement and compensation need detailed examination.

---

[2] ABC electronic audits website traffic, typically for advertising purposes. From conversations with ABCe in the UK, most sites selling advertising have traffic above 1 million page impressions per month.

[3] Technically this is not strictly true as it is possible to delve into the packet level transactions and read information in a similar manner to a packet sniffer. Specialist software is definitely required, and at high volume specialist hardware as well.

4   The Internet as a Technical Environment

The public Internet is not as stable or of the same quality as most organisations' internal networks. The Internet is evolving and it is distributed.

The path between users and a site's web servers is routed across equipment owned and maintained by several commercial organisations. Traffic patterns change minute by minute, bottlenecks develop and are resolved, new routers and fibre are brought on stream every day. Although the hardware itself is mostly extremely reliable, access is mediated by software, and routing tables are configured and maintained by very fallible humans.

The consequence is that what was proving extremely reliable at 3 p.m. on Monday may go alarmingly wrong at 8 a.m. the following day. Overall the distributed nature of the Internet is basically very reliable, but if a router one or two steps out from the website firewall goes wrong, the site is likely to suffer. The fact that several different commercial suppliers are likely involved in the path from the user's browser to the website also gives enormous scope for buck-passing – "not our fault". Proof that the service is not available, preferably backed up by diagnostic information can help resolve the problem rapidly.

5   The Website's Environment

Assuming that the software components have been thoroughly tested at the functional level, many of the problems that will arise are related to the interaction between the various hardware and software components.

Some companies manage their entire web development and environment themselves, and buy a leased line connection from a telco or ISP. At the opposite end others outsource the entire site, including the development and maintenance to outside suppliers. In the middle ground, many host their production environment externally, but manage much of the development and software maintenance in-house.

All three choices have implications for monitoring, in particular the identification of who will manage and solve problems as they occur.

5.1   All In-House

If the servers and software development is all in-house, staff should be available to receive notification of problems. If a reliable 24-by-7 service is to be offered, this requires a rota of staff. This is really only a solution for the largest of companies. Otherwise the internal infrastructure is unlikely to be of sufficient quality, and costs for the number of staff willing and able to respond around the clock is probably prohibitively expensive.

Likely problems include both hardware and software issues:

Table 2: In-house Website Problems

Issue	Consequence	Solution(s)
Power cut	Unavailable website, may require considerable time & expertise to restart the servers.	UPS (battery back-up) can help. Redundant power feeds and diesel generators are expensive. These are standard at good hosting companies.
Bandwidth outage or poor QOS	Unavailable website. If someone has knocked out the line, the classic "a road construction crew dug up the cable", this can take days to solve	Redundant communications lines and, better, redundant suppliers, i.e. two lines from different telcos/ISPs.
Router failure (not at the local ISP)	Partially unavailable website	Can be difficult to diagnose and likely to require in-house analysis.
Operating system crash or standard application crash	Unavailable or partially unavailable website.	Reboot server(s) or applications. Easy and quick during office hours, but may require staff to travel to the office from home.
Custom software problems	Partially unavailable website	There may or may not be a quick solution. The issue is knowing where and how the error occurred

5.2 Fully Outsourced

Full outsourcing is potentially the most attractive solution as then (in theory) the hardware, the software and the content are all managed by a specialist. Unfortunately there are not really any companies who actually do all three well in-house. A typical solution is that the company developing the software and content will itself outsource the production servers and management of them (and the software they have developed) to a third-party hosting company. It is extremely unlikely that a traditional media house has sufficient technical expertise to build and manage a true transactional website. Equally, it is rare that a software house or IT services provider understands marketing and design issues for the Internet.

This can be expensive, but is potentially an attractive solution for any organisation that lacks in-house expertise and has the budget to pay for a comprehensive solution.

All problems with power cuts and other hardware-related problems should disappear. Furthermore when something does go wrong, the "buck stops" with the primary supplier. The problems listed in Table 2 above become the supplier's to solve.

Table 3: In-house Website Problems

Issue	Consequence	Solution(s)
Achieving a robust technical environment	Website unstable, not scalable etc.	Due diligence … exactly where are the servers, who looks after them, what kind of hosting environment.
Assuring SLAs are met	Poor website performance if SLA is broken	Independent monitoring or an SLA that can be audited
Management oversight	Confirming that a good service is being provided at a reasonable price.	Transparency is often difficult to achieve as once committed to a fully outsourced solution there can be high degree of lock-in.

From experience in providing monitoring services to companies that have chosen to fully outsource their website to small design companies who also do hosting in-house, this can be the worst solution. When things go wrong, the only person who can fix the problem is probably on holiday or sick. This solution requires a large supplier.

5.3 Software In-House, Production Facility Hosted

An increasingly popular solution is for the website owner to manage software and content in-house, but to locate the servers in a secure production environment. This is usually known as co-location. Co-location can include the supplier providing basic management of the operating system and database software (aka a "managed service").

Some of the problems noted in Table 2 remain with the website owner, but these are principally related to custom-developed software.

Table 4: Hosted Website Problems

Issue	Consequence	Solution(s)
Managing suppliers	Management headache	Understanding needs correctly. Requires sufficient in-house technical understanding to negotiate the right contracts
Assuring SLAs are met	Poor website performance if SLA is broken	Independent monitoring or an SLA that can be audited
Who resolves problems	Problems not solved due to buck-passing between different suppliers	third- party monitoring solution or trusted in-house monitoring system that all suppliers can access

5.4 Comparison of Website Environments

For all except large organisations, the all in-house solution is probably more expensive and less stable than either of the other two solutions.

A fully outsourced solution is potentially the most expensive, but also the least difficult to manage if the supplier does a good job. The main issue is in assuring the solution, is the website as stable and available as it should be?

The third potential solution, software in house, production facility housed elsewhere, is becoming more and more popular as company websites become more core to the organisation's basic business. It is also the most economic.[4]

6   Types of Website Problems

The possible problems are many, but these can be broken down into manageable issues.

6.1 DNS Mapping Problems

If the name of the website is not mapped to an IP address, e.g. www.yahoo.co.uk mapped to 217.12.6.17, then the website is unavailable (a DNS error). A DNS error can apply to all users, or it can be local to some ISPs. These DNS mappings change and must be maintained. For example one of our customers (a large UK bank) moved their website from one set of servers to another, thus changing the IP address to be used by the user's browser. Our service showed the site as effectively 'down' for a whole day as the DNS mappings were not updated across the Internet properly.

6.2 Connectivity Problems

Network unreliability on the public Internet is a fact of life. Every website suffers occasionally from delays, and unless a website is served by redundant suppliers, it is likely to suffer some outages. Even Yahoo! goes down sometimes. The problem can be at the web server itself or on the network.

At SiteConfidence we see a surprising number of sites where the point of failure is not in the site itself, but in the network connections inside the ISP, i.e. a single router through

---

[4] At the time of writing bandwidth is available at high-quality hosting centres in London at £500 per Mbps. A standard '47u rack' that can contain upwards of 30 computers, which would be easily capable of supporting 200 page downloads a minute (>two million a month) can be rented for £350 per month, with the required bandwidth costing about £1200 per month. Computer servers are dropping rapidly in price, and can often be rented by the month for a few hundred pounds per server (or less in the USA)

which traffic must flow. Judging by the regularity with which ISPs go down, this is clearly a more difficult technical problem than it would seem at first glance. Alternatively one could make assumptions about some ISPs' commitment to providing a quality service.[5]

If a router on the recognised path to a website goes down, this can stop all or some traffic to the website. Whilst the Internet is designed to be resilient, it can take hours to route around a failed router. Problems with network connections to a website can also be intermittent. Pings and traceroutes can diagnose these to some degree, depending on the degree of security implemented by the ISP[6]. As well as total failures, congestion can occur that can lead to a very slow download of web pages. Response times for a ping should normally be under 100 milliseconds from any single device in the route if it is local, perhaps up to 250 to 300 ms if it is on another continent[7].

Some, but not all websites are built with entirely redundant network connections. Many ISPs maintain secondary connections to their servers in the event that the primary one goes down. Unfortunately the secondary connections rarely have enough capacity. Hence traffic is routed through a choke point. One ISP we know has a 2Mbps main Internet pipe, but only a 128k ISDN backup. This is analogous to a three-lane motorway when an accident happens and two lanes are shut. Everything effectively slows to near paralysis.

Hosting in-house almost guarantees that there is single point of telecommunications failure unless the data centre has purchased service from two different ISPs. Where a managed service has been chosen including servers, bandwidth and security, it is important to ask about redundant network connections. Many ISPs offer hosting, but normally all the bandwidth then comes from that same ISP. The alternative is to choose carrier independent hosting and to deliberately buy bandwidth (and network connections over separate cables) from two or more ISPs.[8]

The issue here is diagnosis, i.e. at which point does the problem lie. Although the network provider may not be at fault, their support staff generally know whom to contact at the other supplier. Consequently, allowing the network supplier's support staff to see evidence of problems is the first step is getting the problem solved. Buck-passing at this level is endemic, technical diagnostic information is essential. This can be shown using a traceroute and ping generated manually by in-house staff, some monitoring services (e.g. SiteConfidence) provide these automatically as part of the alerts they generate when an outage is detected.

---

[5] There is a difference between different ISPs. When negotiating with ISPs ask about SLAs and how they can verify their compliance with their SLA over the last three months.

[6] For security reasons, many ISPs block ping/traceroutes on their network. The side effect of this is to prevent the retrieval of diagnostic information.

[7] More information at www.matrix.net. Our experience is that routing to a website that passes across the Atlantic and then back again adds around 170 ms to the 'trip time'. Whilst that is not a lot of time in itself, it applies to each page component (e.g. graphics image). If the page contains 20 images, that can be an extra five seconds for total download time for a page depending on the efficiency of the browser!

[8] SiteConfidence has two separate ISPs, each of which provides a redundant connection.

More difficult to diagnose are failures to create a TCP/IP socket connection between the browser (or testing servers) and the target web server. If the hardware or operating system is not functioning (e.g. server powered down) then a TCP/IP socket connection cannot be established. (The fundamental Http protocol runs on top of TCP/IP). An intelligent network card may respond to a ping, but it is the operating system that manages TCP/IP sessions. An overloaded server may refuse some connections but not all. This would be the equivalent of an overloaded telephone switchboard, where too many people are trying to call simultaneously.

6.3 Technical Hardware Components

It is actually rare for hardware to fail, for example the servers we use at SiteConfidence have a Mean Time Between Failure of four years, and most suppliers offer the same levels of reliability. Hardware failure can be monitored for at the hardware level by inside-the-firewall services or from the outside. The usual solution is to have redundant hardware, e.g. database servers with multiple disks running RAID software.

Although most web servers are configured to auto recover when a power outage occurs, this is not always a smooth procedure. There are ways of allowing remote access to reboot a server which has not recovered properly.

6.4 Technical Software Components

Far more likely than a hardware failure is that software will go wrong. We can distinguish here between custom-built software (high risk) and more stable database and operating system software (low to medium risk).

Based on data gathered by SiteConfidence in decreasing order of stability and reliability are:

Web server > operating system > database > scripted software > custom software

All software is vulnerable to failure, the order shown is basically determined by the degree of standardisation. It is very rare to write a web server or operating system, although these are configured. At the opposite end, custom software is usually very vulnerable to failures as it does not have the equivalent of 1000's of years of usage.

A web server and operating system can be considered a pair of interdependent applications. These are generally configured and it is very rare to actually change the core code. Problems here relate to tuning (changing configuration parameters) rather than bugs.

The failure of a standard application such as an Oracle or MS SQL database is not unknown. Whilst the website itself is still available, it is probably crippled in practice, as no queries can be carried out. If the website is made up of dynamic content, then the failure of the underlying database application is basically the same as a total failure of the website.

Some applications create standard error messages, SiteConfidence traps for these on the pages downloaded on behalf of customers. We can then alert operations staff with more than standard 'your site is down' messages, and provide diagnostic information that makes fixing the problem faster.

It is not only applications that can fail, key processes such as login can also be a cause of failure. The login process can be entirely separate to the rest of the applications for security purposes, and hence if it goes down, the other applications are unavailable.

6.5   Architectural Issues

A large website is usually run on more than one server. There may be tiers of servers each performing their own tasks, e.g. content aggregation, database access, security authentication etc. This requires careful performance tuning and management of load balancing to avoid bottlenecks. For example the author was the R&D director for a large dot-com in early 2000. The company was a pure dot-com, and customers were calling customer service to complain they could not buy. The IT director who also ran production denied that there could be a problem as the system logs and internal performance monitoring showed the system was "running fine". Further investigation using outside-the-firewall testing showed that a single login server was a bottleneck and was denying registered customers access.

The other issue often faced by larger companies is the need to provide web services that draw upon data and applications taken from older systems that were not designed for 24-by-7 operation. This is a typical problem for banks and other companies whose systems have evolved over time. A claim to provide true 24-by-7 availability cannot be supported if the systems are taken offline for maintenance every night.

6.6   Choices of Software

The decisions relating to operating systems, web server software and databases are choosing between vendors. The business-specific software is a buy-or-build decision. This is not always easy, especially when faced with a software-oriented IT department that would much rather write code rather than buy someone else's because that is more interesting.

Broadly speaking the choice is between Microsoft technology and that from other vendors. Microsoft are clearly very successful in the web space and their technology is used by many companies for websites. That said, results from testing at SiteConfidence is that some environments are less stable than others. We are certainly aware of companies all using the same technology who reboot their web servers every night 'just in case', while this is rarely the case with other types of web servers.[9]

6.7 Technical Content Issues

Content can be static or dynamic, and furthermore locally generated or taken from third-party feeds (e.g. news channel) or third-party ad servers. Static content is basically unchanging, or changed by editing pages on a weekly or, more likely, a monthly basis. Dynamic content is held in a database, and is inserted into each page when that page is requested.

In broad terms, in decreasing order of stability and reliability are:

Static local content > dynamic local content > third-party content > banner ads

Although the content from a third party may itself be reliably produced, it may have to cross the public Internet to the website that displays the advert. It is also typically dynamic, links may become broken etc. SiteConfidence experience is that banner ads are unreliable. The COO of one of our customers asked us to exclude banner ads served by one well-known advertising service from our alerts and statistics on the grounds that a) she knows the ad servers are very unreliable and b) she cannot do anything about the unreliability anyway.

6.8 Website Content Design Issues

Even though the content itself may download reliably, the size and composition of web pages is also a frequent problem. Many pages are simply too big, and hence download so slowly that the ordinary user will get bored of waiting and will click elsewhere. Site-Confidence data shows that the average UK commercial home page takes about 15 seconds to download using a standard dial-up modem. US data concurs with this average[10]. Customers will switch off and fail to buy from slow websites. US research[11]

---

[9] Scalability and reliability of NT versus various types of UNIX are controversial topics. See for example: 1. www.kegel.com for links to numbers of references 2. ZDNET Nov 1999 refers to a study by SMARTPART-NER which found that NT crashed on average every six weeks, whereas as Linux had no downtime over a 10 month period. 3. Gartner 7 May, 8 June, 20 June 2001 note IIS is very insecure and recommend that organisations should not use IIS as it not secure as a web server. 4. Smart Reseller Jan 1999 "Linux is the Web Server's Choice" 5. Slashdot.org refers to a Swiss study carried out by syscom that found Apache to be two times more reliable than IIS when comparing 100 commercial websites. 6. Information Week April 16 2001"Wintel servers still have plenty to do before they can equal the power and performance of Unix machines" 7. ZDNET June 18 2001 "Tux built for speed" notes that Tux/Linux is superior to NT/IIS in scalability 8. Ziff Davis Magazines, May 1999, "Solaris superior to NT"

[10] Keynote Systems.

[11] Zona Research, (3 May 2001)

claims that 82% of retail site abandonment is due to the slow loading of pages, the primary cause being too may graphics.

Macromedia Flash is a useful technology, but all too many home pages are created by designers who see the Web as akin to a TV advertising medium. Either the whole page is in Flash, or a significant portion requires the user to wait. Apart from the fact that not every user can (or wants) to download and run Flash[12], the download often takes more than 30 seconds. The Technical Director at one design agency recently told me of a new client whose old site took five minutes to download due to the enormous size of the Flash file that comprised the home page.

Even ordinary html-based home pages can be enormous and therefore slow. At the time of writing (June 2001) a survey of UK supermarket websites offering home shopping showed a variation in home pages between 65 kb and 230 kb in size and hence a variation between 12 seconds and 45 seconds to download their home pages using an ordinary modem. These variations are caused by the use of graphics images (many were not optimised). Given that waiting in checkout queues is a typical bugbear of supermarket customers, it seems odd that the owners of the slower sites did not make this comparison.

6.9 Traffic-Related Problems

Most websites experience different traffic patterns by time of day and day of the week. Not all B2B websites are at their busiest during the business day of course. Published data on working patterns in the UK shows that many managerial staff work in the evenings and at the weekends, and this is no doubt true in other European countries in practice. Other users will be in the USA on the west coast. Four p.m. in the afternoon there is midnight in the UK and the rest of Europe.

Capacity planning comes from experience, and B2C sites probably experience greater surges than B2B sites. The normal causes of massive surges in traffic are promotions and special events. Surges to 10 or 20 times normal levels are not unknown.

Bandwidth is usually purchased on a per GB per month or per Mbit per second[13]. Larger sites will purchase per Mbit per second, this can be purchased with built in

---

[12] At a recent testing conference 75 participants were asked to vote on their like/dislike of Flash. None liked it. See also Jakob Nielsens's Alertbox damning the use of Flash as 99% unusable. (www.useit.com).

[13] Assuming the average user is downloading at 40Kbps (using a dial-up modem), using simple arithmetic, a 1 Mbps connection can support 25 simultaneous page downloads. Depending on the amount of time a user spends looking at a page before downloading the next one, that can represent 100 to 200 simultaneous browsing sessions. Ignoring surges and assuming that a user spends on average five minutes at a website looking at five pages, that could translate to 15,000 unique user sessions in an eight-hour day, and 1.5 million page impressions in a 20-day business month. These numbers are purely illustrative, and the same bandwidth could support many more page downloads, with fewer users depending on traffic patterns. Furthermore, use of caching technology by ISPs can substantially increase this nominal capacity.

surge (aka burst) availability. For example one of our bandwidth suppliers meters our usage, but does not limit it, so we have 100Mbps should we need it.

The obvious techniques to be used for capacity planning and assurance include load testing, a topic outside the scope of this chapter.

6.10 Security

Security is outside the scope of this chapter, but it may not be wise to assume that firewalls are properly configured. If budgets permit, a website should be 'probed' by specialist security consultants.

There is an issue with too much security as well as too little. If something goes wrong support staff might have to connect from home at 1 a.m. to fix a problem. They should not be locked out by overly tight security.

7   Testing Techniques and Technology

To illustrate how testing can be carried out, SiteConfidence is used as an example of the technology that can be deployed, and this is compared to other techniques.

7.1 Inside the Firewall Versus Outside the Firewall

Network monitoring technologies have been available for many years and are well defined. There are well-known tools available in the marketplace such as CA's Unicenter, IBM's Tivoli and HP's OpenView. Possibly for cost reasons, many ISPs run HP Openview.

These tools use SNMP and other techniques to measure the availability of devices at a fundamentally technical level. They have been enhanced to include the availability of services and even applications, but their roots lie in 'pinging' devices such as routers and switches. They are designed to test from an inside perspective, and require that the relevant SNMP software has been installed on all the devices and applications on the network. There is no guarantee that access to a website via the public Internet is available and performant as this type of monitoring stops at the firewall. It is worth noting that although the data is gathered inside the firewall, an external monitoring service can gather the data. The firewall needs to be configured to allow this to happen of course.

By contrast, SiteConfidence tests from outside the firewall at the application level and does not require the installation of any software on the target system. It downloads web pages across the public Internet just as a user does from his own PC. Done on a scheduled basis around the clock (known as 24 by 7) it will be monitored whether a website is really available to actual customers.

7.2 Varieties of External Monitoring: Their Strengths and Weaknesses

There are basically three techniques that can be used to check the availability of a website.

7.2.1 Ping

A ping is the simplest method of checking that a web server is available. A packet of data is sent to the relevant server, and a response is received. This is quick, technically easy to implement, and can show that a connection is down or is degraded (packet loss).

Pings have two weaknesses. Firstly many firewalls are configured to block pinging, they may need to be re-enabled to accept pings from an external testing server. Even more problematic is that if the ping succeeds, it does not prove that the website is itself available. An intelligent network card can respond to a ping even though the server itself has crashed. To serve pages, the website requires that the operating system be alive and functioning (e.g. Windows 2000 or Linux), the web server software be working (e.g. Apache or IIS) and that associated applications that support that website (e.g. Oracle, SQL Server) are working.

7.2.2 HTTP Get to obtain the 1st 1000 bytes

A web page is typically comprised of html text and a number of images. By checking that the page header or first 1000 bytes can be downloaded, we can test that the web server itself is working and at least responding to requests for pages. Technically this is a bit more complex than pinging, but still works well and is fast.

But it is still not a true measure of website availability. Although the server may itself be active, the page returned to a user could contain an error code, e.g. http 404, an http 500 or perhaps a database error code because the database has crashed. Even if the page itself is returned, it may be so slow that in practice a user would give up and go elsewhere. Although the website is in this circumstance 'technically' available, from the user perspective it is not.

Although a good test, a simple http get to download 1000 bytes is not good enough.

7.2.3 Downloading Entire Pages

Downloading entire pages is the definitive test that the website, (or at least the pages tested), are available to end-users across the public Internet. This can be done using either a sophisticated browser emulator or a testing tool layer that sits on top of a true browser such as Internet Explorer.

A further advantage of this type of testing is that problems such as unauthorised changes to content (e.g. as a result of hacking) can be detected., Also failure of standard applications such as Oracle, SQL Server, Cold Fusion can be detected by monitoring for error messages displayed on a web page.

The disadvantages are the time this takes to download the complete page and the difficulty in downloading very sophisticated pages that contain complex JavaScript or other client-side executable code. A true browser may be required to test the availability of a complex page, especially one based on plug-in technologies such as Macromedia Flash.

7.3 Testing Sequences of Pages

Testing the download of a sequence of pages requires a careful test strategy. A typical example would be the completion of a shopping basket transaction. Assume that this is tested four times per hour, or 672 times per week. Test design becomes crucially important as purchasing the same goods for every test can cause serious problems on a live system and reversing financial payments can be complex and problematic.

This type of testing will usually be relatively expensive because it requires a consultant to set it up and debug the testing sequence(s). Testing of single pages can be automated quite quickly. When testing a shopping basket transaction there is no standard transaction flow, this will vary for each website. Consequently, the setup, interpretation and write-up of the results can consume many days, even weeks of consultancy time depending on the complexity of the testing.

7.4 What is the Best Strategy?

Inside-the-firewall monitoring can measure how the various parts of a website are functioning together, and can give diagnostic metrics such as SQL queries per minute, CPU and disk usage on the web server etc., but cannot measure how the website appears to actual users. Generally speaking, it is necessary to install software to do this monitoring and will require some design consultancy to gather the correct types of data.

Outside-the-firewall monitoring can tell the site owner how users are experiencing the website, but cannot produce diagnostic information about some of the problems unless software is installed on the relevant servers and routers.

Consequently, a complete (but probably expensive) monitoring solution requires both.

For outside-the-firewall monitoring, the best strategy is to use downloading of complete pages, and, if that is not feasible, to drop down to using an http get to obtain the first 1000 bytes. When a TCP/IP connection cannot be established, pinging and a traceroute can help to diagnose the problem further.

Feasibility is a function of cost. Most pages can be downloaded completely using a browser emulator, but some pages are sufficiently complex that they can only be downloaded using a true browser. To dedicate a single machine to running one browser to enable the testing of a complex page is expensive, whereas a well-designed browser emulator can download many pages in parallel.

SiteConfidence offers both single and multiple page monitoring. Our basic tool is a browser emulator capable of downloading 98% of all web pages completely.

7.5 Reliability and False Alerts

The reliability of alerts must be a key concern. A false alert is unacceptable if it occurs more than once and, given the generally unreliable nature of the Internet, can be caused by problems local to the testing servers rather than the website being tested. To test from a single server over a single network connection is to leave two single points of failure.

At SiteConfidence we guard against this problem of false alerts by running a cluster of multiple servers that use totally separate network connections from two different telco suppliers. Each telco connection is itself delivered over redundant cables. When we detect a page is down, an alert is issued only after testing from two different servers, over two different routings. As a final check before issuing the alert we also ping yahoo.co.uk to check that there is no generic Internet problem.

7.6 Diagnosis

Once a problem has been identified, it needs diagnosis: where has it occurred, what is the cause?

Walking through the steps necessary to download a page within a time acceptable to the end user, the following has to be achieved.

(1) The name of the website must map to a route across the Internet from the browser.
(2) A path must exist from the browser to the website server, i.e. each router and switch must be up and running.
(3) The website server must be working at the network TCP/IP level (an operating system function).
(4) The web server software must be working, i.e., can receive and fulfil requests for web pages.
(5) The applications upon which the website itself depends(e.g. database) must be working.
(6) The whole chain must be performing/responding within normal parameters.
(7) The web page must be 'normally' downloadable within a standard time, e.g. 30 seconds.

Stage 1 - Name of the Website

A DNS error occurs. This is easy to trap and an alert can be sent.

Stage 2 – Network Path Exists

The tool fails to create a TCP/IP socket connection with the target server. This can be caused by a path failure or an overly busy web server that cannot support the traffic load it is under. A traceroute may be able to diagnose the problem, but may not fully expose the point of failure, as the relevant router may not be configured to respond to a traceroute. An alert can be generated with the traceroute. If a connection fails across two different ISPs the error is very likely in the path from the bandwidth supplier to the website or the website server itself.

Stage 3 - Server Crashed (Hardware or Operating System)

A server crash is probably not distinguishable from a failure in the network path.

Stage 4 - Web Server Crashed or Misconfigured

If the web server application has crashed then no pages will be available. The response will vary by manufacturer and version of web server. A misconfiguration can result in an http error code 500. It may be that no connection can be achieved to the web server, in which a traceroute may be able to show the connection exists. This can be difficult to distinguish from a network path error.

Stage 5 - Application Crashed

If a database has crashed then a standard error message generated by that application and displayed on the web page can be trapped by the testing tool and sent to the website in an alert. Another technique is to trap for error text included on a web page and the send that back to the website owner in an alert. SiteConfidence offers both options.

Stage 6 - Erratic Response Times

Testing the response time of a page over time will show whether there is a consistent time to download the page. An erratic response with large variations in the time taken probably indicates congestion somewhere. A good testing tool will offer daily trend graphs showing the change in download time.

The only way to identify this weak point is to load test.

Stage 7 – Slow Download Speeds

As already noted, the average home page is about 75kb in the UK; that will take approximately 15 seconds over a standard dialup line. Unfortunately, despite the lack of broadband usage across Europe, many web pages are designed to be viewed over a broadband connection, and hence their sheer size makes them very slow to download.

SiteConfidence provides a diagnosis tool that shows the size of a page and the size of its components.

8 Future

There are a number of technologies that will greatly influence the performance aspects of websites. Among the most influential from today's perspective seem to be the following three:

8.1 Broadband

The lack of progress with broadband in the UK and elsewhere in Europe indicates that these problems are not going to go away in the next two to three years. If we look back, five years ago a 28k dialup modem was considered very fast. We had speed problems then. We still have problems now been though today's bandwidth would have solved those problems of five years ago. Despite improving bandwidth, designers continue to find 'creative' uses for all that extra performance. That overloads the available capacity, and users will continue to experience pages that take 30 seconds to load.

8.2 Mobile Data

At some point mobile phones will offer a reliable, high-bandwidth platform for mobile services. WAP was a commercial disaster, and the current prototypes of GPRS and 3G phones don't yet offer a reliable scaleable service. Consequently, this does not seem likely to replace most forms of Internet usage in the near future.

8.3 Digital TV

Digital TV is a different technical and commercial environment to the standard Internet. We must distinguish between Internet delivered via a cable connection (i.e. the cable company is providing a wire over which an Internet connection is running) and Interactive TV where the TV set itself is the 'browser'.

When the TV itself is the browser, then the cable or satellite provider controls the end-to-end experience. Currently in the UK these 'TV shops' have tended to be provided within a 'closed garden' and do not offer general Internet browsing. That should be very reliable but is outside the scope of this chapter.

Where the cable company is providing the Internet connection, then broadband is on tap, and the customer should experience a good high-speed connection. Many of the other problems are still of course present. The servers and the network connections between the website and the cable company are still a potential problem.

Applying a Control Loop
for Performance Testing and Tuning

ARNIM BUCH, STEFAN ENGELKAMP, DIRK KIRSTEIN
sd&m software design & management AG (Germany)

Abstract: This article introduces an approach that allows software developers to implement a system's functionality in a very short time frame and simultaneously optimise or tune its performance. We call this the control loop approach, and its elements include performance measurement, analysis, tuning and re-measurement. This control loop is part of the development process. The approach is applicable to projects that require a high level of parallelism regarding further development, correction of errors (bug fixing) and performance tuning. To illustrate the approach, we will reference experiences from a project that reached a severe crisis level. In the project, there were serious performance problems discovered by the end users through subjective observation. These problems could not be quantified due to the lack of an environment suitable for performance measurement and to the lack of test scenarios. At this point we gradually introduced the control loop approach, thus ensuring the success of the project.

Keywords: Performance test, performance tuning, quality requirements

1 Introduction

After the end user had refused to sign-off a software project, we were asked to support the required consolidation of the project. The end users – we will simply call them "the customer"– had found serious bugs and lacks of functionality. Furthermore, the customer considered the system performance to be insufficient for later operation. Due to the lack of an environment suitable for measuring performance and test scenarios, the system performance could not be quantified in any way.

Once a system has been finished, its quality can be increased only to a limited extent. So we started with a short study in order to determine whether the system's functional and non-functional features at least basically met the requirements. In this situation, stopping the project had been a serious alternative.

The basic situation of the project was not that bad. Hence, our task was to achieve the required target performance in a way transparent to the customer. This had to be synchronised with parallel bug fixing and further development. To this purpose, we introduced the control loop for performance tuning step by step. It enabled the team to achieve the functional and non-functional quality objectives under great time pressure within five months. This article focuses on the performance aspects of the control loop. Experiences from other projects supplement the individual chapters.

2 Starting Point

At the time we took over the responsibility for the project, a sub-team was already exclusively working on the topic of performance. This team had already substantially accelerated the presentation of the GUI (graphic user interface) on the client computers. However, the environment in which performance was measured had no resemblance to the later operational environment because work was essentially performed based on the following:

- Inaccurate system performance requirements
- Single-user operation instead of multi-user operation
- Test scenarios without foundation in the customer's business
- A database filled with master data only
- Unrealistically well-equipped computer workstations

These factors supported the customer's doubts concerning the software's operational capability. In order to regain the customer's lost confidence in the team and in the system, the performance team first concentrated on designing a realistic environment for measuring performance. To achieve this, the following actions were taken:

- Precise performance requirements motivated by the needs of everyday business were established.
- Close-to-business performance scenarios were determined with the customer.
- Realistic data stocks were designed in close co-operation with the computer centre which was later to operate the system.
- The technical environment for performance measurement was accurately documented in order to recognise and eliminate differences to the operational environment.
- The scenarios agreed upon were automated.

3   A Control Loop for Performance Tuning

If there are only a few months to complete a software project in which functional scope, error correction and performance must progress simultaneously, the approach selected must allow for fast results and short control cycles. The project described here reached a particularly high level of difficulty due to the complexity of the software (approximately 16,000 Java classes).

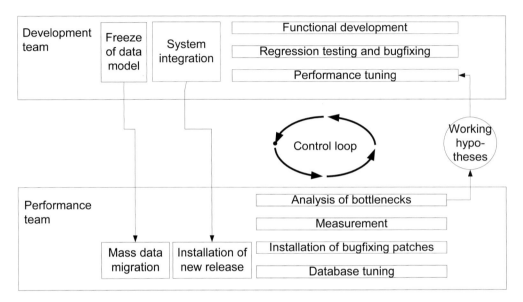

Figure 1: A control loop for performance tuning

The performance team in this project selected an iterative approach, namely a control loop consisting of measurement, analysis, tuning and re-measurement. The individual cycles were driven by each new integration of the software. For this reason, the performance team had to react to model changes, new or revised functional specifications and bug fixes.

In the beginning, an individual cycle lasted two weeks. Shortly before the delivery of the first release this time decreased to one week. In the performance team, such a cycle consisted of the following steps (see Figure 1), done partly in parallel:

- Create or update mass data due to changes in the data model
- Install the new software version in the performance test environment
- Perform measurements or re-measurements
- Analyse weaknesses using the profiler tool in a lab environment

- Analyse source code and define possible measures as working hypotheses (what has to be done, expected benefits - with proof, if possible -, expected costs, etc.)
- Discuss measures with development team
- Tune databases (indices, etc.)

Scenario for delivering items
07/28/2000

Absolute

Items 2000	Start/Finish	Requiremet [s]	Progress R0.4 Average [s]	Progress R0.9 Average [s]	Progress R1.0 Average [s]	Status im Detail Release 1.0 Number	Min [s]	Max [s]	Average [s]	Acceleration factors compared to R0.4 R0.9	R1.0
Use Case 1: Set up delivery	S	3	4,6	99,5	2,2	5	1,3	5,5	2,2	0,0	2,1
	F	20	75,0	42,0	17,5	5	15,7	19,1	17,5	1,8	4,3
Use Case 2: Add items	S	3	0,8	0,5	1,0	5	0,5	2,1	1,0	1,6	0,8
	F	5	5,6	0,3	0,7	5	0,2	2,8	0,7	18,7	7,9
Use Case 3: ...	S	3	1,2	0,4	0,6	100	0,4	2,9	0,6	3,0	2,1
	F	5	21,2	0,9	0,5	100	0,2	1,8	0,5	23,6	43,4
Use Case 4: ...	S	3	1,9	0,5	0,6	100	0,6	2,4	0,6	3,7	2,9
	F	5	49,1	1,9	1,5	100	1,0	3,7	1,5	25,8	32,0
Use Case 5: ...	S	20	201,0	170,2	3,2	5	2,4	5,0	3,2	1,2	63,2
	F	1.600	4970,0	892,5	834,8	5	797,3	882,5	834,8	5,6	6,0
Use Case 6: Quality test	S	3			1,3	5	0,7	2,3	1,3		
	F	5			1,0	5	0,6	2,8	1,0		
SUM		1.675	5330,4	1208,7	864,9		820,8	933,0	864,9	4,4	6,2

Percentage

Items	Start/Finish	[%]	R0.4 [%]	R0.9 [%]	R1.0 [%]	[%]	[%]	[%]	Status R0.4	R0.9	R1.0
Use Case 1: Set up delivery	S	100	153	3317	74	43	184	74	nok	nok	ok
	F	100	375	210	87	79	96	87	nok	nok	ok
Use Case 2: Add items	S	100	27	17	35	18	71	35	ok	ok	ok
	F	100	112	6	14	3	55	14	nok	ok	ok
Use Case 3: ...	S	100	40	13	19	14	98	19	ok	ok	ok
	F	100	424	18	10	3	37	10	nok	ok	ok
Use Case 4: ...	S	100	62	17	21	19	81	21	ok	ok	ok
	F	100	982	38	31	20	74	31	nok	ok	ok
Use Case 5: ...	S	100	1005	851	16	12	25	16	nok	nok	ok
	F	100	311	56	52	50	55	52	nok	ok	ok
Use Case 6: Quality test	S	100	0	0	42	23	78	42	ok	ok	ok
	F	100	0	0	21	11	56	21	ok	ok	ok
SUM		100	318	72	52	49	56	52	nok	ok	ok

Detail

Progress UC5/Finish		R0.4	R0.5	R0.6	R0.7	R0.8	R0.9	R1.0
Total time	No. Of items	4970	2595	1746,1	1746,1	1746,1	892,5	834
Per item	2000	2,49	1,30	0,87	0,87	0,87	0,45	0,42
Requirement per item	0,8	0,80	0,80	0,80	0,80	0,80	0,80	0,80

Figure 2: Results of an example performance test scenario

The development team then implemented the measures, often by heavily cutting into the highly complex interwoven class structure or substantially changing business algorithms. In addition, these tuning measures were integrated into further functional development and finally tested for correctness in the functional regression test.

In the beginning, only about one of the entire two weeks could be used for analysis and tuning during each cycle. The rest of the time was spent in the performance team on data migration, start-up of the new release in the performance test environment, adjustment of measuring scripts as well as performing measurements. Implementing the measures in the development team was limited due to the integration deadlines. As the process continued to mature and the functional behaviour of the software began to stabilise, the preparation activities, including data migration, installation and adaptation of the test scripts, could be advanced and even automated to such an extent that almost the entire two weeks could be used for analysis and optimisation.

After establishing the control loop, we were able to inform the customer in regular intervals of new results that were usually an improvement compared to the previous update. This also included the potential of planned, but not yet realised tuning measures.

Re-measuring the previously analysed and successfully tuned or optimised scenarios was highly significant because the run times sometimes deteriorated again due to further functional development and bug fixing. In the example described, the starting time for the first use case increased dramatically between releases 0.4 and 0.9. This was discovered during the re-measuring phase and was rectified in the delivered release 1.0.

4   Step by Step

In this project, it was not possible to establish the underlying conditions for realistic measurements "all at once." However, in order to be able to enter the control loop quickly, the environment was gradually set up and expanded. The following steps proved to be reasonable and easy to manage:

1. Design of an operation-oriented environment (hardware, operating system, network, database)
2. Volume-oriented, automated test scenarios (regarding frequency as well as the data volume to be processed within the use case)
3. Mass data with realistic quantity structure
4. Synchronous exchange with upstream or downstream systems, e.g. workflow
5. Multi-user operation

Steps 1, 2 and 5 required significant effort before tests could be performed. In general, the measured times substantially deteriorate with steps 2, 3 and 5, because the magnitude of the data to be processed increases (2, 3) or the number of parallel accesses increases (5).

The step-by-step approach to realistic conditions allows us to achieve even the earliest, initial results that can point to weaknesses in the system. If use cases already take a long time on an empty database, one can immediately begin the analysis without first establishing a complete environment for performance measurement.

In order to obtain results based on mass data even earlier, we did the initial mass data measurement in the project at a data volume of 2% of the expected overall volume (a ratio of 100,000 customer data records to 5 million), still in single-user operation. Despite this, the numbers were sobering, but had been recorded early enough in order to begin further expansion of the performance test environment with analysis and tuning simultaneously.

The step up to multi-user operation represents a difficult hurdle. However, in many critical projects the application is tested for functionally correct behaviour, but there is often no time to perform multi-user tests in order for example to find dead locks. This is why a true multi-user situation often does not emerge until stress tests are performed.

In the case of Internet projects, the requirements for multi-user capability with regard to throughput, availability and locking conflicts are barely describable, not to mention the fact that they are difficult to be tested reliably. That is why special strategies are necessary for such cases. For example, server accesses via WAN connections have to be ensured and simulated, instead of using the company LAN or local network. In addition, there are considerably more intermediate stations on the test track between the server and the end user. Furthermore, some of these stations are out of reach for the project team.

In the project being discussed, we performed an additional step in which we ran individual performance scenarios that were already in the tuning control loop while others were still under discussion. This "quick-win" effect proved to be extremely valuable in tense project situations because it allowed us to present early results and to demonstrate to the customer that the control loop worked.

5 Working Hypotheses

The performance team founded their work on clear hypotheses. These helped to make the implicit explicit and set objectives towards which the work was directed: The hypothesis should be either verified or refuted.

An example of a working hypothesis that refers to a tuning measure is:

- "Merging the xy and yz classes saves two INSERT statements for each item generated and reduces the run time of the use case by 30%." A lab test was performed to confirm the above hypothesis so that the measurement could be performed with a greater certainty of success.

In this way, the performance potential already recorded and verified but not yet realised could be presented to the customers (see figures 3, 4). This procedure paid off in

Scenario for "Batch run 1"
07/29/2000

Items 24000

Absolut

Items	S/F/T	Requirement [s]	Progress R0.8 Average [s]	Progress R 1.0 Average [s]	Progress Potential Average [s]	Status in detail Release 1.0 Number	Min [s]	Max [s]	Average [s]	Acceleration factors compared with R0.8 — R 1.0	Potential
Use Case: Set up batch run	S	3	1	1,2	1,2	10	0,8	3,0	1,2	0,9	0,9
	F	5	0,4	0,6	0,6	10	0,4	0,8	0,6	0,7	0,7
Use Case 2: Define batch run	S	3	0,6	0,8	0,8	5	0,5	1,4	0,8	0,8	0,8
	F	5	0,2	0,2	0,2	5	0,2	0,3	0,2	1,0	1,0
Use Case 3: Set starting time	S	3	2	1,5	1,5	5	1,1	2,0	1,5	1,3	1,3
	F	5	0,2	0,3	0,3	5	0,3	0,3	0,3	0,7	0,7
Batch run part 1	T	3.456	1270	312	250	1	312	312	312	4,1	5,1
Batch run part 2	T	10.368	30131	21402	9000	1	21402	21402	21402	1,4	3,3
Sum		**13.848**	**31.405**	**21.719**	**9.255**		**21.717**	**21.722**	**21.719**	**1,4**	**3,4**

Percentage

Items	S/F/T	Requirement [%]	Progress R0.8 [%]	Progress R 1.0 [%]	Progress Potential [%]	Status in detail Min [%]	Max [%]	Average [%]	Status R0.8	R 1.0	Potential
Use Case: Set up batch run	S	100	33	39	39	27	99	39	ok	ok	ok
	F	100	8	11	11	8	16	11	ok	ok	ok
Use Case 2: Define batch run	S	100	20	25	25	16	48	25	ok	ok	ok
	F	100	4	4	4	3	7	4	ok	ok	ok
Use Case 3: Set starting time	S	100	67	51	51	37	65	51	ok	ok	ok
	F	100	4	6	6	5	6	6	ok	ok	ok
Batch run part 1	T	100	37	9	7	9	9	9	ok	ok	ok
Batch run part 2	T	100	291	206	87	206	206	206	nok	nok	ok
Sum		**100**	**227**	**157**	**67**	**157**	**157**	**157**	**nok**	**nok**	**ok**

Figure 3: Results of an example performance test scenario with tuning potential

this project. Although the requirements for the described sample scenario had not been achieved by the agreed deadline (the only one), the customer could be convinced of the feasibility because sufficient measurements had been found and were planned for the subsequent release.

By concentrating on the essentials, hypotheses are also helpful in analysing weaknesses. The following are examples of this:

- "The run time to build up a screen presentation is independent of data volume". If this hypothesis can be verified, the tuning measures that will be necessary due to the increased data volume can concentrate on the software components that are not used for screen display.
- "In use case xyz, the run time increases by the power of two with the number of items to be processed." Relevant measurements, e.g. with 100, 200, 400, 800 items, would have the goal of verifying the relevant connections and of focusing further analysis on possible nested loop designs.

Thus there are two parallel issues: first to work on the basis of the hypotheses and second to verify or refute them.

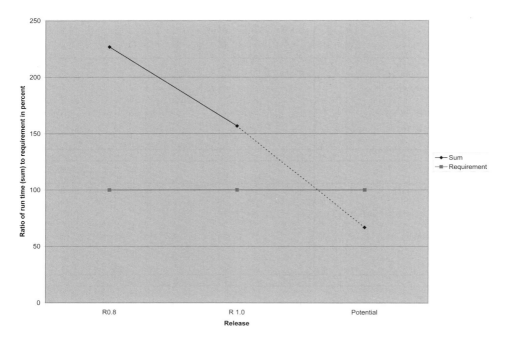

Figure 4: Results and potential

6 Requirements and Underlying Conditions

The foundation for any work on performance is the definition of what performance exactly means in the respective project. This chapter describes our experiences from the project outlined above and several other projects.

6.1 Measurements

Performance requirements, if there are any, are often only vaguely defined. In the project described above, definitive response times of no more than three seconds when starting and no more than five seconds when finishing were required for all use cases. Such a requirement can neither be measured nor verified when it comes to signing off.

Each measurement is made under certain clinical conditions; reality itself cannot be simulated at a justifiable cost – if at all. Of course, it is recommended to create an environment which is as realistic as possible in which the measurements can be performed, reproduced and assessed afterwards. If the difference between the performance test environment and reality is too large, the conclusion of the test results concerning later operation will be highly risky. Such risk should be minimised at reasonable expense and taken only after much thought. We recommend to produce at least realistic data volumes and ensure a realistic number of simultaneous system accesses. In exchange, one can abstract from correctly simulating the whole business, as long as the load produced is comparable.

Furthermore, it has to be defined how often a measurement is to be repeated and which criterion the results must meet. Does the average value have to be below three seconds, should 90% of these be below this threshold, or do all measured values have to remain below three seconds? How many measurements are needed? How high can the variance be?

In the project described here, the mathematical average consisted of five measurements. A maximum and a minimum value were also specified. In another project, the customer explicitly requested the variance data.

These questions must be worked out together with the customer (user, operator). In our discussions with the customer concerning these issues, we were able to increase their understanding of the complexity of performance measurements. Even here, working hypotheses can emerge, many of which were not tested or were even ignored when the performance test environment was set up – maybe because they were not yet known or because they were considered irrelevant. Together with the customer, one has to assess how high the probability of a mistake is, its impact and the cost and effort required to test the hypothesis.

6.2 Technical Environment

Operational environment, network bandwidth (nominal and available) and the workstation equipment for the end user are typical and important technical parameters. In addition, there are Internet specifications such as provider as well as browser type and version. Overall, one has to consider and establish the entire track between the server's processor and the user's monitor.

In one intranet project it was necessary to install a Java run-time environment on the end user's workstation to enable the operation of the client. It turned out later that these workstations had only a maximum of 128 MB memory and there were no plans for upgrading them. Though a corresponding adjustment to the performance test environment had no effect on the measured run-times, it considerably increased the customer's confidence in obtaining realistic test results.

Since the software in the project under discussion was used for the first time under operations-oriented conditions during the performance tests, many problems not related to performance appeared for the first time. The team's lack of experience with aspects of operation and the idiosyncrasies of new software, which often arise due to the lack of installation or operating manuals, were just a few of the things that delayed the measurements from being performed for the first time. Setting up the database's rollback segments, never-ending test runs due to missing indices as well as the not-yet-tested delivery and installation process are just a few examples of these types of idio-syncrasies.

6.3 Data Stocks

The quantity structure to be dealt with is a central business aspect that has to be clari-fied early. This concerns not only the data volumes to be processed in individual use cases, but also the magnitude of the managed data stocks. In contrast to tests regarding functional correctness, here the emphasis is exclusively on data volume and frequency of data use. Typical questions are which business entities exist how often, how often are they accessed and how often are they changed through which use cases. Therefore, smaller data volumes (except master data such as item types, etc) can be ignored in this context, if necessary, because they do not significantly influence the run-time behav-iour (working hypothesis).

If large, old data stocks have to be migrated prior to deployment of the software, tools are often created to initially fill up the database of the new system. With their help, a realistic test data stock can be set up. Alternatively, data can be generated. If this is done according to a regular production pattern, it will possibly lead to an unrealistic system and database access behaviour.

Data stock at the beginning of the measurements	Number
Item	3316598
Order	48300
Order position	48300
Item type	7822
Address	3341402
Customer	3456789
...	...

Figure 5: Measurement template that the tester prepares for each measurement

In the case being considered, a "hybrid solution" was used due to unsatisfactory performance of the tool that was developed for migration of the old data: First, the old data stocks were imported at a volume of approx. 10,000 data records. Then, the data was replicated using a database script which replaced the primary and the foreign keys according to a fixed pattern. In this way, entire networks of data could be replicated. In addition, the distribution of the most frequent search fields – e.g. of the customer name – was obtained through rotation of the characters within a text field.

6.4 Test Scenarios

In the project we first prioritised the business test scenarios. Criteria were the frequency of performance and of the typical data conversion (are there 10 or 10,000 items to be determined during each scenario?) expected in later operation as well as the computing intensity and other time restrictions. For example, some batches had to be completed within a weekend. Time buffers for possible repetitions had to be planned for, further reducing the available time.

These questions were clarified using so-called user profiles. Typical users are administrators, company representatives, and group managers. It was identified who was going to use the system, when, how often and in which way. The time of day is relevant because usually the system load is not evenly distributed throughout the day. Added to this are backup procedures and batch windows; especially for systems available 24 hours a day.

At this point, it is important to achieve a common understanding with the customer as to what a complete, thorough measurement of the software would mean in terms of completely simulating reality regarding cost and deadline. Therefore, in the project here, some use cases were purposely not measured and analysed, especially administrative use cases. Instead, eleven of approximately sixty business scenarios were selected according to the previous prioritisation. Test scenarios with specific user data, just like the functional test cases, were agreed on for these use cases. Then, the expected response times were determined precisely, for example, "For 2,000 items of type 123, closing the new system with "OK" may take 100 seconds."

The functional test scenarios originally planned for the performance tests were unsuitable because the data quantities within the test scenarios were too small. For example the scenario in Figure 2 was performed with ten different items during functional testing. In operation, there would be 2000 identical items processed each morning within a single execution of the use case. Therefore, the existing test scripts had to be heavily adapted.

Data is required to perform the test scenarios. This data can be taken from the functional tests, if necessary, but for performance testing there are additional requirements:

- Since the measurements have to be performed numerous times one after the other, "repeatable" test scenarios are necessary. To do this, independent starting data records have to be provided or the data changes within a scenario have to be "undone" afterwards. The last approach has the advantage that the test data are never "used up". Under certain circumstances, this makes the time-consuming task of refilling the performance test environment with large amounts of data obsolete.

- For multi-user tests, interdependencies between the test data and test scenarios should be avoided if at all possible. Otherwise, the test complexity increases to a point that the tests become nearly impossible to perform.

7   Use of Tools

In the project under discussion, right at the time we took over, WinRunner [WINR01] was used as the capture/replay tool for automating the functional regression test. We also decided to use WinRunner, so that on the one hand we were able to make use of existing knowledge in the team and one the other hand we could save costs. This enabled us to adapt the already existing scripts to the performance tests. However, there were a few technical difficulties. For example, in some scenarios, there was some irregular long-running processing that the tool reacted to by issuing timeout messages. This then required manual intervention for the measurements to continue. Finally, we were even able to successfully use WinRunner scripts for the multi-user tests.

Even for this project, it paid off to have external consultants provide special know-how, which was needed in the short term, instead of having the team itself spend valuable time to acquire it. In order to increase productivity when adapting the scripts, experts from SQS AG were brought in.

In another project, a concept for a test track had to be worked out and implemented within only a few days. We were able to secure this procedure for the customer, again with the help of SQS as an external expert. Since, in this project, the server performance was the focus, we selected the WebLoad tool [WEBL01], which communicates directly with the web server via HTTP.

Further tools that were specifically created during the project described here and have proved to be useful were:

- SQL scripts for database quantification, meaning output of the quantity structures (see measurement template in Fig. 5), contained in the database.
- PL/SQL scripts for replicating data,
- PL/SQL scripts for migrating data to a new integration update,
- Shell scripts for delivering and installing new integration updates into the performance test environment and
- a performance monitor that permits time measurement without seriously influencing the test results (in contrast to profiling tools).

8   Summary

Serious performance problems in a project should not be discovered for the first time when the customer refuses to sign off or after deployment. This is a legitimate requirement, but not always easy to fulfil. Based on our observations we recommend the following, particularly for Internet projects with a short time frame in which a high level of parallel development has to be achieved:

- The requirements analysis must include performance requirements:
  - How many users will do what with the system and how often (user profile)?
  - How much data should the system process (structure quantities)?
  - What is the target platform (test track)?
  - Which additional restrictions must be taken into consideration for later operation (e.g. 24-hour operation, duration of the batch window, online archiving)?
- The software design has to be geared toward meeting these requirements.
- The iterations to test the functional level of completion that are often performed in projects with a short time frame should also be used for testing system performance. The control loop that we have presented shows how this goal can be achieved. It is important to set up the performance test environment early and to invest adequately in test automation. It is helpful to approach operational conditions gradually in order to establish a balance between fast results and invested effort and cost.
- Project planning should be set up in such a way that the performance-critical system components are completed as early as possible. This way, proof that the architecture can bear the load is produced early. Alternatively, a technical prototype can be produced as proof of the load capacity.

Despite the fact that these fundamental principles were not previously addressed properly in the projects described, we were still able to ensure project success by introducing them later with the help of the described control loop.

Software Quality Assessments for System, Architecture, Design and Code

FRANK SIMON
SQS AG (Germany)

CLAUS LEWERENTZ
Technical University Cottbus (Germany)

WALTER BISCHOFBERGER
Wabic GmbH (Switzerland)

Abstract: In this chapter we introduce the concept of structural quality assessments for industrial software systems (especially object-oriented code). Such a quality assessment can be used both to determine the current state with respect to quality and to plan further actions, i.e. reengineering steps, process adjustments or further education of engineers in an ongoing project. The assessment itself is based on an innovative software analysis workbench that integrates multiple interdependent views on a software system into a coherent analysis environment. These views provide information on four aspects: user-defined metrics and query results with high-level information about the system, detailed cross-reference information, browsing views and diagrams to support efficient understanding of the structure. The workbench applies powerful static analysis techniques on the source code under consideration and uses it to generate, access, visualise and browse the different views and analysis results. For practical assessments the workbench is used in a well-defined process such that a first quality assessment of large systems can be done within a very short period of time.

The quality assessment described here has been applied in various projects. In order to illustrate the results that such an assessment gives for project management, developers or managers of an outsourced project this paper ends with a short description of a typical example project. This is one of the projects supported jointly by SQS and the Software Systems Engineering Research Group Cottbus.

Keywords: Software metrics, software quality assessment, design system architecture, software code, object-oriented programming

1   Introduction

In today's software development one of the major goals – besides developing economically successful software – is to produce high quality software: In a recent survey by TechRepublic (sponsored by MKS) "[...] *more than half of the respondents endorsed quality as the single most important factor for their development team*" ([MKS01]).

Quality is one of the most important factors for the commercial success of a software system (especially when looking at its whole life-span, i.e. including maintenance activities).

Usually the multi-dimensional concept of quality can be differentiated with respect to the view on the system: Whereas the end user of a system is primarily interested in the usability and user-friendliness of the product – which depends on criteria like ergonomic look and feel, consistency with other products or ease of understanding (cf. e.g. ISO 9241) – the developer of a system is primarily interested in typical engineering goals such as maintainability, efficiency and portability (cf. e.g. ISO 9126). Corresponding to these two views, quality can be divided into *external quality* to cover the end users' interests and *internal quality* to cover the engineers' interests (cf. [GHEZ91]).

The quality assessment described in this article concentrates on internal quality. This internal quality is particularly important for large long-living systems, especially object-oriented systems that are often created in an iterative and evolutionary way. A project with low internal quality typically causes, among other issues, high maintenance risks, high maintenance costs and high training effort for new SW engineers. These disadvantages become even more important with increased life span of the software.

One of the major issues to ensure internal quality is of course to concentrate on quality aspects from the very first stages of the software development process. Many processes support this constructive quality assurance (e.g. eXtreme programming or Cleanroom technique). Nevertheless, none of these techniques prevents the system from loosing structure during further evolution. The *law of increasing entropy* [LEHM85] states that the entropy of a system increases with time, unless special care is taken to maintain the system. In the software industry this special care is often impossible due to release pressure, bug fixing and resource shortage. Management has to handle these two issues and depends on answers to the following questions (excerpt):

- What is the current quality of the system (e.g. for planning maintenance activities)?

- Is a software system which is developed within an outsourced project easy to maintain (especially if further bug-fixings, modifications, extensions, etc. should be done in-house)?

- Which software has better quality (e.g. to support decisions between different versions/types of a system)?

- When does the loss of structure of a system exceed a specific but not necessarily before-known limit (e.g. to be able to identify problems as soon as possible)?

- Do the developers adhere to any pre-defined rules (especially important if other documents such as architecture specs or design specs have to remain valid)?

- Where should a limited effort for reengineering activities be spent (e.g. to get maximal benefit)?

One practicable method to answer these questions efficiently is the use of static analysis techniques. The software analysis workbench provides tools for obtaining information on deep internal structures by focusing on specific aspects of a software system. The vision behind this flexible in-depth analysis and diagnostics technique can be described with the term *software tomography*, borrowing a metaphor from the medical field of diagnostics. A tool set to supply the basic analysis data and interactively create and explore diagnostic views could be called a "software tomograph". After adjusting this software tomograph to specific goals and needs it allows for an efficient assessment of large systems and so provides valuable insights into systems with respect to their internal quality.

The rest of the article is structured as follows:

Section 2 gives an overview of different aspects and granularity levels that are potential candidates for a quality assessment and which have to be selected and defined in advance. Every aspect/level has its own typical management problems and questions to be answered by the assessment.

Section 3 describes a process for quality assessments of large object-oriented systems. It also sketches the efforts required for the refined sub-steps.

Section 4 introduces a software analysis workbench[1]. This powerful tool is an important pre-requisite for the presented quality diagnostics. The work presented in this article is based on this tool.

Section 5 describes experiences in a typical project developing a large JAVA system. SQS performs projects of this type, and BTU gives support for example through the adjustment of tools to special needs.

Section 6 gives a summary and an outlook.

2   Aspects and Granularity Levels for a Quality Assessment

When performing quality assessments, the term quality must be well understood and precisely defined. ISO 8402 gives the following definition:

"The totality of features and characteristics of a product or service that bear on its ability to satisfy stated or implied needs."

Definition 1: Quality (taken from ISO 8402)

---

[1] The workbench is developed at the Software Engineering Research Group at BTU Cottbus in co-operation with an external software development company.

3 Quality Assessment Process

The following quality assessment process is to some degree just an extension of the ISO 14598 (cf. [PUNT97]) which is concerned with the evaluation of software product quality. So we only sketch it and focus on a few particular process parameters we applied.

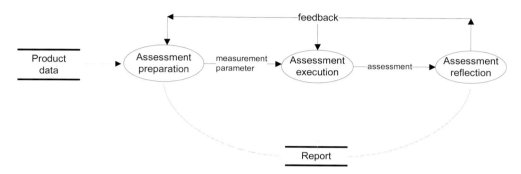

Figure 3: Process for quality assessments

1. The *assessment preparation* corresponds to the three ISO-sub-processes analysis, specification and design. ISO calls the process output *evaluation plan*. The goal of this task is to set the goals of the assessment (e.g. to get an overview for management, or to get constructive reengineering hints for engineers) and to prepare the tool environment. The single tasks are:

    1.1 Interview with project[2] to set focus (which parts of the software have to be assessed; for example it might make sense to exclude some libraries or frameworks), the granularity to be considered and aspects used for the assessment.

    1.2 Adjustment of tool environment to specific requirements (called *quality profile* in ISO 14598), given by the I-QR or Sota-QR.

    1.3 Preparation of analysis, i.e. getting access to source code, parsing it, starting data extraction and automated analysis (cf. Section 4).

2. In the step *assessment execution* (called *evaluation execution* in ISO 14598) the assessment itself is performed and the report to the project is prepared. This step is carried out with the help of the software analysis workbench (cf. Section 4). The tasks are:

---

[2] In the following the quality assessment is introduced as an external service offered by SQS (as assessor) to a customer (having the assessed product). Especially the examples described come from such project situations. In general, the process used for the quality assessment itself can also be applied as an in-house service.

2.1 Exploring the system by analysing measurements and high-level information (e.g. package view, inheritance view, call graphs, etc.).

2.2 Comparison of current state (given by source code) with desired one (given by specifications).

2.3 Development of the quality assessment report.

2.4 Development of a presentation for the customer.

3. *Assessment reflection*: In this step the results are presented to the project (after agreement) and further actions are planned. The results of the quality assessment can be used as input for further assessments (e.g. for trend analysis to get insights into the effects of applied reengineering activities based on a previous quality assessment). The tasks of this step are in detail:

3.1 Interview with project to check identified quality anomalies (because some might be well known but not communicated to the quality assessor) and to agree on final report and perhaps result presentation (because there might be some political constraints to be considered).

3.2 Presentation of final report to project.

3.3 Discussion of further action plans; this might for example contain plans for further quality assessments, more specific requirements, more concrete artefacts to be considered (given by the granularity levels), the development of a reengineering action list or education of engineers.

The quality assessment report contains the quality requirements considered, the granularity level(s) viewed and the results from the quality assessment. One point in a typical quality assessment of a software system's implemented architecture (based on the sources) with respect to the specified architecture might be the following:

On the left side, the target architecture (a typical layer architecture) is presented. Every component consists of many packages/classes of a large JAVA system. On the right side the "real" structure of the corresponding packages is presented; the identified deviation of target structure from actual structure will require special maintenance effort because the architecture document is not up-to-date or/and the software engineers did not adhere to it. So the quality of the assessed software system is not optimal with respect to this aspect.

Architecture
Spec

Architecture
extracted from
source code

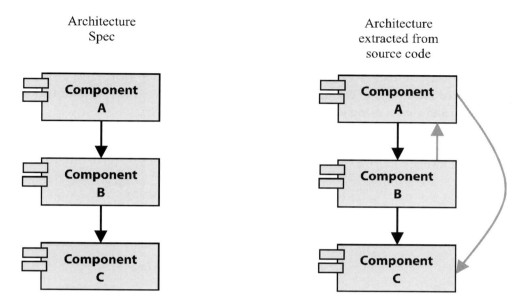

Figure 4: Quality assessment of an architecture with respect to a project-specific architecture spec

4   Software Analysis Workbench

In the following, the Software Analysis Workbench is presented. Currently extensions to this tool set are being developed by the BTU. Conventional software development or programming environments are very well tailored to support the construction of software and related tasks such as debugging or version management. However, they offer little help for code comprehension, quality assessment and exploration of large software systems.

Based on years of experience with the development and use of software metrics tools [ERNI96], [SIMO98], [SIMO01] the Software Engineering Research Group at BTU in co-operation with an external software product company developed a tool platform and – based on this platform – a set of tools which address specific software analysis issues for object-oriented software. The core of this software analysis workbench consists of a relational database system, containing all relevant structural and measurement data of the software system being assessed. Basically, the database comprises the classical symbol table and cross-reference information of a program. The database is initially filled with information derived from parser interfaces. In the current version, Wind River's SNiFF+ programming environment is used [PFEI97] because SNiFF+ provides a versatile and robust parser implementing the workbench's parser interface and because it provides good tool integration facilities. This information is used, evaluated and augmented by various analysis tools.

Conceptually, the database could be filled from any information source that provides the required information. The database can manage complete structural information about Java and almost complete information about C/C++.

The overall architecture of a software analysis workbench that integrates multiple interdependent views on a software system into a coherent analysis environment looks like the following:

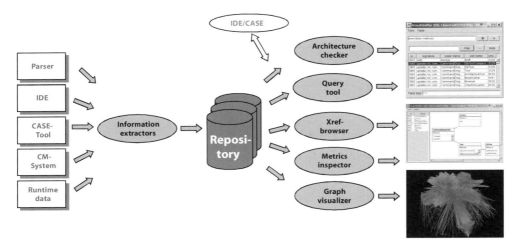

Figure 5: Overall architecture of the software analysis workbench

In addition to the database the workbench platform provides a number of frameworks, which make the development of new analysis components a straightforward process. The frameworks provide standardised solutions for menu and shortcut handling, for visualisation of information in tables and graphs, for accessing the database through an extended version of SQL and for integrating a number of tools into a coherent environment. The platform provides a generic IDE integration to support seamless context switching between micro and macro analysis tasks.

A number of analysis tools were implemented on top of this platform:

- The *ArchitectureChecker* provides a language for describing the architecture of a system in terms of a set of layered architecture models. Based on these models the ArchitectureChecker checks whether there are illegal relationships in the source code. This helps to prevent the typical decay of architectures during maintenance.

- The *QueryTool* manages the definition and execution of powerful queries and their representation according to the underlying data model. This allows the definition of problem-specific sets of queries that describe the generation of both basic as well as complex analysis views.

- The *XrefBrowser* provides high-level cross-referencing functionality between flexibly definable abstraction levels. It supports queries for the following relationships: call, read, write, containment, inheritance and type access. These relationships can be queried from an entity on any abstraction level to another entity on any abstraction level. Abstraction levels are package, file, class and symbol. It is possible to navigate flexibly between abstraction levels. Aggregated results (e.g., relationships between packages) can be unfolded at any time in order to investigate the primitive relations in the source code.

- The *MetricsInspector* is an enhanced software metrics tool. It overcomes the typical weak points of most existing software metrics tools (i.e. producing overwhelming amounts of data) by providing a user with comprehensive support for browsing and filtering metrics values. Data for entities that are not of interest at a certain time or for future analysis can be filtered away on different levels. Metrics values of interest can be annotated. At a later point in time these annotations can be used to retrieve entities for which further actions are necessary. Entities with metrics values of interest can be investigated at any time with the other tools or with the integrated IDE. Overviews of the metrics values for entities and the entities they contain are available in any workbench tool at any time.

- The *GraphVisualizer* allows the creation of 2D and 3D graph representations of entity sets as UML-like class diagrams or inheritance trees. It also implements a novel 3D visualisation approach for large graphs, which is particularly well suited to obtain overview representations of systems on different abstraction levels. The tool provides interactive exploration mechanisms for the resulting 3D structures that help to navigate and understand large virtual information spaces [SIMO01]. For the work presented in this article only 2D visualisations were used.

5   A Typical Software Quality Assessment

Some typical experiences with quality assessments are presented in the following. Due to non-disclosure agreements the data in the following was rendered anonymous. The results presented are taken from a single project. However, other quality assessments led to similar results.

The project developed an industrial software system, implemented in JAVA, with about 500.000 LOC. The very first assessment done in this project was divided into three subtasks (cf. Figure 3). It was done to get a very general impression of the overall quality:

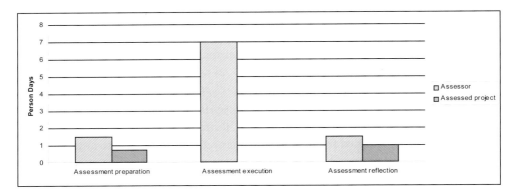

Figure 6: Efforts for single steps of quality assessment (for the assessor (in this example: SQS) and for the assessed project (in this example an external customer))

According to the quality assessment process described above the first step was to prepare the assessment by specifying the quality requirements. These were the decisions taken in the preparation step:

- The assessment was to be done on all four granularity levels to get an overview of the system's quality ("what is the current quality, is there any quality improvement necessary, where are risks for later maintenance tasks").

- In the assessed project there was no technical architecture document and no technical design document that could be used as architecture/design spec for the quality assessment of the corresponding level (even this fact was new for some project members). However, an engineer's handbook was used to extract some system specification (e.g. rare usage of nested classes) and to extract some coding conventions (e.g. only use explicit imports like import <package>.<class>). For all other levels some state-of-the-art quality requirements were considered (e.g. demand for cohesive packages, data hiding, low coupling, abstraction to make similar behaviour explicit, etc.) All these requirements (specific ones and state-of-the-art ones) were used for customising the software analysis tools.

- The assessment focused on an important subset of the sources of the project. This excluded class libraries and some parts of the code not so relevant for the overall quality.

5.1 The System Assessment

In addition to the exact size of the project (e.g. number of classes, number of inheritances, number of interfaces, number of methods – basically management information typically not available in many software projects) some points on this level are:

- Some files of different packages had the same name and the same content (in JAVA this is possible because the package defines a scope level above the file level). Many of these files were just copies, so redundant code was identified; additionally, some of these files had already been modified separately; so some files with the same content occurred in different versions in the same system. These files are very difficult to maintain, because a bug fixed, for instance, in one file has to be fixed in other copies too which is very error-prone.

- One requirement of the engineer's handbook, namely to rarely use nested classes, was fulfilled (only 200 of the 2000 classes were nested; in other projects this proportion of 1:10 often is larger, e.g. 1:5).

- Another requirement of the engineer's handbook, namely to avoid direct data usages (data hiding), was not satisfied, as shown in the following viewgraph:

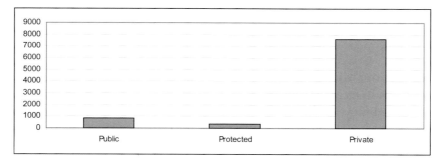

Figure 7: Number of attributes in the system (classified by their visibility)

It became obvious that almost 1000 public attributes existed. A more detailed analysis revealed that those did not just have the wrong visibility but were really used directly. So, with respect to this system spec the quality was not optimal.

- Another important aspect is the distribution of couplings between classes in a system (e.g. to examine if attributes are used directly). The following distribution was found by the MetricsInspector tool :

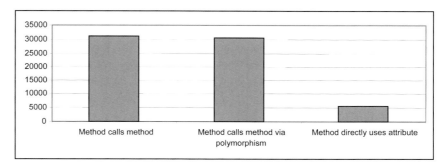

Figure 8: Number of couplings between classes, classified by direct or polymorph method call and attribute usage

On the one side it became apparent that public attributes were really directly used. The other interesting fact was the relatively low number of method calls via polymorphism: This value counts for a method call, how many different methods can be executed by this call at run-time due to polymorphism. One call to one interface here is considered as calls to all implementation classes of the interface. Usually this number is many times higher than the direct method-call number. This fact demonstrates that inheritance and with it the concept of polymorphism was rarely used in this particular system. One of the consequences for this system was duplicated code because of missing abstractions, expressed by inheritance in object-oriented languages.

5.2 The Architecture Assessment

Because there was no explicit architecture spec some Sota-QR were used for the assessment. Some points of this level are:

- The distribution of functionality into packages is one of the most important source code structures for identifying an architecture. A package should provide a well defined high-level functionality of the entire project. For this examination the distribution of classes/interfaces into packages has been viewed:

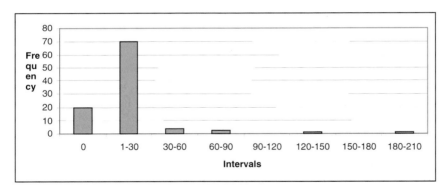

Figure 9: Distribution of number of classes/interfaces in a package

It became apparent that many of the packages were empty: Usually these are just container packages for other packages (nodes within the package hierarchy), but in this case these were also filled with functionality. Here superfluous packages forcing extra maintenance effort (because e.g. for a new engineer it takes some time to see that many packages are superfluous) were identified.

Additionally, there were few packages that contained too much functionality; an architecture component containing more than 200 classes is very difficult to un-

stand whether the development teams are actually on the right track. Are they using OO concepts as they should? Will the final software product be maintainable?

Questions like these are easily answered by a quality assessment. Currently SQS is running several projects where the structural software quality analysis is used to develop reengineering action plans, setting quality profiles for contracts with third-party software developers or estimating maintenance efforts.

"The Back-End Side of Web Testing": Integration of Legacy Systems

Katrin Severid
CSC Ploenzke AG (Germany)

Jan-Gerold Winter
Deutsche Bank AG (Germany)

Abstract: Due to the enormous growth of securities transactions in Germany, fast and efficient transaction processing is extremely important for a bank. In order to meet this challenge Deutsche Bank uses the settlement system db trader MVS. This system was improved by a new web-based front-end called NetTrader.
The challenging task for the developers was to connect two systems which are based on completely different architectures and languages. The challenge for the QA and Test team was to ensure a complete and functionally correct re-implementation of business logic, that was available at the legacy system's front end, for the web front end. Also the connection of this new front end business logic to the back end legacy system had to be quality controlled.
After considering different alternatives the db trader team decided to use a code generator for the development of the web front end. With the help of this tool the NetTrader was developed within a relatively short time. The code generator was a kind of constructive QA means and also increased testing efficiency.
In this article we describe the functionality and features of the db trader MVS and NetTrader systems. We highlight the functionality of the code generator which was used for the development of NetTrader and we discuss the use of regression tests in QA of the resulting product. Thereby we show that the connection of new and traditional technologies is possible and requires an acceptable amount of time and costs.

Keywords: Software testing, web-based front-end, code generator, settlement system

1 Introduction

In the long run the German securities market will be facing enormous growth. The current slack time seems to be only a temporary phenomenon. Studies have found that the number of securities transactions will grow until 2005 by 20% per year. There are several reasons for this growth, for example, the increased interest of private investors in securities, their improved knowledge about securities, the faster information gathering via internet and the convenient use of online banking. Due to the globalisation of markets cross-border transactions become more and more important. Therefore, fast and efficient transaction processing for banks will become increasingly important . The quality of information technology will become a key competitive element ([MOOR99]).

2   The Settlement System db trader MVS

Deutsche Bank AG uses the system db trader MVS for the settlement of securities transactions ([DEUB01]). Its focus is on a high degree of automation and standardised functionality in order to realise economies of scale. The system is not only offered to internal customers but also to customers outside Deutsche Bank through the subsidiary European Transaction Bank (etb) as a distribution channel.

The system supports the complete process chain of the securities business. db trader MVS operates in a transaction-oriented manner, i.e. after "one-off entry" of the transaction, it is further-processed fully automatically. First, the transaction is read in via an interface which is standardised but nevertheless can be modified client-specifically. After various plausibility checks, the functions of billing, position-keeping, settlement and clearing are performed automatically. Finally, the required postings, reports and the client notifications are provided at the output interface. db trader MVS supports all types of securities such as shares, warrants, funds, repos and (convertible) bonds. It includes direct interfaces to Clearstream and Euroclear as well as to other custodians via integrated S.W.I.F.T. links.

db trader MVS is a real-time system. This means that securities processing is completed within only a few seconds ([WINT01]). Integrated processes ensure high-quality standards together with a low-cost burden. The system is able to process large transac-

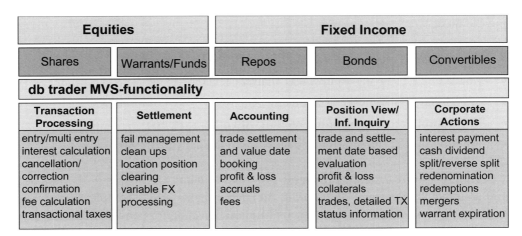

Figure 1: db trader MVS – functionality model

tion volumes. Currently, approximately 350,000 transactions are processed daily with a clearing volume of approximately 70 billion Euro. In peak times db trader MVS has already processed 1.6 million transactions per day. Currently, there is no quantity limitation in sight. Manual processing, failures and costs are reduced by straight-through processing. The STP Rate at national level is around 95-99 % and the trans-border figure is around 75-80 %.

db trader MVS is a mainframe application system that runs on OS/390. It is implemented in COBOL and uses DB2 as a database. The system consists of more than 2,000 programs, more than 4,500 load modules and over 500 DB2 tables.

3   Test Environment of db trader MVS

db trader MVS can not be considered as a complete, finished system. Because of continuously changing legal and institutional restrictions like the introduction of the Euro or the introduction of Central Counterparty by Deutsche Börse AG, constant extensions and adaptations of the system are necessary. These changes must be tested intensively. In order to minimize the risk of failures software quality management at Deutsche Bank AG has been extensively investigated during the last years. The focus has been on regression testing and configuration management. An advanced test bed was developed that has significantly contributed to the improvement of software quality management and quality assurance.

Regarding Software-Quality and Testing the db trader team has been supported by SQS Software Quality Systems AG. For test case specification, test data definition and test automation the tool SQS-TEST was used ([WINT01]) to ensure that tests are complete, transparent, maintainable and repeatable at any time.

The tests for db trader MVS are performed on different program levels ([BALZ98], pp. 426-503):

- Programmer Test (testing on programmers' level)
- Analyst's Test (testing on business analysts' level)
- Functional Test (functional test using SQS tools)
- Integration Test (testing of interaction with other systems)
- Production Test (integration of changes into the daily processes)

Currently approximately 20 different test environments are hosted in the test bed and maintained by a small central unit. All environments have a complete set of files and database tables, run under dedicated transaction monitors and can contain data for different test items or scenarios.

Each test environment supports a test archive providing storage space for complete time-stamped data, including all file and database contents for specific test scenarios. Automated procedures enable a complete load-execute-store cycle for each environment, freeing testers from the necessity to consult technicians. This contributes to achieving highest software quality within reasonable time.

Test preparation and analysis of test results can be done outside of the test environment, thus not affecting parallel test operations of different test teams in the same environment and maximising throughput and efficiency.

Reliable test methods are not only important for system changes but also for the development of new applications. An example for this was the development of a new web-based front-end for db trader MVS: NetTrader.

4   Development of NetTrader

The development of NetTrader was driven by the necessity of maintaining the existing system components in the back-end while using new technological opportunities.

NetTrader was designed to make the usage of db trader MVS easier and thereby improving market positioning as well as market chances. It is a web-based, platform-independent, adaptable application with an intuitive graphical user interface to db trader MVS.

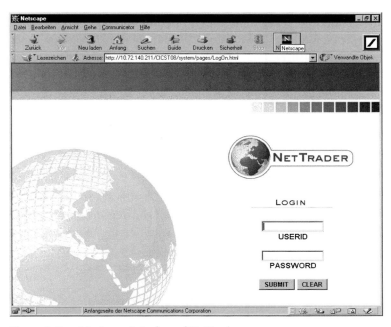

Figure 2: Graphical user interface of NetTrader

NetTrader is a multi-channel platform, accessible by browser, WAP, PDAs and other PC-based applications, which feeds all transactions directly to db trader MVS. Data validation is performed at the point of transaction entry into the back-end system. NetTrader replaces the presentation layer of the db trader MVS 3-layer architecture, making full use of the existing data and processing layers.

5   Challenges for the Development of New Front-Ends

Connecting the new front-end with the existing back-end meant crossing technological borders. While db trader MVS is based on COBOL and CICS, NetTrader makes use of new programming-languages. NetTrader's business logic was maintained by COBOL programs, but the presentation logic which is independent of the business logic was to be implemented using Java and HTML. Both solutions are based on completely different systems, philosophies and architectures.

When developing NetTrader it was necessary to test the presentation logic, the connectors to the host and the business logic while maintaining full compatibility to the old ISPF interface and not compromising existing business logic. This had to be done with high quality, in short time and at low costs – the magic triangle for all developers.

COBOL is a proven programming-language, but the market has developed in a different direction. This issue may force the hiring of Java specialists for the development of NetTrader. But such a programmer must not only know the programming-language but also the exact functionality of the db trader MVS presentation layer logic – a requirement which can hardly be found in one person. The manual transformation process of re-implementing COBOL business logic in JAVA was expected to be error prone. This was the main reason why quality of the result was a challenge and why another way was chosen – the development and use of a code generator.

6   Use of a Code Generator

The task of the code generator is direct translation of the requirements defined by business analysts into Java, JSP or HTML. That is why it can shorten the development process and make it less error-prone. The advantage over traditional manual coding is that less time and human resources are needed [BALZ98, p 302-303]. The hiring of additional staff is not necessary; rather, the skills of the existing employees can be used in an optimal way.

When using a code generator there are no syntax errors. In manual coding syntax errors can always appear – especially when working under time pressure – and are often hard to find. Programmers and analysts only have to put the business logic in, but they do not need to code it in detail. They therefore have more time left for working on the business logic. The following table compares the two approaches:

Table 1: Comparison of manual coding and using code generators

Manual Coding	Code Generator
Takes much time to implement	Fast and easy implementation of requirements
Prone to syntax errors	No syntax errors
Possible deviation from code standards	No deviation from code standards
Testing is focused on syntax errors, correct presentation and correct business logic	Testing is more focused on the correct business logic
Changes in specification take much time to implement	Fast changes of specification
Changes done on programs are difficult to monitor	Easy monitoring with version control capability
No central place where source codes are generated	One central place where source codes are generated and archived
New product releases require modifying each existing program manually	Need only to modify generator to implement changes

The use of the code generator showed that new and traditional technologies do not exclude each other and "Correctness by Construction" is a viable alternative in shortening development cycles. The effort necessary when using the code generator was much lower than when coding manually. Development of the code generator took only six months. This relatively short period was possible due to the existing experience with code generators in the db trader development team.

The code generator is to be used for further developments within Deutsche Bank thereby contributing to further cost savings in software testing. By reducing test times and error rates, considerable increases of efficiency and quality of systems can be achieved. This is an important requirement for gaining a competitive advantage and making systems ready for the future.

7   Regression Testing

In addition to code generation, existing regression tests were used to ensure uncompromised transaction processing. The automated handling of different test environments with consistent data configurations proved extremely valuable at this level of application development.

The regression test suite and the test environments were developed with the help of SQS AG. For test preparation the test specification module of SQS-TEST was used in order to ensure full coverage of the business by the test cases. For automation of the tests the component for test process automation within SQS-TEST provided the backbone while additional standard tools for capture/replay, compare and other testing tasks were included where necessary.

Based on validated test data collected during the development of db trader MVS, testers could verify business logic and transaction processing for the new front-end without investing in test case specification or test data definition. Quality assurance concentrated on the added presentation layer logic and its integration with the legacy system resulting in meaningful savings in time and money.

8 Configuration Management

Design, development, test and deployment of complex application systems can not be accomplished without relying on accepted concepts of software configuration management. This holds true for db trader as it does for similar applications. Due to the application system's complexity and the depth of the different development environments (five different levels!) the use of a configuration management system is mandatory. To support this approach in a OS/390 environment Deutsche Bank AG uses the SCLM tool.

Tight integration with test environments and matured build procedures provide a stronghold on which to base test and deployment decisions. This necessarily implies a PULL process rather than a PUSH process to populate test environments on different development levels and leaves testers and decision boards in a controlling and managing position as opposed to being forced to operate in ever-changing system and test configurations.

9 Conclusion

New paradigms in application development due to new technologies and procedures imply several challenges for the existing development teams. This is especially true for test methods and strategies.

db trader MVS was to be improved by a new web front-end based on a completely new technology. This was to be integrated into the existing system environment (including a proven test environment).

The experience showed that it is possible not only to connect technologies with each other; furthermore, one can still use the test methods based on traditional technologies when adding a new web-based module.

The db trader team decided to trust in the existing staff and their skills (COBOL, DB2, CICS) and to meet the requirements of new technologies by using code generation on the presentation layer level and extensive regression testing on the data and processing levels.

Thereby time- and cost-intensive recruiting activities were avoided while generating new and interesting tasks for the existing staff.

Part V

Test Automation Techniques and Tools

Automated Testing of mySAP Business Processes

Efficient Usage of the SAP Test Workbench

CHRISTOPH MECKE
SAP AG (Germany)

Abstract: SAP AG is the world's leading provider of e-business software solutions that integrate the processes within and among enterprises and business communities. SAP's ability to deliver customer-centric, open, personalised, and collaborative e-business software is the foundation of mySAP.com®. Through the mySAP.com e-business platform, people in businesses around the globe are improving relationships with customers and partners, streamlining operations, and achieving significant efficiencies throughout their supply chains.

Today, more than 13,000 companies in over 100 countries run more than 30,000 installations of SAP software. SAP employs over 6,500 software developers around the globe. In addition to the main development center at the company's headquarters in Walldorf, Germany, SAP has a network of development labs at locations around the world including: Palo Alto (California); Tokyo (Japan); Bangalore (India); Sophia Antipolis (France); and Tel Aviv (Israel); as well as in the German cities of Berlin, Karlsruhe, and Saarbruecken.

From this point of view it becomes obvious that the quality management of the development process is a huge task of enormous importance. This article describes the aspect of the quality assurance that deals with automated testing of the mySAP business scenarios. The methodology and tools, with the focus on functional testing, are explained in detail.

Keywords: Business processes, test tools, test automation

1 Introduction

The business solutions provided by the mySAP.com e-business platform enable customers to run their businesses more efficiently, productively, and effectively in the new New Economy, regardless of industry or sector, by helping companies collaborate for mutual benefit. The mySAP.com cross-industry solutions include:

- mySAP Workplace
- mySAP Supply Chain Management
- mySAP Customer Relationship Management
- mySAP E-Procurement

- mySAP Business Intelligence
- mySAP Product Lifecycle Management
- mySAP Financials
- mySAP Human Resources
- mySAP Mobile Business
- mySAP Marketplace by SAPMarkets

In addition to these common scenarios there are special solutions for industries and a large number of services and technologies. Due to the very large number of business processes of mySAP.com, all of which can be adapted to the special needs of a single customer, it is a great challenge for testers to identify those business processes that will guarantee a high test coverage. Therefore, an effective test strategy has to be developed and automated tests have to be implemented wherever possible.

The need for automation becomes clear when it is considered that SAP supports several releases of every product. This means that bug fixes, which are shipped by support packages, have to be tested for each product in each release. Often the same error affects more than one release resulting in test efforts for many releases in parallel. Given the number of releases and support packages each year, the problem of whether a correction has no negative influence on other functionality (negative test) can only be solved through the high coverage of automated testing. Furthermore, we have to avoid running into the maintenance trap for the test scripts themselves. This can be achieved with a high reuse of test modules.

SAP uses many in-house-developed tools. These automated test tools cover the aspects of formal, functional, load and performance testing. Some of these tools are of static and others of dynamic character. There are also tools for test administration, code coverage measurement and other metrics. In this paper we focus on functional testing.

2 Methodology

2.1 Motivation for Testing in an SAP Environment

The reasons for functional testing in a SAP environment depend on the point of view. From SAP's point of view, we have to make sure that the products and corrections are delivered free of errors to the customers and therefore fulfil the requirements of quality standards like every other product. Testing is also a part of the DIN ISO 9001 certification process that SAP guarantees.

The need for testing at the customer side can arise from customer modifications and development. Customers adapt SAP software to their specific business processes, which have to be verified before usage. Possible changes are customer-modified internal business processes, which make it necessary to change organisational data like cost centres, or enforcement due to legal requirements (e.g. Food and Drug Administration – FDA). Furthermore, modifications of the SAP standard can be due to changes which cannot be handled with a change of settings or an upgrade of an existing software to a new release with more functionality. Typical questions the customer has to answer after an upgrade are:

- Was the upgrade basically successful?
- Does the new release affect my modifications?
- Does the release upgrade affect the results of my transactions?

Also, any new implementation of a software component makes it necessary to test the affected business processes. Implementation can mean an installation of a new SAP product (e.g. the New Dimension Applications like "Advanced Planner and Optimizer" – APO), implementation of a R/3 module that was not used in the past (e.g. Quality Management – QM), or an integration of third-party software by means of the SAP Workplace as an enterprise portal.

2.2 Advantages of Automatic Testing

Transactions of a SAP system react in a very flexible way. In our context, this stands for a dependence of the specific reactions of the program on the input a user makes on a screen. A certain value in a field can determine the number and type of fields on the next screens. Very often, the screen sequence or the number of screens also depend on a value of a previous input. Consequently, there is a large number of paths through a SAP transaction or through a complete business process. From a pragmatic standpoint it becomes clear, that it is nearly impossible to be absolutely sure what a manual tester really did, even if he has a very detailed test description including the test data. Thus, automatic testing is the only way to get really reproducible and reliable results, including exact test documentation through the log of the testing tool, which is essential for auditing purposes especially in the pharmaceutical sector. A regression test with minimal administration effort becomes possible in combination with the possibility of an automatic and scheduled start at a time with low system load.

Another important advantage is of course the saving of costs when we see automated testing as part of a long-term strategy. There is not only a reduction of manual test costs like manpower or equipment but also the problem of motivation for a monotonous task, which has to be done with high accuracy again and again. Finally, we get the benefit of the synergy due to an easier implementation of new test procedures when we produce test modules as described in the next section.

2.3 Test Strategy

Testing in a SAP environment requires a system landscape that supports the testing process and ensures the significance of the test results. An example of a simple system landscape suitable for a test is shown in Figure 1. For safety reasons the productive system should never be changed or modified directly; rather, changes should be transported from a quality assurance system after a test has been carried out there successfully. The reason for the transport from a development system, where changes are done, to the quality assurance system, where the test is performed, is that there might also be problems from the transport itself, for example due to the incompleteness of the transported package.

In a more complex environment the productive system landscape can consist of several different systems communicating with each other (see Figure 2). Here it turns out to be very helpful to use a dedicated system where the test tools and test scripts are located and which is used as a driver and logging system. This strategy helps a lot in keeping the test scripts, test documentation, and test logs well organised. In combination with the SAP archiving tool, a reliable storage for auditing purposes can be ensured.

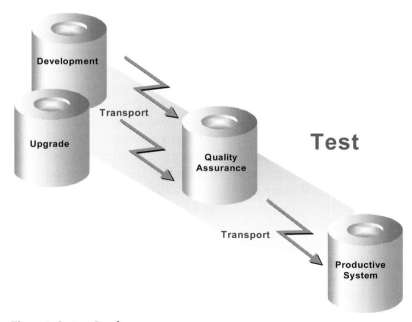

Figure 1: System Landscape

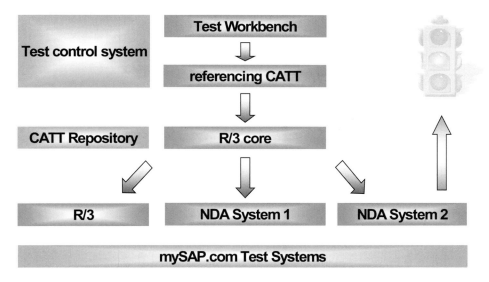

Figure 2: Central Test Control System (NDA = New Dimension Application)

The SAP Test Workbench supports this system strategy through the generic "Remote Function Call" (RFC) technology. This allows running test scripts on one system for the target (remote) systems and retrieving the results from the remote systems to the driving system. Because the idea of mySAP.com is a landscape with many collaborating systems, this functionality of the Test Workbench becomes an essential feature.

2.4 The Modular Concept

Automated test tools are drivers for certain interfaces of the Application Under Test (AUT). After or during the test run, automated test tools allow checking and verifying expected results. Examples for expected results from a technical point of view are values on the database, output values on screens or intermediate results from an internal calculation.

Examples of drivable interfaces of a SAP system are the Graphical User Interface (GUI), Business Application Programming Interfaces (BAPIs) or further SAP-specific technologies. The maintenance of existing test scripts is mostly caused by changes in these interfaces. This is unavoidable during development or implementation. A part of the ideal strategy to minimize maintenance efforts is to encapsulate every interface only once in one test module, and use this test module in every test process where the functionality is needed as a part of the corresponding business process (see Figure 3). Notice that the test script, which represents the whole business process, is symbolised by the outer box and will be referred to as "CATT procedure" while the two smaller boxes, which represent single steps (transactions) of a business process, will be referred

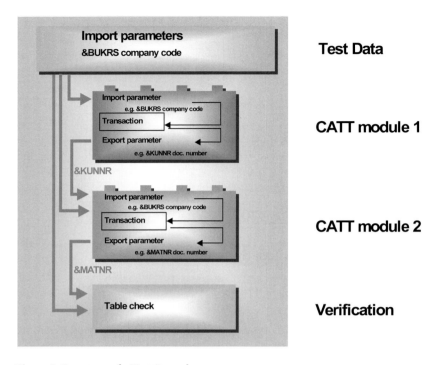

Figure 3: Structure of a Test Procedure

to as "CATT modules" (CATT = Computer Aided test Tool). Changes in the interface can then be handled in only one test script without the need to change the referencing scripts. This corresponds to the strategy of modular programming in order to avoid unstructured code and leads to a clear internal structure of test scripts.

In practice this ideal strategy cannot always be implemented in a SAP test because the transactions, as the smallest units of a business process, are very often too powerful and variable themselves. A single test script for a large transaction would result in a very complex internal logic of the script in order to cover every possibility that a business process could use this transaction for. Powerful transactions therefore are often represented by two or three different test scripts with different forms for the benefit of clarity.

As a result, SAP has internally built up a reuse library with a very large number of CATT modules, which are administrated in a hierarchy of business applications (financials, logistics, ...). There are agreed standards that a new CATT module must fulfil when it is added to the reuse library. These standards include the release of the module by the developer with the name of the responsible person in case of questions; documentation containing a description for purpose, parameters and interface; a complete parameterisation of all input fields of the encapsulated transaction; and an internal logic to improve the robustness of the script for language differences or the use of small or capital letters. Before implementing a new test process the developer checks the availability of suitable CATT modules in the library. In the case of a minor lack of functionality, a module is enhanced in order to avoid having CATT modules with similar functionality.

2.5 Robustness and Adaptations

A stable test environment is a crucial factor for the efficiency of an automated test project. If the effort for maintenance or troubleshooting of the test scripts themselves rises, the advantages of automated testing are lost. In this context stability means on the one hand the reliability of all (relevant) data in the system and on the other hand the ability of the tool and the individual test script to cope with irrelevant differences to the expected system state.

The stability of the system data can be achieved by the combination of a copy and a data creation process. An SAP system is a client system, which means that there are widely independent data areas where, for example, different companies can use the same SAP system without data interference. It is therefore possible to store the data state in one client and use it as a master for another dedicated test client with a periodical refresh from the master client. Recovery of data via data base tools is not recommended when testing in a SAP environment, because the dependencies of data are very close and there is a high potential for producing inconsistent data with tools which work without the control of the SAP system.

The opposite strategy would be to start with an empty client and generate all relevant data with CATT scripts that act purely as data generators. Experience has shown that a combination of both concepts is the most efficient, because a build-up with a client copy only would not be flexible enough and a build-up with CATT only is time-consuming and generates additional test scripts needing maintenance effort.

In a SAP system there is a lot of customising data, which determines the look and the behaviour of screens and screen sequences. Fields can be turned on and off, or they can be changed from optional to mandatory input fields. The screen sequence can be adapted to user-dependent needs or unnecessary screens can be deleted. Obviously, such changes have an enormous influence on any capture/replay tool. Unfortunately, these activities are unavoidable during an implementation process and can even occur a very short time before a going-live date.

Due to its integration in the system, CATT can support the user with these changes more than other tools can. If we take the worst case, where a transaction has to be re-recorded because of too many changes, CATT automatically finds the fields where a previous parameterisation was done and maps parameters to the same fields even if the fields are now on totally different screens or positions. This is possible because CATT maps values or parameters to the technical names of fields, which normally remain unchanged and can therefore be recognised in the new transaction automatically. The re-

recording is a matter of a few minutes and the tool does the parameterisation, which is the difficult and time-consuming part.

Another measure to reduce the maintenance of test scripts due to these changes is to use non-GUI interfaces of the SAP system, which are much more constant. If master data of a creditor is needed in order to use it in a business process, it is normally of no interest to check the creation of the creditor itself but the results of later steps (e.g. a posting transaction which uses the creditor). Therefore, we do not have to use the user transaction but can instead use the corresponding BAPI, which can easily be found in the BAPI repository. If we want to ensure that for some reason we do use the user transaction, we can insert a condition that decides from a control parameter the path to be taken. SAP guarantees the stability and compatibility of BAPIs over a period of several releases. CATT scripts which use these BAPIs will therefore remain valid even after a release upgrade, whereas a CATT script with the corresponding user transaction would have to be adapted due to changes in the transaction.

3   Tools

3.1   The SAP Test Workbench

For test administration and functional testing, SAP has developed the Test Workbench, which is fully integrated and shipped with every SAP system. The usage of the Workbench tools is free of charge, because SAP positions these tools not as a product, but as a service for the customers in order to support their testing efforts.

The Workbench is fully integrated in the SAP system and developed with the SAP programming language ABAP, still the language in which most SAP applications are implemented. This leads to significant advantages for the test strategy. The integration enables the tool to drive the SAP system in a very effective, fast and specific way by using SAP native interfaces for the test of ABAP function modules and other interfaces besides the usual capture/replay functionality. This enables the test co-ordinator to use the tool according to the common test strategy of starting with tests on a modular basis and continuing up to an integration test (bottom-up test).

Another advantage of the integration is the shipment of ready-to-use testing modules by SAP. This is done with any SAP system as well as with the shipment of the Accelerated SAP (ASAP) methodology. This shipment includes a large number of ready-to-run test processes and descriptions and enables the customer to test, build up test data, or run the test process for training.

A general question on the delivery of test contents is, of course, whether the effort for adapting the shipped test scripts is easier or more difficult than developing them on one's own. This question can only be answered for an individual installation and it turns out that there are implementations where it is extremely helpful but there are also customers with a very individual setup of their business processes which makes it necessary to start with the creation of test cases on an individual basis.

In the next sections we describe the main functions of the Test Workbench. We will see that the Test Workbench consists of two parts; firstly, there is a test administration and monitoring tool, the Test Organizer; secondly there is the CATT for implementation of manual or automatic test cases.

3.1.1 Test Organizer

The Test Organizer is used by the test co-ordinator in order to define the structure of a test project and to monitor the test process. The tester uses it to find the test cases that the test co-ordinator assigned to him, to execute them and to report the results. The Test Organizer includes three main structures (see Figure 4):

- Test Catalogue
- Test Plan
- Test Package

The Test Catalogue is a library containing and structuring all test cases. Of course, it is possible to create an arbitrary number of Test Catalogues, for example, according to the number of modules or other criteria the user thinks to be useful. The hierarchy of a

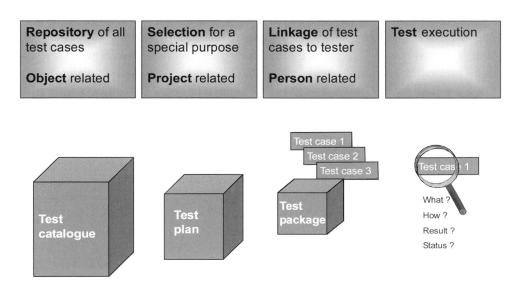

Figure 4: Objects of the Test Organizer

Figure 5: Test Catalogue

Test Catalogue is user defined (see Figure 5) and should correspond to the structure of the test project. A well-structured Test Catalogue is a crucial success factor for the test project itself. Because the idea of the Catalogue is to have a repository for the test objects it is considered as an object-related matter.

With a special test project in mind it becomes necessary to derive another structure of the Test Organizer from the Test Catalogue. This is done with the Test Plan, which is a project-related matter. It can be derived from one or several Catalogues by selecting the nodes in the hierarchy, which are relevant for the project. The Test Plan therefore inherits the structure and the test cases from the catalogues above it. Although the Test Plan is an independent structure which can be changed and maintained separately, it is strongly recommended to do changes in the Test Catalogue and regenerate the Test Plan from there in order not to lose the modifications for later projects.

Test Packages are subsets of a given Test Plan and specify a hierarchy with Test Cases for a single tester. For manual test cases, the Test Package defines the task that was assigned to an individual tester. For automatic tests, the test package is the unit which can be scheduled for execution at an arbitrary time.

The test process is monitored by the test co-ordinator using the status information system. He can watch the percentage of processed test cases with the corresponding results together with additional information such as comments, time needed and errors

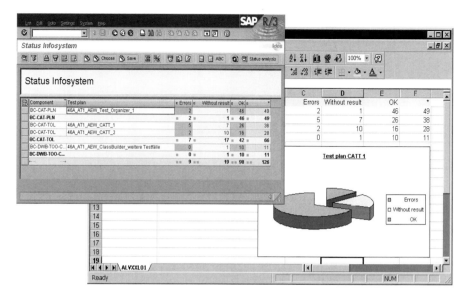

Figure 6: Status Information System

found. There is an integration with several SAP error-tracking and workflow systems, which can be set up in a user-defined way. Because there is an enhanced download possibility it is very easy to generate a state-of-the-art management report via standard spreadsheet applications (see Figure 6).

3.1.2 Computer Aided Test Tool – CATT

CATT Types
CATT is the tool used to edit test cases of any type. Apart from the obvious difference of a manual test case and an automatic test case, from a technical point of view it is only a certain attribute within the test case which indicates the type. CATT has the following main test case types:

- Manual
- Automatic
- External

Due to the minor technical differences it is very easy and intuitive to handle all types in a similar way as far as the usage and administration of test cases by the Test Organizer is concerned (see 3.1.1). When the user selects the manual type, the editor of the CATT is a simple text editor with a user-defined template for the test case description.

Figure 7: CATT Function Screen

The tester has to work through the description, create error messages or notes if necessary, and set a status which is relevant for Test Organizer reporting.

For the automatic type the editor contains an additional function screen, where the CATT language can be used. This language is very simple and has no similarities with other well-known programming languages. It has only about a dozen, but very powerful, commands (see Figure 7: CATT).

CATT Commands

The most important command is the "TCD" statement, which is used for the capture and replay of transactions. Because of the integration of CATT in the SAP system there is no need for any GUI-map third-party tools to identify and map screens or fields. There is also no need for using language-dependent screen titles or other characteristics, which can be session or resolution-dependent. All required information comes from the global SAP repository to which CATT has full access. Therefore, even changes which might be done by the developer of a certain screen are found within the CATT recording automatically (see Figure 8).

It is also very important to understand that the CATT capture/replay does not work at a GUI level (on the front-end PC) but at a deeper layer on the SAP application server. When running in background mode, this means that performance is at least three times higher than with other capture/replay tools. In addition, the application does not

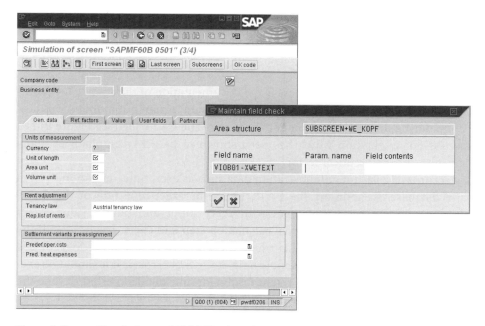

Figure 8: Screen Simulation and Field Check Maintenance

block the PC during replay; the PC need not even be turned on. Performance is of great importance, not only for the testing purposes, but also because CATT is very often used for mass changes or data migration.

Besides the common control commands for loops, conditions, or exits, there are also statements for the access to ABAP function modules for a low-level test and, especially important, check functions. Again the integration of CATT in the SAP system allows a very easy verification of values directly in database tables, which is obviously the most rigorous test. In addition, values can not only be read and verified but also be changed if necessary.

The verification of screen output is especially user-friendly because CATT allows a screen simulation without running the test case. Checks can be inserted via double click on any output field from the CATT screen simulation editor (see Figure 8).

Another important feature is the test of system messages like "Access denied" or "Material 123 was created successfully". The first example can be found in a user-profile test in order to ensure that a new user profile will not allow the corresponding users to access a certain transaction. This task must be done very carefully but at the same time it is very monotonous. Because CATT has access to the internal number of a SAP system message it is very easy to check the existence of this message in a language-independent way. The second example shows another useful feature of CATT: because CATT knows the internal structure of the message "Material 123 was created successfully" it can easily identify the variable part "123" of the message and check the number without the problem of finding the "123" using complicated string operations.

CATT Log

A very important part of the test process is the documentation of the results, for example, for auditing purposes. With an automatic test this important but monotonous task can be done during the test execution automatically. The CATT log (see Figure 9) is a complete test documentation which has been shown to be FDA-compliant at many customers in the pharmaceutical sector.

The log records all relevant administration data such as user, time, operation, system name, and database. In addition, the CATT log is the exact reflection of the CATT script by documenting every statement with every input and output value, every screen, that was used, and every internal calculation step and check result. Even if the test run fails all results up to the point where the problem occurred are logged. The user can choose whether the test run should stop at the first error or if it should be executed to the end anyway. In order to retain results for an extended period of time the standard SAP archiving tool can be used to archive all relevant logs.

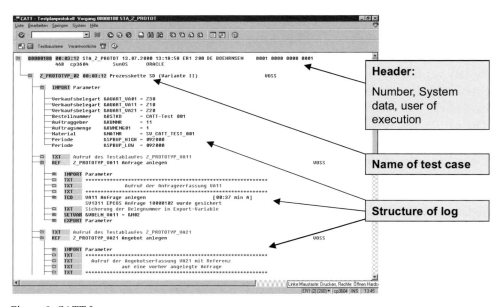

Figure 9: CATT Log

Creation of a CATT procedure

The creation of a SAP business process via CATT follows a simple scheme:

1. Identification of the business process

The business process must be defined in a very specific way including test data. Therefore the "n" single steps of the process have to be examined carefully in order to prepare for the recording. Unnecessary data or screens should be avoided in order to minimize sources of errors and maintenance. On the other hand, extensibility to a more general usage of the step should be considered in order to maximise the reusability of the modules.

2. Creation of CATT modules

If not already available in a reuse library the single transactions have to be recorded into "n" CATT modules. It is convenient to use a naming convention for the test scripts in order to remember them when they are needed. Sometimes it is necessary to have additional commands in the script for example when a certain preparation or formatting of the data is needed. A specialised logic should be avoided because it reduces reusability. Good documentation, which can be added to tests scripts as an attachment, is a precondition for other users to include the module into their test procedures. The documentation should explain the purpose of the module and list the parameters with their usage.

3. Parameterisation of values

Parameterisation is essential for the interface definition of the modules and in order to achieve more flexibility. There are import parameters which are filled by the referencing test script, export parameters which are sent back to the referencing test script, and local parameters which are only used for calculations inside the test script.

4. Combination of the CATT modules to a CATT procedure

The CATT modules, which represent the single steps of the business process, have to be referenced in the correct order in a test procedure. The proper supply of values for the import and export parameters has to be ensured and logic for necessary loops or conditions added. In order to improve the maintainability, comments should be added and documentation should be written as an attachment with a description of the purpose and structure.

5. Insertion of Checks

There is no general rule whether checks should be inserted into the test modules or in the test procedure. Both strategies can be useful. Inserting the checks into the procedure keeps the modules lean and avoids unnecessary or unreasonable checks. A disadvantage is that the interface must be larger in order to pass the necessary information for the check to the test procedure. Sometimes the knowledge of what has to be checked is with the person who created the module so information exchange becomes necessary. A possible solution could be to insert the checks normally in the modules and add a special control parameter which turns the checking on or off.

6.   Creation of variations

The import parameters of a test procedure represent the interface for the input of external test data. CATT allows "variants", value sets for these parameters, to be defined. These variants can be exported to a local PC in order to edit them with a local editor and imported from an ASCII file after editing or from a program which generates those files, for example, for data migration purposes. In this way a generic interface to tools which generate test data, for example, by test case analysis is realised.

3.2 Outlook

Before we have a look what is coming up soon in the test tool area, we have to understand the reasons why SAP develops its own test tools whereas many other companies which had their own test tools in the past now use third-party tools instead. For SAP a very important reason is that its own development platforms, programming models and languages (e.g. ABAP) are used and continually improved. As a consequence changes of any test tool become necessary in order to handle the new features shortly after they are introduced. Because the third-party vendors of tools cannot react to these requirements before the new SAP Release is available, it is too late for a SAP internal test by the final assembly department of SAP. This department ensures the quality of the SAP Release on the more than 200 different platforms (hardware, operating systems and databases) that SAP supports. The number and complexity of these test systems at the final assembly could not be handled with PC-based tools. Additionally, they are not fast enough for the short time schedule in this department.

As we saw above, an integrated tool has many advantages due to the direct and full access to the SAP system that is crucial for really significant tests. We also saw that SAP wants to support its customer with the free usage of the tools and corresponding business content. This can only be achieved with a certain degree of independence.

In order to cope with the challenges of new technologies where platforms are not developed at SAP like Internet, Java, or XML, it becomes clear that SAP has to co-operate in the test tool area. Figure 10 shows that every technology requires its own "driver". Some of them can be developed with higher efficiency at SAP like the driver for the SAP non-GUI interfaces or the SAP GUI for Windows. On the other hand drivers for other applications (for example legacy systems, Java or Visual Basic applications) can be covered more efficiently by companies that are specialised in these areas and are in very close contact to the suppliers of these applications and standards.

In a current project CATT is being developed further and will provide certified interfaces where third-party tools can be integrated in order to cover business processes which use more than one technology or environment. In the mySAP.com solution this is what normally happens. From a user standpoint, there is a central test repository with all advantages of a SAP system such as a client server architecture, data security,

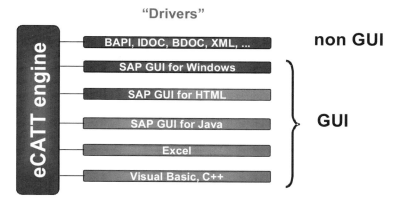

"Drivers"

non GUI

GUI

Coverage of all business processes with „environment hopping"
- Single point of entry
- Central test repository

Figure 10: eCATT Drivers (enhanced Computer Aided Test Tool)

and a single test script for each business process comprising modules from other test tools including data exchange.

Other goals for the project are an enhanced support of the SAP ActiveX Controls in the SAP GUI for Windows, an improved usability (see Figure 12), and the reuse of test and system data. Furthermore, there will be a closer integration to SAP's tools for performance analysis and the capability of using CATT for generating load on a system.

As is shown schematically in Figure 11, there is a new object, the Test Configuration, as a container for three sub-objects. The Test Data is stored separately as a sub-object, which allows a reuse of often-needed data such as cost centres. Changes in the Test Data will then automatically take effect in all scripts in which they are referenced. This is an enormous simplification and increase of transparency.

The System Data as sub-object allows an efficient redirection of all test scripts when the physical mySAP.com system landscape, or part of it, changes in any way. The script itself contains the commands which manage the different drivers for the different interfaces to the AUT. It becomes obvious that in the future, due to the rising number of technologies, the developer of a test script will have to consider more things than the business process he wants to test. He also has to select the appropriate drivers for a special purpose. Without knowing the exact circumstances there is no best choice. Every driver has advantages and disadvantages like stability, performance, ease of use and so on.

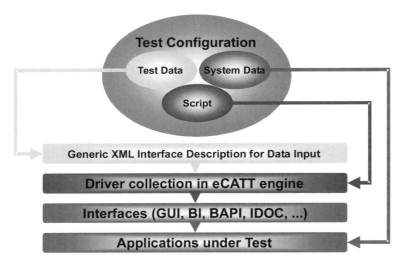

Figure 11: eCATT Test Configuration

Some of the concepts outlined above can be found in Figure 12. We see that all test scripts have a versioning for the requirement of different script versions of different AUT releases. This happens at SAP internally and at large customers.

Structured parameters such as tables can be used and maintained in a generic XML editor. This editor also allows the maintenance of the driver interfaces. In spite of the technically very different structures of the drivers the user always has the same editor

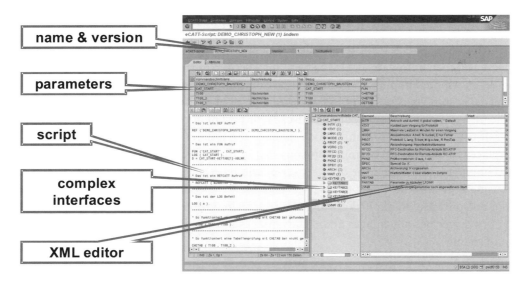

Figure 12: eCATT Script Editor

for them. This is an enormous improvement in usability and an investment for future technologies. The script language was adapted with attention to common state-of-the-art programming languages. In a later version the language can be visualised in a graphical display, in order to get a better overview of the underlying business process.

4 Summary

Automated tests are the only efficient way to cope with the specific needs for testing in a SAP environment. From an internal point of view, it ensures the quality of products and corrections. From the customer point of view it greatly reduces the effort required during periodic tests due to upgrades, support packages, or changes during implementation projects. Practice shows that many customer implementation projects would have been less successful or more time-consuming without the deployment of the integrated SAP Test Workbench. Questions like "What would happen if we changed this setting?" or "What impact would this change have on our defined business processes?" can be answered within hours. Without automated testing every small change would result in a large manual test project and a lot of flexibility for last-minute changes would be lost. SAP will continue developing its own test tools in order to deliver a test solution for customers and to ensure its own internal testing processes. For the integration of non-SAP platforms and legacy systems third-party test tools will be integrated in the test solution in order to allow customers a best-of-breed choice and to react quickly on future technologies.

Acknowledgements: Many thanks to the eCATT Team for supporting this article through fruitful discussions, Franz Schreiner for reviewing the draft and Martin Plummer for stylistic and grammatical improvements.

Part VI

Appendix

References

AGIL01   The Agile Alliance: http://www.agilealliance.org

AKAO90   Y. Akao et.al.: *Quality Function Deployment (QFD)*, Productivity Press, 1990

AMBL00   S.W. Ambler: *Writing Robust Java Code. The AmbySoft Inc. Coding Standards for Java*, v. 17.01.d, available at http://www.Ambysoft.com

ANDE99   M. Anderson: *The top 13 mistakes in Load Testing Applications.* In: Software Testing and Quality Engineering Magazine, Vol. 1, Issue 5, pp. 30-41, 1999

BACH00   J. Bach: *Session-Based Test Management*, In: Software Testing and Quality Engineering magazine, 11/2000

BACH01   J. Bach: *What is Exploratory Testing? And How it Differs from Scripted Testing*, column feature at http://www.StickyMinds.com, January 2001

BACK95   K. Backhaus, M. Voeth, K.B. Bendix: *Die Akzeptanz von Multimedia-Diensten – Konzeptionelle Anmerkungen und empirische Ergebnisse*, Arbeitspapier Nr. 19 des Betriebswirtschaftlichen Instituts für Anlagen und Systemtechnologie der Universität Münster, Germany 1995

BALL00   G. Ball, J. Breese: *Emotion in personality in a conversational agent*, In: [CASS00]

BALZ98   H. Balzert: *Lehrbuch der Software-Technik 2: Software-Management, Software-Qualitätssicherung, Unternehmensmodellierung*, Spektrum Akademischer Verlag, Heidelberg/Berlin, 1998

BALZ98-a   H. Balzert: *Lehrbuch der Software-Technik: Software-Entwicklung*, Spektrum Akademischer Verlag, Heidelberg/Berlin, 1998

BASK01   R. Baskerville, L. Levine, J. Pries-Heje, B. Ramesch, S. Slaughter: *How Internet Software Companies Negotiate Quality*, In: IEEE Computer, Vol. 34, No. 5, pp. 51-57, May 2001

BAUE00   C. Bauer, A. Scharl: *Tool-supported Evolutionary Web Development: Rethinking Traditional Modeling Principles.* In: [HANS00] pp. 282-289, 2000

BECK99   K. Beck: *Extreme Programming Explained: Embrace Change.* Addison-Wesley, Reading, MA, 1999

BECK00   K. Beck, M. Fowler: *Planning Extreme Programming*, Addison-Wesley, Reading, MA, 2000

BEIZ90   B Beizer: *Software Testing Techniques*, 2nd Edition, Van Nostrand Reinhold, New York, 1990

BEVA97   N. Bevan: *Quality and usability: a new framework*, In: E. van Veenendaal, J. McMullan (Eds.), *Achieving Software Product Quality*, Tutein Noltehnius, s Hertogenbosch, The Netherlands, 1997

BIND00   R. Binder: *Testing Object-Oriented Systems*, Addison-Wesley, Reading, MA, 2000.

BOOT01   Bootstrap 3.2, Model documentation, http://www.bootstrap-institute.com

284 References

BOS98	R. Bos, E. van Veenendaal: *Quality of Multimedia Systems: The MultiSpace approach* (in Dutch), In: Information Management, May 1998
BUSC96	F. Buschmann, R. Meunier, H. Rohnert, P. Sommerlad, M. Stal: *Pattern-Oriented Software Architecture, Vol. 1, A System of Patterns*, John Wiley & Son Ltd., 1996
CASS00	J. Cassell (ed.): *Embodied Conversational Agents*, MIT Press (MIT Media Lab), Cambridge/London, 2000
CASP99	S. Caspers, D. Meyerhoff: *Performance and Robustness Test – Factors of Success for Development and Introduction of Commercial Software*, Conquest – Conference on Quality Engineering in Software Technology, ASQF, Nuremberg, Germany, 1999
CLAR01	D. Clark: *Visual Basic and the Future of Web-Application Development.* IEEE Computer, Vol. 34, No. 8, pp. 16-18, August 2001
CLEG99	B. Clegg, P. Birch: *Instant Creativity*, Kogan Page Ltd., 1999
COHE95	L. Cohen: *Quality Function Deployment, How to Make QFD Work for You*, Prentice Hall, Engineering Process Improvement Series, 1995
DEUB01	Deutsche Bank Web Site, Transaction Systems, http://www.deutsche-bank.de/tx
DUST99	E. Dustin, J. Rashka, J. Paul: *Automated Software Testing*, Addison Wesley, Reading, MA, 1999.
ELTI01	A. Elting, W. Huber: *Immer im Plan? Programmieren zwischen Chaos und Planwirtschaft*, In: c't, pp.184-191, 2001
ENGE95	E. Engeler: *The Combinatory Programme*, Birkhäuser, 1995
ERNI96	K. Erni, C. Lewerentz: *Applying Design Metrics to Object-Oriented Frameworks*, In: Proceedings of Software Metrics Symposium, IEEE Computer Society Press, pp. 64-74, 1996
FEHL00-a	T. Fehlmann: *Measuring Competitiveness in Service Design; Decisions based on Customer's Needs.* In: QFD Institute (Ed.): 12th Symposium On Quality Function Deployment, Novi, MI, 2000
FEHL00-b	T. Fehlmann, C. Hauri: *Measuring Project Management Excellence.* In: 3rd European Conference on Software Measurement and ICT Control, FESMA – AEMES, Madrid, Spain, 2000
FEHL01	T. Fehlmann: *QFD as Algebra of Combinators.* In: 7th International Symposium in QFD, Tokyo, Japan, 2001
FEWS99	M. Fewster, D. Graham: *Software Test Automation (Effective use of text execution tools)*, London, 1999
FISC01	R. Fischbach: *Die im Schatten ...... – Programmieren: Stand der Dinge jenseits der Softwarekrise,* In: iX-Magazin für professionelle Informationstechnik, pp. 60-65, May 2001
GAMM95	E. Gamma, R. Helm, R. Johnson, J. Vlissides (The Gang of Four): *Design Patterns: Elements of Reusable Object-Oriented Software*, Addison Wesley Professional Computing Series, Reading, MA, 1994
GHEZ91	C. Ghezzi, M. Jazayeri, D. Mandrioli: *Fundaments of Software Engineering*, Prentice Hall International, London, 1991
GILB99	T. Gilb und D. Graham: *Software Inspection*, Addison Wesley, Reading, MA, 1999.
GRIS01	M.L. Griss, G. Pour: *Accelerating Development with Agent Components*, In: IEEE Computer, Vol. 34, No. 5, pp. 37-43, May 2001

HANS00   H. Hansen, M. Bichler, H. Mahrer (Eds.): *Proceedings of the 8ᵗʰ European confer-ence on Information Systems (ECIS)*, Vienna University of Economics and Busi-ness Administration, Austria, Vol. 1, 2000

HENR96   M. Henricson, E. Nyquist: *Industrial strength C++: Rules and Recommendations*, Prentice Hall, London, 1996

HERZ97   G. Herzwurm, S. Schockert, W. Mellis: *Qualitätssoftware durch Kundenorien-tierung. Die Methode Quality Function Deployment (QFD). Grundlagen, Praxis-leitfaden, SAP R/3 Fallbeispiel*, Vieweg – Verlag, Braunschweig – Wiesbaden, 1997

HOWC00   D. Howcroft, J. Carroll: *A Proposed Methodology for Web Development*, In: [HANS00], pp. 290-297

HUNT01   A. Hunt, D. Thomas: *The Pragmatic Programmer – from journeyman to master*, Addison Wesley Longman, Reading, MA, 1999

IFPU00   International Function Point Users Group: *IFPUG Function Point Couting Prac-tices Manual*, Release 4.1.1, Troy, Michigan, April 2000

ISO9126-1   ISO/IEC FCD 9126-1: *Information technology – Software product quality – Part 1: Quality model*, International Organization of Standardization, 2001

ISO9126-2   ISO/IEC PDTR 9126-2: *Information technology – Software quality characteristics and metrics – Part 2: External metrics*, International Organization of Standardiza-tion, 1997

ISO9241-10   ISO 9241-10: *Ergonomic Requirements for office work with visual display terminals (VDT's) – Part 10: Dialogue principles*, International Organization of Standardiza-tion, 1996

ISO9241-11   ISO 9241-11: *Ergonomic Requirements for office work with visual display terminals (VDT's) – Part 11: Guidance on usability*, International Organization of Standardi-zation, 1998

JACO92   I. Jacobson: *Object-Oriented Software Engineering: A Use Case Driven Approach*, Addison Wesley, Reading, MA, 1992

JEFF00   R. Jeffries, A. Anderson, C. Hendrickson: *Extreme Programming Installed*, Addison Wesley, Reading, 2000

JUNI01   Junit, IBM Public Licence, http://www.junit.org

JUTI99   U. Jutila, A. Dehnel: *Acceptability: Focus on the user/customer*, QSDG Magazine, Vol. 2, No. 1, 1999

JWAM01   The JWAM Framework: http://www.jwam.org

KANE99   C. Kaner, J. Falk, H.Q. Nguyen: *Testing Computer Software,* John Wiley & Sons Inc., New York, 1999

KANE01   C. Kaner, J. Bach: *Exploratory Testing in Pairs*, STAR East Conference – Software Testing Analysis & Review, Orlando, CA, 2001

KEES01-a   P. Keese: *Scalable Acceptance Testing.* In: [WIEC00]

KEES01-b   P. Keese, D. Meyerhoff: *Experiences from Business Integration Testing in Large Software Projects.* In: Proceedings of the 5ᵗʰ Conquest – Conference on Quality En-gineering in Software Technology, ASQF, Nuremberg, Germany, 2001

KIRA93   J. Kirakowski, M. Corbett: *SUMI: the Software Usability Measurement Inventory*, In: British Journal of Educational Technology, Vol. 24, No. 3, pp. 210-212, 1993

KIRA96   J. Kirakowski: *The Software Usability Measurement Inventory: Background and Usage*, In: P. Jordan, B. Thomas, B. Weerdmeester (Eds.), *Usability Evaluation in Industry*, Taylor and Francis, 1996

KOOM99   T. Koomen, M. Pol: *Test Process Improvement – A Practical Step-By-Step Guide to Structured Testing,* Addison Wesley, Reading, MA, 1999

LEHM85   M.M. Lehmann, L.A. Belady: *Programm Evaluation,* Academic Press, New York, 1985

LEON97   A. Leonard: *An insightful historica. Overview. The Origin of a new Species,* Pinguin book, Computers/Science & Technology, New York, 1997

LIPP01-a   M. Lippert, S. Roock, R. Tunkel, H. Wolf: *Stabilizing the XP Process Using Specialized Tools,* Proceedings of XP 2001 Conference, Villasimius, Sardinia, Italy, 2001

LIPP01-b   M. Lippert, S. Roock, H. Wolf, H. Züllighoven: *XP in Complex Project Settings: Some Extensions,* In: Proceedings of XP, 2001 Conference, Villasiumius, Sardinia, Italy, 2001

LJUN00   J. Ljungberg: *Open Source Movements as a Model for Organizing.* In: [HANS00], pp. 501-508

LOEB01   http://www.loebner.net

MAZU93   G. Mazur: *QFD for Service Organizations,* Japan Business Consultants, Ltd., 1993

MCCA76   T. McCabe: *A Complexity measure.* In: IEEE Transactions on Software Engineering, Vol. 2, No. 4, pp. 308-320, 1976

MECK01   C. Mecke: *Automated Testing of mySAP.com,* In: [MEYE01-a]

MELI98   R. Meli: *SAFE: A method to understand, reduce, and accept project risk,* European Software Control and Metric (ESCOM)-ENCRESS 98 – Project Control for 2000 and Beyond, Rome, Italy, May 1998

MELL01   W. Mellis: *Process and Product Orientation in Software Development and their Effect on Software Quality Management.* In: [WIEC01]

MEYE95   S. Meyers: *Effective C++: 50 Specific Ways to Improve your Programs and Design,* Addison Wesley, Reading, MA, 1995

MEYE99   D. Meyerhoff, M. Timpe: *Vom Entwurfs- bis zum Systemtest: Objektorientierte Anwendungsentwicklung verändert die Testprozesse,* In: OBJEKTspektrum, SIGS, Germany, Vol. 1, 1999

MEYE01-a   D. Meyerhoff (Ed.): *Proceedings of the 2nd ICSTEST – International Conference on Software Testing 2001,* SQS AG, Cologne, Germany, 2001

MEYE01-b   D. Meyerhoff, D. Huberty: *Testing Internet Based Home Banking Software,* In: [MEYE01-a]

MIZU88   S. Mizuno (Ed.): *Management for Quality Improvement, The 7 New QC Tools,* Productivity Press, 1988

MIZU94   S. Mizuno, Y. Akao (Eds.): *QFD: The Customer-Driven Approach to Quality Planning and Deployment,* translated by Glenn Mazur, Tokyo, Asian Productivity Organization, 1994

MKS01   Mortice Kern Sytems Inc.: *Changing Application Development Needs,* a TechRepublic Survey, Sponsored by MKS, available at http://www.mks.com

MOOR99   J. Moormann: *Umbruch in der Bankinformatik – Status quo und Perspektiven für eine Neugestaltung.* In: J. Moormann T. Fischer (Eds.): *Handbuch Informationstechnologie in Banken,* pp. 3-20, Wiesbaden, 1999

MOOR00   S. Moore: *Application Analysis and Mining Tools: Big Payback Potential.* Giga Information Group (www.gigaweb.com), Cambridge, MA, 2000

MULT97   Multispace: *Report on demand oriented survey*, Multispace Project [ESPRIT 23066], CEC, Brussels, 1997

MYER76   G.J. Myers: *Software Reliability: Principles and Practices*, John Wiley Publications, 1976

MYER79   G. J. Myers: *The Art of Software Testing*, New York, 1997.

NASS00   C.K. Nass, K. Isbister, E. Lee: *Truth is Beauty: Researching Embodied Conversational Agents*. In: [CASS00]

NGUY01   H.Q. Nguyen: *Testing Applications on the WEB*, John Wiley & Sons Inc., New York, 2001

NIEL93   J. Nielsen: *Usability Engineering*, Academic Press, 1993

NIEL94   J. Nielsen, R.L. Mack: *Usability Inspection Methods*, John Wiley & Sons Inc., New York, 1994

NIEL01   J. Nielsen's Website: http://www.useit.com

NPL95   National Physical Laboratory (NPL): *Usability Context Analysis: A Practical Guide*, Version 4.0, NPL University Services, UK, 1995

PARN72   D.L. Parnas: *On the criteria to be used in decomposing systems into modules*, Communications of the ACM, 1972

PFEI97   A. Pfeiffer: *SniFF+: Eine einheitliche Arbeitsumgebung für große Softwareprojekte*. In: OBJEKTspektrum, pp. 30-34, March/April 1997

PREE94   J. Preece et.al: *Human Computer Interaction*, Addison Wesley Publishing Company, Readint, MA, 1994

PUNT97   T. Punter, R. van Solingen, J. Trienekens: *Software Product Evaluation*. In: *Proceedings of the 4^{in} European Conference on Evaluation of Information Technology (EVIT97)*, Delft, The Netherlands, 1997

RUBI94   J. Rubin: *Handbook of Usability Testing: How to Plan, Design, and Conduct Effective Tests*, John Wiley & Sons Inc., 1994

SACH99   L. Sachs: *Angewandte Statistik*, 9th Edition, Springer, Berlin, 1999

SAMU98   P.A. Samuelson, W.D. Nordhaus: *Economics,* 16th Edition, McGraw Hill, Boston, 1998

SAND00   G.A. Sanders, J. Scholtz: *Measurement and Evaluation of Embodied Conversational Agents*. In: [CASS00]

SCHU92   G. Schulmeyer, J. McManus (Eds.): *Handbook of Software Quality Asscurance*, 2nd Edition, Van Nostrand Reinhold, pp. 297-319, Zurich, Switzerland, 1992

SHIL00   M.L. Shillito: *Acquiring, Processing, and Deploying Voice of the Customer*, CRC Press, 2000

SHIR01   C. Shirky: *What is P2P.... And what isn't!* The O'Reilly Peer-to-Peer and Web Services Conference, Washington D.C., http://www.conferences.oreilly.com/p2p/

SIMO98   F. Simon, C. Lewerentz: *A product metrics tool integrated into a software development environment*. In: Proceedings of the European Measurement Conferences (FESMA), p. 603-608, 1998

SIMO01   F. Simon: *Meßwertbasierte Qualitätssicherung – Ein generisches Distanzmaß zur Erweiterung bisherigeer Softwareproduktmaße*, Dissertation at the Institute for Computer Sciences, Brandenburgische Technical University Cottbus, Germany, 2001

SING01   M.P. Singh: *Peering at Peer-to-Peer Computing*, IEEE Internet Computing, pp. 4-5, January/February 2001

STAH99   P. Stahlknecht, U. Hasenkamp: *Einführung in die Wirtschaftsinformatik,* 9th Edition, Springer, Berlin, 1999

STAL99   R. Stallmann: *The GNU Operating System and the Free Software Movement.* In: C. DiBona, S. Ockman, M. Stone (Eds.): *Open Sources – Voices from the Open Source Revolution,* O'Reilly, 1999

STAL01   M. Stal: *Im Rahmen bleiben,* In: iX-Magazin für professionelle Informationstechnik, pp. 72-77, Mai 2001

TRIE97   J. Trienekens, E. van Veenendaal: *Software Quality from a Business Perspective,* Kluwer Bedrijfsinformatie, Deventer, The Netherlands, 1997

TURI50   A.M.Turing: *Computing machinery and intelligence.* In: Computing machinery and intelligence, Vol. 59, No. 236, pp. 433-560, 1950

V-MOD01   V-Modell, http://www.v-modell.iabg.de

WALK97   M.A. Walker, D.J. Litman, C.A. Kamm, A. Abella: *PARADISE, A Framework for evaluating spoken dialogue agents.* In: Proceedings of the 35th ACL and 8th EACL, Madrid, Spain, San Francisco, Calif., Association for Computational Linguistics and Morgan Kaufmann, pp. 271-280, 1997

WALL01   E. Wallmüller: *Software – Qualitätsmanagement in der Praxis,* 2nd Edition, Carl Hanser Verlag, May 2001

WARG01   M. Warg, G. Scholz: *Großprojekte erfolgreich managen (Successful Management of Major Projects), Mit der Informationsfabrik Oskar in die IT Echtzeit (Oskar, the information factory paving the way for real-time IT),* FAZ-Verlag, Frankfurt/Main, 2001

WEBL01   WebLoad, Product of Radview, http://www.radview.com

WIEC00   M. Wieczorek, D. Meyerhoff (Eds.): *Software Quality – State of the Art in Management, Testing, and Tools,* Springer, Heidelberg, 2001

WINR01   WinRunner; Product of Mercury, http://www.mercuryinteractive.de

WINT01   J.G. Winter: *Schnelligkeit und Qualität.* In: Bankmagazin, pp. 78-79, No. 10/00, 2000

WYSS01   C. Wyss: *Tief im Osten – Ruby: Objektorientierung aus Japan,* In: iX-Magazin für professionelle Informationstechnik, pp. 78-81, May 2001

YU01   E. Yu: *Agent orientation as a modelling paradigm,* Wirtschaftsinformatik 43, Vol. 2, pp. 123-132, 2001

ZAHR98   S. Zahran: *Software Process Improvement: Practical Guidelines for Business Success (SEI Series in Software Engineering),* Addison Wesley, Reading, MA, 1998

ZULT92   R.E. Zultner: *Quality Function Deployment (QFD) for Software: Structured Requirements Exploration.* In: [SCHU92]

List of Contributors

STÅLE AMLAND
Amland Consulting
Hulda Garborgsv. 2, 4020 Stavanger,
Norway
E-Mail: stale@amland.no
Web: www.amland.no
Tel: + 47 51 580587
Fax: + 47 51 585524

WALTER BISCHOFBERGER, DR.
Wabic GmbH
Brüttenweg 11, 8052 Zürich,
Switzerland
E-Mail: wbischofberger@acm.org
Tel: + 41 1 3030079

ARNIM BUCH
Sd&m software design & management AG
Am Schimmersfeld 7a, 40882 Ratingen,
Germany
E-Mail: Arnim.Buch@sdm.de
Web: www.sdm.de
Tel: + 49 2102 99 57 937
Fax: + 49 2102 99 57 50

ASTRID DEHNEL
T-Systems Nova GmbH, Berkom
Goslarer Ufer 35, 10589 Berlin,
Germany
E-Mail: Astrid.Dehnel@t-systems.de
Web: www.t-systems.de
Tel: + 49 30 34970
Fax: + 49 30 3497 3541

TESSA DÖRING
Dresdner Bank AG
Fehlandtstr. 3 / 4. OG, 20354 Hamburg,
Germany
E-Mail:
Tessa.Doering@dresdner-bank. com
Web: www.dresdner-bank.de
Tel: + 49 40 3501 0
Fax: + 49 40 3501 2415

STEFAN ENGELKAMP
Sd&m software design & management AG
Am Schimmersfeld 7a, 40882 Ratingen,
Germany
E-Mail: Stefan.Engelkamp@sdm.de
Web: www.sdm.de
Tel: + 49 2102 99 57 48
Fax: + 49 2102 99 57 54

THOMAS FEHLMANN, DR.
Euro Project Office AG
Zeltweg 50, 8032 Zürich,
Switzerland
E-Mail: Thomas.Fehlmann@e-p-o.com
Web: www.e-p-o.com
Tel: + 41 1 2531306
Fax: + 41 1 2531364

ELMAR FICHTL
T-Systems Nova GmbH, Berkom
Goslarer Ufer 35, 10589 Berlin,
Germany
E-Mail: Elmar.Fichtl@t-systems.de
Web: www.t-systems.de
Tel: + 49 30 34970
Fax: + 49 30 3497 3541

STEPHAN FRIEDRICH
Dresdner Bank AG
Fehlandtstr. 3 / 4. OG, 20354 Hamburg,
Germany
E-Mail:
Stephan.Friedrich@dresdner-bank.com
Web: www.dresdner-bank.de
Tel: + 49 40 3501 0

ULRICH HASENKAMP, PROF. DR.
Universität Marburg
Universitätsstraße, 35032 Marburg,
Germany
E-Mail:
Hasenkamp@wiwi.uni-marburg.de
Web: www.uni-marburg.de
Tel: + 49 6421 28 22 230
Fax: + 49 6421 28 26 554

DIRK HUBERTY
SQS Software Quality Systems AG
Stollwerckstraße 11, 51149 Cologne,
Germany
E-Mail: dirk.huberty@sqs.de
Web: www.sqs.de
Tel: + 49 2203 9154 0
Fax: + 49 2203 9154 15

PAUL KEESE
SQS Software Quality Systems AG
Stollwerckstraße 11, 51149 Cologne,
Germany
E-Mail: paul.keese@sqs.de
Web: www.sqs.de
Tel: + 49 2203 9154 0
Fax: + 49 2203 9154 15

DIRK KIRSTEIN
Sd&m software design & management AG
Am Schimmersfeld 7a, 40882 Ratingen,
Germany
E-Mail: Dirk.Kirstein@sdm.de
Web: www.sdm.de
Tel: + 49 2102 99 57 0
Fax: + 49 2102 99 57 54

ANDREAS KRAMP
Dresdner Bank AG
Fehlandtstr. 3 / 4. OG, 20354 Hamburg,
Germany
E-Mail:
Andreas.Kramp@dresdner-bank.com
Web: www.dresdner-bank.de
Tel: + 49 40 3501 2420
Fax: + 49 40 3501 2415

BEGOÑA LAIBARRA
SQS Software Quality Systems S.A.
Avd. Zugazarte 8,1
48930 Las Arenas, Vizcaya,
Spain
Web: www.sqs.es
E-Mail: blaibarra@sqs.es
Tel: + 34 94 480 4617
Fax: + 34 94 480 4247

JENS LEHMBACH
Philipps-University Marburg
Universitätsstraße 24, 35032 Marburg,
Germany
E-Mail: lehmbach@wiwi.uni-marburg.de
Web: www.uni-marburg.de
Tel: + 49 6421 28 23174
Fax: + 49 6421 28 26554

CLAUS LEWERENTZ, PROF. DR.
Technical University Cottbus
Ewald-Haase-Str. 12/13, 03044 Cottbus,
Germany
E-Mail: cl@tu-cottbus.de
Web: www.tu-cottbus.de
Tel: + 49 355 693880
Fax: + 49 355 693810

MARTIN LIPPERT
It – Workplace Solutions GmbH,
Universität Hamburg
Hummelsbütteler Landstr. 137,
22339 Hamburg,
Germany
E-Mail:
lippert@informatik.uni-hamburg.de
Web: www.informatik.uni-hamburg.de
Tel: + 49 40 42883 2306
Fax: + 49 40 42883 2302

CHRISTOPH MECKE, DR.
SAP AG
Neurottstr. 16, 69190 Walldorf,
Germany
E-Mail: Christoph.Mecke@sap.com
Web: www.sap.com
Tel: + 49 6227 748248
Fax: + 49 6227 758248

MICHAEL MEYER
T-Systems Nova GmbH, Berkom
Goslarer Ufer 35, 10589 Berlin,
Germany
E-Mail: Michael.Meyer07@t-systems.de
Web: www.t-systems.de
Tel: + 49 30 3497 3540
Fax: + 49 30 3497 3541

DIRK MEYERHOFF, DR.
SQS Software Quality Systems AG
Stollwerckstraße 11, 51149 Cologne,
Germany
E-Mail: dirk.meyerhoff@sqs.de
Web: www.sqs.de
Tel: + 49 2203 9154 0
Fax: + 49 2203 9154 15

TREVOR PRICE
SIM Group Ltd.,
Systems Integration Management,
Albion House, Chertsey Road,
Woking, Surrey GU21 1BE,
United Kingdom
E-Mail: trevor.price@simgroup.com
Web: www.simgroup.com
Tel: + 44 483 740 289
Fax: + 44 483 720 112

WERNER SCHMITZ-THRUN
FTT – Future Technology Team GmbH
Sophienstr. 1, 51149 Cologne,
Germany
E-Mail: Werner.Schmitz-Thrun@ftt.de
Web: www.ftt.de
Tel: + 49 2203 9154 8910
Fax: + 49 2203 9154 88

KATRIN SEVERID
CSC Ploenzke AG, Strategy Consulting
Finanzinstitute
Bahnhofstr. 27–32, 65185 Wiesbaden,
Germany
E-Mail: KSeverid@cscploenzke.de
Web: www.cscploenzke.de
Tel: + 49 611 1662359

FRANK SIMON, DR.
SQS AG, Stollwerckstr. 11, 51149 Cologne,
Germany
E-Mail: Frank.Simon@sqs.de
Web: www.sqs.de
Tel: + 49 2203 9154 476
Fax: + 49 2203 9154 58

DAVID SINGLETON †
Contact: Bill Kirkwood
Siteconfidence
Paper Mews Court, 284 High Street,
Dorking, Surrey RH4 1QT,
United Kingdom
Web: www.siteconfidence.co.uk
Tel: + 44 1483 813876
Fax + 44 1306 644940

JARLE VÅGA
TietoEnator Consulting A/S
P. O. Box 233 Økern, 0510 Oslo,
Norway
E-Mail: Jarle.Vaga@tietoenator.com
Web: www.tietoenator.com
Tel: + 47 22076368
Fax: + 47 22076200

ROB VAN DER POUW KRAAN
SQS Software Quality Systems B.V.
Van Voordenpark 5A,
5301 KP Zaltbommel,
The Netherlands
E-Mail: pouwkraan@sqs-group.nl
Web: www.sqs-group.nl
Tel: + 31 418 655 888
Fax: + 31 418 655 889

ERIK VAN VEENENDAAL
Improve Quality Services BV
Waalreseweg 17, 5554 Valkenswaard,
The Netherlands
E-Mail: eve@ImproveQS.nl
Web: www.Improveqs.nl
Tel: + 31 40 2089283
Fax: + 31 40 202 1450

MICHAEL VETTER
ComValue Internet Consulting
Joinvillerstr. 44-46
63303 Dreieich-Sprendlingen,
Germany
E-Mail: michael.vetter@comvalue.com
Web: www.comvalue.com
Tel: + 49 6103 7333 400
Fax: + 49 6103 7333 401

ALAN WALLET
SIM Group Ltd.,
System Integration Management,
Albion House, Chertsey Road,
Woking, Surrey GU21 1BE
United Kingdom
E-Mail: alan.wallat@simgroup.com
Web: www.simgroup.com
Tel: + 44 1483 733 100
Fax: + 44 1483 733 101

STEVE WILLIS
Build & Test
Barclaycard IT
1234, Pavilion Drive, Northampton NN4,
United Kingdom
E-Mail: Steve.Willis@barclaycard.co.uk
Web: www.barclaycard.co.uk
Tel: + 44 1604 251265

JAN-GEROLD WINTER
Deutsche Bank AG
Frankfurter Str. 84–90,
65760 Eschborn/ Ts.,
Germany
E-Mail: Jan-Gerold.Winter@db.com
Web: www.deutsche-bank.de
Tel: + 49 69 910 69003
Fax + 49 69 910 68341

HEINZ ZÜLLIGHOVEN, PROF. DR.
It – Workplace Solutions GmbH,
Universität Hamburg
Hummelsbütteler Landstr. 137,
22339 Hamburg,
Germany
E-Mail:
zuelligh@informatik.uni-hamburg.de
Web: www.informatik.uni-hamburg.de
Tel: + 49 40 5004 8914
Fax: + 49 40 5004 8915

Copyrights